PHILOSOPHERS ON
SHAKESPEARE

PHILOSOPHERS *on* SHAKESPEARE

Edited by

PAUL A. KOTTMAN

Pg 89, 91 good Quote
97, 100
Pg 114

STANFORD UNIVERSITY PRESS

Stanford, California 2009

Stanford University Press
Stanford, California

Library of Congress Cataloging-in-Publication Data

Philosophers on Shakespeare / edited by Paul A. Kottman
    p. cm.
    Includes bibliographical references and index.
    ISBN 978-0-8047-5919-9 (cloth : alk. paper) —
    ISBN 978-0-8047-5920-5 (pbk. : alk. paper)
    1. Shakespeare, William, 1564–1616—Criticism and interpretation.
2. Shakespeare, William, 1564–1616—Philosophy.   3. English drama—Early
modern and Elizabethan, 1500–1600—History and criticism.   4. English
drama—17th century—History and criticism.   5. Philosophy in literature.
I. Kottman, Paul A.
   PR2976.P45 2009
   822.3'3—dc22

                                          2009007181

Printed in the United States of America on acid-free, archival-quality paper.
Typeset at Stanford University Press in 10/14 Minion.

Contents

Acknowledgments

I am grateful to Eugene Lang College, the New School for Liberal Arts, for funds provided for the purpose of securing rights and permissions for this volume. The students in my Fall 2006 seminar on Shakespeare and modern philosophy in liberal studies at the New School for Social Research helped me to think in new ways about some of the material collected in this volume. Julia Reinhard Lupton offered very helpful suggestions along the way. My gratitude extends as well to Meghan Robinson and Kaija Matiss for their kind assistance with the transcription of these writings. Finally, I would like to thank Emily-Jane Cohen and Sarah Crane Newman at Stanford University Press for helping to guide this project to publication.

About the Authors

Walter Benjamin (1892–1940) was a literary critic, essayist, translator, and philosopher. He moved to Paris to escape the Nazis and later committed suicide while attempting to cross into Spain from occupied France.

Andrew Cecil Bradley (1851–1935) was an English literary theorist whose writings have exerted an impressive influence on Shakespeare scholarship and literary criticism more generally.

Stanley Louis Cavell (born 1926) is the Walter M. Cabot Professor Emeritus of Aesthetics and the General Theory of Value at Harvard University. He is the author of over fifteen books, most recently *Philosophy the Day After Tomorrow* (Harvard University Press, 2005). His writings on Shakespeare are collected in *Disowning Knowledge in Seven Plays of Shakespeare* (Cambridge University Press, 1987).

Jacques Derrida (1930–2004) was an Algerian-born French philosopher, renowned as the founder of 'deconstruction.' His voluminous writings, which have had a profound influence upon literary studies and philosophy, include other reflections on Shakespeare's drama, notably, in *Specters of Marx* (Routledge, 1994) and in his essay "The Time Is Out of Joint" in *Deconstruction Is/In America* (New York University Press, 1996).

Johann Wolfgang von Goethe (1749–1832) is widely regarded as the most influential writer in the German language. His writings include works of poetry, drama, literature, theology, and science.

Georg Wilhelm Friedrich Hegel (1770–1831) was a German philosopher who broke with the rational, skeptical, and scientific foundations of modern philosophy by offering what he called a "ladder" to a standpoint of knowing achievable only through experience, or transformations in social-historical forms of consciousness. His work has influenced the direction of modern philosophy, political science, anthropology, economics, aesthetics, and other areas of inquiry over roughly the past two centuries.

Agnes Heller (born 1929) is Hannah Arendt Professor Emeritus of Philosophy at the New School for Social Research in New York City. The author of more than twenty books in the fields of political philosophy, social theory, literary criticism, social history, and aesthetics, she has written about Shakespeare most recently in her book *Immortal Comedy: The Comic Phenomenon in Art, Literature, and Life* (Rowman & Littlefield, 2005) in addition to her book-length study of Shakespeare, *The Time Is Out of Joint: Shakespeare as Philosopher of History* (Rowman & Littlefield, 2002), from which this essay is taken.

Johann Gottfried von Herder (1744–1803) was a German philosopher, poet, and literary critic.

Georg Lukács (1885–1971) was a Hungarian philosopher and literary theorist. His political writings elaborated and deepened Marx's reflections on class-consciousness, and his writings on literature contributed broadly to influential theories on realism and the novel.

Karl Heinrich Marx (1818–83) was a German philosopher whose works of political and economic theory, and whose analyses of class struggle, are widely regarded as foundational for modern social theory, as well as for many subsequent political movements.

Friedrich Wilhelm Nietzsche (1844–1900) was a German philosopher whose writings on morality, science, religion, and philosophy have had lasting influence on various strains of contemporary thought.

Carl Schmitt (1888–1985) was a German jurist, political theorist, and professor of law whose work has influenced many contemporary political theorists. He was also a proponent of Nazi ideology and argued for the compatibility between his own philosophy and Nazi authority.

Peter Szondi (1929–71) was a Hungarian literary scholar and philologist of some renown, and a professor of comparative literature at the Free University in Berlin from 1965 until his death by suicide. He is known chiefly for his writings on literary hermeneutics, on the theory of drama, and on poets such as Hölderlin and Paul Celan.

PHILOSOPHERS ON
SHAKESPEARE

Introduction

1

This volume assembles for the first time writings composed by philosophers from the middle of the eighteenth century to the present day in Europe and the United States that engage the dramatic work of William Shakespeare. It is intended to provide an introduction to, and overview of, a compelling tradition of grappling with Shakespeare's work. Although philosophical approaches to Shakespeare's work have long appeared in various quarters—especially, and increasingly, in recent years[1]—before the present volume no substantial anthology of core philosophical writings on Shakespeare has been made available to students and scholars wishing to engage the insights these works offer.

Philosophical interpretations of the plays have never really ceased to be produced, of course; new essays of this sort are continually written, and students of the plays invariably find themselves wrapped up, by the very nature of Shakespeare's work, in philosophical questions. Although historicist and cultural materialist approaches to the study of Shakespeare have been predominant in colleges and universities for the past thirty years or so, Shakespeare's work continues to provoke—even within the very studies that might be identified as 'historicist'—reflections on politics, religion, theatricality, sexuality, ethics, nature, and a host of other aspects of human existence and sociality.[2]

The first organizing principle of this volume, therefore, has been to include essays that think alongside, and in a certain struggle with, Shakespeare about matters by which the plays are understood to be bound and determined. None of these essays begin by taking for granted Shakespeare's works, life, historical context, or linguistic innovations as objects of scholarly worth. Nor do they necessarily aim to deepen our philological or historical knowledge about the language of Shakespeare's plays or their historical context of origin, any more than they furnish particular revelations regarding the dramaturgical techniques of Shakespeare's era. It is true that most of the essays in the following pages offer novel interpretations of the plays or of Shakespeare's accomplishments as a dramatist more generally. However, I would suggest that such hermeneutical efficacy is an effect, and not a cause, of the extent to which these writings struggle alongside Shakespeare with matters by which the plays and their protagonists are also seen as being gripped. Like Shakespeare's *Timon of Athens*, Karl Marx is engrossed by the power of money to determine the life of its possessor; like Romeo and Juliet themselves, Jacques Derrida seeks to articulate an understanding of how our names divide us.

Secondly, I have tried to select writings that might also be read fruitfully beside one another, in at least some of the ways that I will try to suggest and outline in this introduction. My hope in offering these writings in this arrangement is that students of Shakespeare might begin not only to discern a tradition of philosophical engagement with Shakespeare but also, and especially, to envision new ways of revitalizing that tradition. Section I thus tracks readings of Shakespeare within the philosophy of the tragic, from J. G. Herder to Peter Szondi; Section II collects individual entries that offer interpretations of particular plays, or of Shakespeare's dramatic work as a whole.

In selecting works for inclusion within the limited space of this volume, I have opted for essays that have received relatively little attention in scholarly work published on Shakespeare over the past century or so. This has meant leaving out, among others, writings by Samuel Johnson, F.W.J. Schelling, and A. W. Schlegel, which through their influence on Samuel Coleridge's interpretations of Shakespeare constitute a significant part of early-twentieth-century Anglophone scholarship on Shakespeare. Likewise, because the interpretations of Shakespeare's work by Sigmund Freud and his followers in psychoanalytic thought have themselves been a focus of numerous studies and have long permeated the teaching and study of Shakespeare, I have chosen not to reprint them here.[3] This choice led me to omit two other important studies: Jacques Lacan's essay "Desire and the Interpretation of Desire in *Hamlet*" and Jean-François Lyotard's essay on *Hamlet*, "Jewish Oedipus." Also missing are brief but illuminating passages devoted to Shakespeare's plays written by philosophers from Immanuel Kant, Søren Kierkegaard, and Ralph Waldo Emerson to Ernst Bloch, Theodor Adorno, Michel Foucault, and Emmanuel Levinas. The list of texts one might wish to include could easily extend to writings by critics like T. S. Eliot, G. Wilson Knight, Jan Kott, Northrop Frye, Ernst Kantorowicz, or W. H. Auden, to say nothing of writings that have appeared in recent decades. I can only emphasize that I have tried, within the space available, to bring to the attention of students of Shakespeare a set of texts that, not having been anthologized before, might suggest new horizons for thinking alongside Shakespeare's plays.

2

By the time that Hegel composed his *Lectures on Fine Art* in the 1820s, Shakespeare was venerated as the bard of northern Europe such that "a life without Shakespeare was, in Goethe's phrasing, barely a life at all."[4] However, when Gotthold Ephraim Lessing (1729–81) asserted in a text written in 1759 that Shakespeare's tragedies were the equal of Sophocles', he was the first European critic to do so.[5]

It is within an essay on Shakespeare written by Johann Gottfried von Herder (1744–1803) that the debate over how, or even whether, to engage Shakespeare's drama becomes something more than a polemic over whether, or by how much, Shakespeare broke the rules of French classicism or was sufficiently cognizant of the view of art laid out in Aristotle's *Poetics* and the multifarious espousals of that text, which had circulated for centuries.[6] The final version of Herder's essay—the one included in this volume (published in 1773)—had been rewritten twice in the preceding years[7]; and in the progression from the earlier drafts to the final version it is possible to follow the emerging recognition of the questions that Shakespeare's work had suddenly come to pose.[8]

Breaking with those who had read Shakespeare from the perspective of a prephilological and ahistorical understanding of Aristotle's *Poetics*, typical of classical aesthetics in the period, Herder observed that not only could Shakespeare's drama not be read in terms of received notions of genre, but moreover formal rules were useless for understanding a body of drama like Shakespeare's that had to solve for itself, again and again with each play, what it meant to be a dramatic work. In this way, Herder was able to introduce a new problem not only into the study of Shakespeare but also into the philosophy of modern art more broadly—with Shakespeare, no less, as the very impetus for the question. Now that "the work *itself* is forced to carry the responsibility of justifying its own existence," as is the case in Shakespeare's poetics, we have to ask not only whether Aristotelian poetic categories could govern Shakespearean drama but moreover whether they could suffice to provide our own understanding of artworks henceforth.[9]

It is thus probably not too much to say that Shakespeare's drama offered to

German aesthetics of the period something that would become emblematic of modern art more generally; namely, the vanishing of presumed universality in social roles, norms, and ideals, and the concomitant experience of freedom and self-determination in both modern individuals and in the works of art that represent them. "Shakespeare narrated the experience of individuals etched by the absence of a governing culture"—which amounts to saying as well that a Greek philosophy of art cannot help us comprehend it.[10]

It is in this spirit of "expounding and rhapsodizing" that Herder—observing himself to be "closer to Shakespeare than the Greek"—suggests that Shakespeare needs something like his own Aristotle, one capable not of establishing new rules for poetry but rather of coming to terms with works that now make their own rules, and with what this means for we who stage these works. But this suggestion contains within it yet another that is more far-reaching, which is where Herder's essay finally leads. In Shakespeare the distinction between genres—comedy, tragedy, pastoral, historical drama—is confounded not because Shakespeare is merely an unruly or disobedient artist with little regard for Greek principles; Shakespeare confounds genre because the historical world itself, in which and of which Shakespeare writes, knows no "unity of action, time or place."[11] Shakespeare does not give us, as Aristotle's Sophocles did, poetic genres perfectly suited to the world in which he composed them; rather, says Herder, Shakespeare gives us "History in the widest sense" in all of its complexity and disunity. Herder's intuition is that Shakespeare is scripting our world, our fragmented and disjointed history, which might sound close to Harold Bloom's claim that Shakespeare invented the modern human being. But Herder is not claiming that Shakespeare has thereby accomplished an achievement that could be legitimately classified as art, as poetic, from the start. For what Herder means by emphasizing that what Shakespeare gives us is not tragedy, comedy, or romance but "history itself" is that this achievement forces us to rethink art as self-legitimating, when such self-determination comes to be seen as our problem as modern subjects as well.[12]

3

Peter Szondi begins his study *An Essay on the Tragic* (excerpted in this volume) by claiming that "Aristotle's powerful and monumental sphere of influence, one that knows neither national nor epochal boundaries," meets a certain limit with the "philosophy of the tragic" that begins with Schelling and "rises like an island" above this influence.[13] Given what I have just said about Herder, one might offer Herder's essay on Shakespeare as an earlier and alternative pro-genitor to Schelling in this regard; but Szondi's overall point is well taken. The rediscovery of tragedy—primarily Attic tragedy, and above all Sophocles—as a wellspring of the 'tragic', a theme that runs through Idealist and post-Ideal-ist German philosophy,[14] revealed something for which, in the ancient drama, Aristotle's categories had not fully accounted.[15]

Still, that it is Schelling, for Szondi, and not Herder who stands at the beginning of the "philosophy of the tragic"—as distinct from the "poetics of tragedy" (Aristotle)—is significant for our purposes in one further respect. For starting with Schelling's *Philosophical Letters on Dogmatism and Criticism* rather than Herder's essay on Shakespeare is symptomatic of the occlusion of Shakespeare in most accounts of the turn to the 'tragic' in German philoso-phy.

Indeed, Shakespeare's place in the German "philosophy of the tragic" has yet to be adequately investigated or explained. This introduction is not the place to make amends for that, although many selections in Section I of this volume might themselves be approached with an eye toward such an explana-tion. I will limit myself to indicating a few places where such an understanding might begin, precisely in the writings of Hegel.

Crucial to the "philosophy of the tragic," as Szondi points out, is the reve-lation of a "more or less concealed structural element that is common" to tragic situations—the richest articulation of which is to be found not in Schelling but in Hegel.[16] For it is Hegel who identifies tragedy with the dialectic of ethics, and the guilt and transgression it entails, as an essential part of what it means to be a doer of deeds. Because Hegel came to see Sophocles' *Antigone* as "the most magnificent and satisfying work of art of this kind," the "philosophy of the tragic" took as its chief model Attic tragedy and not Shakespeare.[17] Indeed, it is supposed that Hegel came to see Shakespeare's relative modernity in light of a contrast with the Sophoclean model.

But could this trajectory not be viewed from the reverse perspective? That is to say, was it Shakespeare's work that explained Sophocles for Hegel?

We might consider as evidence Hegel's early essay "The Spirit of Christianity and Its Fate" (excerpted in this volume), written when he was in his twenties. It is in this essay that Hegel's conception of Greek tragedy begins to take shape through the idea of a causality of fate, gleaned from a juxtaposition of the spirit of Judaism to Christianity.[18] Hegel's thought, which he elaborates in this essay through the second part of a twofold interpretation of Shakespeare's *Macbeth*, is "an ethical logic of action and reaction: to act against another person is to destroy my own life, to call down upon myself revenging fates."[19]

The essay itself unfolds as a radical critique of morality, with Hegel showing how ethical life is not to be found in any particular moral law, principle, or end; instead, true to the tragic vision implied in the essay, ethical life is bound to the ways in which actions lay bare our social ties and relationships and, therefore, our relation to the realm of what the young Hegel simply calls "life."

Hegel tests this by looking at the different ways in which transgression is dealt with by, on the one hand, a penal code rooted in the moral law (which Hegel identifies with Kant's moral philosophy and, in the context of the essay, with the "spirit of the Jewish people") and, on the other hand, punishment as fate. Whereas the penal code is structured through the sacrifice of the individual to the universal—such that transgressors must be treated as having excluded themselves from the conviviality of others, and therefore as being as good as dead (if not literally subject to the death penalty)—punishment as fate reveals, on the contrary, that trespass of this sort is not the transformation of life into death but rather what Hegel calls life's "diremption." Fate punishes by wrecking the webs of human relationships that are the very conditions for the transgressor's own actions, indeed for his own life. And for this reason, the pain fate brings is not separable from a heightened and keener sense of one's dependence on these conditions; that is, a deepened and renewed understanding of what exactly this diremption means. Here is Hegel making this point by means of Shakespeare's *Macbeth*:

> The illusion of trespass, its belief that it destroys the other's life and thinks itself enlarged thereby, is dissipated by the fact that the disembodied spirit of the injured life comes on the scene against the trespass, just as Banquo, who came as a friend to Macbeth, was not blotted out when he was murdered but immediately thereafter took his seat, not as a guest at the feast, but as an evil spirit.

If in the penal code it is the law that demands the alienation or death of the one who substitutes his individual will, act, or desire for the universal norm, then what Macbeth's fate reveals is that he has alienated himself by his murder of his friend and moreover, as Hegel puts it, by his destruction of the very "friendliness of life."[20]

In this sense, punishment as fate invokes a less superable authority than the pain of death upon which the penal code rests. For what the return of fates augurs is not the death of the transgressor or murderer, the cancellation of his life, but rather the fact that he could not transcend life by killing another. "The trespasser intended to have to do away with another's life, but he has only destroyed his own, for his life is not different from life. . . . In his arrogance he has destroyed indeed, but only the friendliness of life; he has perverted life into an enemy." Rather than being sentenced to death, Macbeth is thus thrown back into life, but now as a stranger to it. "You make me strange, / Even to the disposition that I owe," cries Macbeth following the appearance of Banquo's ghost (3.4.111–12). Here the punishment that Macbeth suffers is not due to the administering of the penal law but rather a fate that "he himself has armed . . . an enemy made an enemy by himself." Nothing makes this clearer than the fact that Banquo's ghost appears in Macbeth's *own* seat, effectively alienating Macbeth from his position, from his place in life with others, before he himself can occupy it.

Strikingly, Hegel reads *Macbeth* not solely as a tragedy that is emblematic of the causality of fate that, for him, characterizes Christianity's repudiation of the strict dualism of universal and particular, law and life, that lies at the heart of "the spirit of Judaism." Earlier in the same essay, he also identifies the fate of Macbeth with the fate of the Jewish people. "The fate of the Jewish people," he writes in a stark formulation, "is the fate of Macbeth, who stepped out of nature itself, clung to foreign beings, and thus in their service had to trample and slay everything holy in human nature, had at last to be forsaken by his gods (for they were objects and he their slave), and be crushed to pieces on his faith itself." Thus, it is as if Shakespeare's tragedy contained within itself both Judaism and Christianity, both penal code and punishment-as-fate, both law and life—as if Shakespeare's tragedy were therefore the sublation of their opposition. Commenting on this double reading of *Macbeth*, Szondi suggests that it be understood as an anticipation of the "synthesis that Hegel achieved in the *Phenomenology of Spirit* with his interpretation of *Antigone*."[21] Pushing Szondi's observation a step further, we can wonder if Hegel does not discover first in Shakespeare's tragedy the genesis of the very dialectic that will later be located by him in Greece, in *Antigone*.[22]

Szondi is not the only one to see Hegel's "Spirit" essay as anticipating the ethical pathos of the reflections on *Antigone* in the *Phenomenology of Spirit*.[23] But Szondi's suggestion is particularly intriguing for our purposes, for he seems to regard Hegel's eventual privileging of *Antigone* not as a function of its antiquity, as opposed to *Macbeth*'s modernity. Rather, Szondi seems to imply that for Hegel, Sophocles' play simply makes more succinct the same sublation of the opposition of law and love (Judaism and Christianity; penal law and fate) already afforded by the double reading of *Macbeth*.[24] Only then, subsequently, did Hegel come to recognize that this relative clarity—a perceived *poetic* difference between Shakespeare and Sophocles—might itself be indicative or revelatory of the difference between ancient tragedy and modern tragedy.

4

More than any other work by Shakespeare, it is *Hamlet* that has garnered the most critical attention, in large measure because of the importance of the play to its philosophical readers in the eighteenth century.

When Goethe's Wilhelm Meister (excerpted in this volume) read the "significant ejaculation—'The time is out of joint / O cursed spite, / That ever I was born to set it right,'" he saw in these words the "key to Hamlet's whole procedure." Probably the single most influential interpretation of the character of Hamlet, this passage grounds Hamlet's predicament not only in what Goethe calls Hamlet's disjointed "inheritance"; rather, Wilhelm Meister understands these lines as arising from a "soul unfit for the performance" of what is being asked. Not that what is being asked of Hamlet is impossible; on the contrary, the deeds are "not in themselves impossibilities"—only "for him," Hamlet himself, are they impossible.[25] To cite Hegel's re-elaboration of Goethe's thought, Hamlet's "noble soul is not made for this kind of energetic activity."[26] The problem, on this reading, lies not so much with Hamlet's external predicament as with Hamlet himself. For Goethe's Wilhelm Meister, as for Hegel, Hamlet *is* his own predicament. "Full of disgust with the world and life, what with decision, proof, arrangements for carrying out his resolve, and being bandied from pillar to post, he eventually perishes owing to his own hesitation and a complication of external circumstances."[27]

Extrapolating from this account of *Hamlet* in his *Lectures on Fine Art*, Hegel arrives at his account of modern tragic *personae tout court*. According to Hegel, modern protagonists like Hamlet "are from the beginning in the midst of a wide field of more or less accidental circumstances and conditions within which it is possible to act in this way or in that." That is to say, the fragmentary, disjointed nature of the "time" robs the protagonist of the "ethical pathos" that, according to Hegel, retrospectively animated the actions of Greek tragic heroes.

The problem is therefore not only Hamlet's noble soul or his disgust with the world; rather, it is what Hamlet discovers over the course of his days and nights in the play. And what he discovers, by means of his "antic disposition," is that it does not matter what he does. Whatever he may do, his choices, his words and deeds do not—whether by accident or design—produce ethical conflicts on the order of, say, Antigone and Creon. No deed done by Hamlet, not even his summary, albeit accidental, killing of Polonius, generates any meaningful response, let alone ethical opposition, from anyone else in Denmark; at most, he is simply sent away by Claudius.[28] Thus, Hamlet discovers, there is no external, meaningful 'conflict', no ethical relation on offer; there is only accident, contingency, complicated external circumstances.

At this point, Hegel extrapolates even further, seeing in *Hamlet* the tragedy of a new, modern subjectivity that is irrevocably alienated from the world and isolated in a manner not at all unlike Hegel's reading of the Cartesian subject. (Stanley Cavell, excerpted in this volume, has perspicaciously expanded and enriched this Hegelian connection into a theory of Shakespearean tragedy as staging the "advent of skepticism."[29]) In his own account of *Hamlet*, philosopher Franz Rosenzweig offers a culmination of the German Idealist reading when he suggests that Shakespeare offers us a tragedy "where the hero is to all intents and purposes a philosopher."[30]

Whereas individuality in the Greek tragic hero is generated, in Hegel's account, through its necessarily ethical 'pathos' (Antigone violating the beautiful ethical totality by burying her brother), "in modern tragedy it remains a matter of chance whether the individual's character is gripped by something intrinsically justified or whether he is led into crime or wrong." Because it is chance—sheer accident—that determines not only the protagonist's field of action but also the ethical stakes of those actions, Hegel concludes that in modern tragedy, as in *Hamlet*, "character and an ethical end *may* coincide, but . . . this coincidence is not the *essential* foundation and objective condition of the depth and beauty of a [modern] tragedy."[31] Fate is revealed to be perhaps no more than mere accident.

What then is the "depth and beauty" of Shakespearean tragedy if not the beautiful ethical totality that it shatters or the ethical stakes that it reveals? It is here that Hamlet's subjectivity becomes important, for the conflict that matters lies no longer in the ethical world outside the actor; rather, it "lies essentially in the character to which the individuals adhere in their passion, not because of any substantial justification but because they are what they are once and for all."[32] Shakespeare's protagonist is, so to speak, the internalization of tragic conflict—"the progress of a great soul, its inner development, the picture of its self-destructive struggle against circumstance, events and their consequences."[33]

This internalization, this new subjectivity, is problematic, however, because its conflicts are not determined by anything "substantial" or "universal" (to stick for a moment longer with Hegel's parlance).[34] It is not as though the Sophoclean conflict between family and state were now played out on the field of Hamlet's *psyche* instead of the Greek *polis*. Rather, the deeper problem is that the internalization of tragic conflict now signals that nothing more is at stake than the individual's *passion*, what Hegel calls "the formal inevitability of their personality." It is precisely "*without* ethical justification" that the Shakespearean protagonists are led by their very personality to do whatever it is they do, with the result that Shakespeare's characters appear to us as "the finest examples of firm and consistent characters who come to ruin simply because of this decisive adherence to themselves."[35] What makes Shakespeare's characters so real to us, as moderns ourselves, is not simply the poetic verisimilitude that Shakespeare accomplishes; rather, it is that his protagonists pick the fruits of their own deeds—not because their deeds have ethical consequences but because their actions are *theirs*, because they reveal who they are.

Actions are thus compelled, not because of broader ethical stakes they may carry or by which they can be forced; rather, actions become the way in which the irreducibly individual (that is, internal, psychological, subjective) passions, thoughts, or aims underlying them are manifested. In this way, the "external" world disappears, so to speak, as the orienting horizon of meaning. Or better, the world (or history) becomes a stage for the dramatization of individual passions at war with themselves, the dramatization of the "internal" conflict of the individual.

What this interpretative tradition of *Hamlet* offers, therefore, is nothing other than the articulation of modern subjectivity as a new kind of agency rooted in the internalized conflicts of one's own passions, thoughts, desires. Indeed, the problem of subjectivity—as Shakespeare invents it or as modern philosophy has come to understand it—is bound to a deepening anxiety about the very possibilities of acting, doing, saying, or performing. For many today, as for Hamlet, subjection is an irresolvable psychic conflict of powers whose substantiality can be tested only by acting in the world; and yet, insofar as no external ethical substance is revealed by these actions, it turns out that the dramatic self or "antic disposition" may be all there is.

5

Shakespeare offers, so says Hegel, "the finest examples of firm and consistent characters who come to ruin simply because of this decisive adherence to themselves."[36] A. C. Bradley, whose older brother was the Hegelian philosopher F. H. Bradley, composed lectures on Shakespeare (one is excerpted in this volume) and on Hegel's theory of tragedy that offer the most sustained and influential elaboration of this thought. In Shakespeare's tragedies, Bradley writes, "action is essentially the expression of character." Although Bradley claims that Hegel is the only writer on tragedy to compare with Aristotle, in a sense it is really Bradley who accomplishes the fullest reversal of Aristotle through his reading of Shakespeare. Whereas Aristotle maintained that character is a function of action and therefore of the *mythos*, Bradley suggests that plot in Shakespearean tragedy is a function of character. The very sequence of Bradley's lectures on *Hamlet* appears to bear this out: the first lecture sweeps aside all other considerations of the play to address first "the central question of Hamlet's character," whereas the second argues that the plot can only be made intelligible by grasping Hamlet himself. In short, Bradley's chief insight in his lectures was to elaborate, and make convincing by the force of his readings of the plays, the thought that in Shakespearean tragedy "character is destiny."

And yet on precisely this point Bradley finds something missing in the Hegelian-German reading of Shakespeare—a sense of lack that he repeatedly attributes to the failure of the Hegelian reading to account for that which *moves us* in Shakespeare's plays.[37] This attention to our affective response to the plays is perhaps the greatest virtue of Bradley's writings, however tendentious his suppositions in this regard may be.

If Shakespeare's characters come to ruin—*pace* Hegel—because of a "decisive adherence to themselves" and because there is no indisputable governing set of social norms and principles to make their deeds consequential, then what Bradley wants to know—*contra* Hegel—is why, if this is all true, these plays are not "depressing" like so many "mis-called tragedies"? For Bradley, Hegel perceived roughly half of the picture, namely, the notion that Shakespeare's protagonists are "free artists of themselves." But what Hegel failed to account for was how Shakespeare managed to conjure a compelling drama of these free artists that does not simply leave us with "the reflection that all is vanity." How did Shakespeare manage to take characters whose fate derives from a decisive adherence to *themselves* and make them meaningful and moving to *us*?

More to the point, Bradley wonders, how did Shakespeare manage this without falling back upon moralistic caricatures, protagonists with whom we identify because they are basically "good" people (the way Aristotle requires that tragic heroes be neither reprobates nor saints, but closer to the latter)? Indeed, crucial to Bradley's suggestions is the observation that Shakespeare's tragic heroes are cruel (Lear), willful criminals (Macbeth), or murderers (Hamlet, Othello).[38] And yet, writes Bradley, "no one ever closes the book with the feeling that man is a poor mean creature." Instead, at the close of the drama, he writes, our "central feeling is the impression of waste"; and this impression, he offers, "makes us realize so vividly the worth of that which is wasted that we cannot possibly seek comfort in the reflection that all is vanity." Departing from the Aristotelian inheritance, Bradley notes that Shakespeare's protagonists are not compelling because of their moral righteousness. For this reason, Shakespeare's plays reveal our 'moral' judgment of the protagonists' actions to be detached, or detachable, from our affective response to the plays. Our feelings about Hamlet or Lear or Othello cannot be understood solely as expressions of a judgment of them, or their deeds; which means, again, that our sense of meaningfulness or loss in relation to Shakespeare's protagonists is not a moral disposition. The "impression of waste" we are left with means simply that we feel that these lives matter—independently, as it were, from the rightness or wrongness or the deeds they perform or the sufferings they endure. Moreover—and this may be Bradley's larger point—if we affectively sense meaning and "worth" in these lives (and perhaps, by extension, in our own lives) through "the impression of waste" elicited by the dramas, then in Shakespeare ethicality appears in a 'negative' form, as it were, through the experience of its resounding lack or defeat.

Returning us to *Macbeth*—and claiming it to be "of one nature" with Hegel's reading of *Antigone*—Bradley thus proposes a revision of the notion of the 'causality of fate' that the young Hegel first detected in Shakespeare's play.[39] Whereas the young Hegel conceives of fate in *Macbeth* along the lines of Aeschylus' *Eumenides*, Bradley understands the actions and sufferings of Macbeth himself—of *this* particular doer and sufferer—to be the sole way in which the conflicting forces by which he is torn can be presented as a conflict that can move us. What Bradley is intimating is that Shakespeare's dramatic representations are the fullest reconciliation of the fate of the individual and the collective (or universal) that we have. The plays show the full weight of universality being borne by individuals, as it were; and this, he offers, is why they move us the way they do.

6

If audiences are moved by Shakespeare's representation of "the mystery of life," to stick for a moment with Bradley's phrase, then others urge us not to regard Shakespeare's protagonists as invested in life in an enchanted way. Anticipating a host of commentators from Freud to Harold Bloom, Nietzsche in the *Birth of Tragedy* (excerpted in this volume) understands Hamlet's disgust to be the result of an "insight into the truth" of life's harsh cruelty, an insight that disables the "illusion" necessary for a livable life, and for agency generally. Theodor Adorno likewise sees in Hamlet the introduction of a gulf between "insight" of this Nietzschean sort—which turns the subject into a "being for itself"—and the "actions a man might play," to use Hamlet's own formulation.[40]

Calling *Hamlet* "the tragedy of tragedy," Emmanuel Levinas takes these thoughts a step further by suggesting in *Time and the Other* that Shakespeare's undoing of the conditions of possibility for an agency that masters fate signals, to us, that there is no longer any way out for the protagonist. Whereas tragedy in its classical sense, says Levinas, implied that the victory of fate over human freedom could be mitigated by the hero's assumption of his own death—such that "mastery through the possibility of suicide is a constant fact of tragedy"— Hamlet contrarily understands that "the 'not to be' is perhaps impossible" and therefore he "can no longer master the absurd." Life is therefore fully disenchanted for Hamlet, not because it is finite and one wishes to leave it but because "it is without limits."[41] Hamlet's anxiety is not only the wisdom of Silenus, namely, that it is better not to have been born; rather, concludes Levinas, the insight is that "it is impossible to die."

7

The spirit of modernity in Europe, as Hegel indicates in the *Phenomenology of Spirit*, takes an uneven course as it passes from land to land. Carl Schmitt's political-historical reading of *Hamlet* (*Hamlet or Hecuba*, excerpted in this volume) takes its initial cue from the fact that early-seventeenth-century England took a comparatively anomalous path out of the Middle Ages.[42] What attracts Schmitt's attention is the fact that unlike France, for example, England does not follow the model of monarchical absolutism; rather, in James I, England had a ruler and political theorist who stubbornly refused to leave behind medieval or feudal notions of sovereign power. James's obstinate (albeit highly informed and idiosyncratic) defense of these political principles is the chief characteristic of his writings, most notably in his *Trew Law of Free Monarchies* (1598); and James's personal identification with these principles is part of what doomed the House of Stuart. For Schmitt, therefore, James I was a tragic figure who was, at the same time, historical. James is not a protagonist in a play, as Hamlet is; but re-deploying Benjamin's formulae and terminology, Schmitt reckons that it is James's historical-tragic fate that allows tragedy to break into the play (*Spiel*) *Hamlet*.[43] Moreover, it allows Schmitt to correct Benjamin's argument in the *Origin of German Tragic Drama* (excerpted in this volume) and to assert that *Hamlet* is not *Trauerspiel* but, precisely, *Tragik*.[44]

The parallel of James and Hamlet sets up Schmitt's argument; but it is important to underscore that his argument is by no means reducible to a proof or elaboration of this parallel. Not unlike Hamlet, James I was the son of a queen who took part in her husband's murder—James's mother, Mary, Queen of Scots, married her husband's assassin only three months after the murder. Schmitt supposes that the ambiguity surrounding Gertrude in Shakespeare's play in fact alludes to this history, and that it is partly responsible for Hamlet's delay.

What Schmitt aims to demonstrate through this recourse to "historical actuality," however, is that Shakespeare's *Hamlet* "is no closed unity of time, place and action" but rather—through the taboo that surrounds the queen, and the deferral of revenge—"historical time breaks into the action of the play [*Spiel*] . . . elevating it" to tragedy. It should thus quickly be emphasized that Schmitt's larger purpose is not to 'historicize' *Hamlet*; although he shares with cultural-materialist readings of Shakespeare the criticism that a certain tradition of aesthetic thought has produced the imperative to approach works of art on their own terms only, thereby obscuring—in the case of *Hamlet*—precisely that which makes *Hamlet* more than a mere artistic-literary-imaginative 'play'.

Schmitt's purpose, rather, is to grasp what makes *Hamlet* not only a play but moreover what makes it "tragic" in a full sense. And, for Schmitt, literary invention or the autonomy of art cannot, on its own, amount to tragedy in this special sense. The "seriousness of tragic action," according to Schmitt, is "impossible to fictionalize . . . and also impossible to play," because to be moved in a tragic way (as opposed to simply weeping, since "one can weep for many things") means being conscious of "an ineluctable reality which no human mind has conceived" but to which we are all bound.

Schmitt's claim—for which *Hamlet* stands as proof—is therefore, in its very historicism, general and categorical. And by the same token, *Hamlet* stands for Schmitt as proof of Shakespeare's eminence as a poet—not because he made poetry, or pure art, but rather because he was capable of making tragedy, of making "from his contemporary political situation" a fully tragic myth, *Hamlet*. Implicitly comparing Shakespeare to Sophocles, Schmitt argues that Shakespeare's artistic greatness lay in his "tact" and his "respect," as it were, for the limits of human art.

For his part, Schmitt does not hesitate to define these limits. "An invented fate," he writes, "is no fate at all." For the "core of tragic action, the source of genuine tragedy, is something so irrevocable that no mortal can invent it."

In his essay "Shakespeare and Modern Drama" (included in this volume) Georg Lukács offers something like the exact reverse of Schmitt's claim about Shakespeare. Lukács was, of course, a great admirer of Hegel, but in his essay he takes issue with Hegel's reading of *Macbeth*, in which Hegel "traces the conflict to disputes between different systems of hereditary rights" and complains that Shakespeare, in representing Macbeth as a criminal, omits the fact that Macbeth suffered a kind of injustice when Duncan named his own son as successor to the throne.[45] In other words, Hegel's complaint is precisely that in *Macbeth* Shakespeare failed to do what Schmitt claims Shakespeare managed in *Hamlet*, namely, the production of a full tragic myth out of a contemporary, historical-political crisis.

Like Bradley before him, Lukács suspects that Hegel underestimates Shakespeare's accomplishment in *Macbeth* and that he therefore misunderstands something fundamental to Shakespearean tragedy. Following the Austrian dramatist Friedrich Hebbel (1813–63), Lukács emphasizes that Shakespeare's poetic achievement lies in the construction of "a powerful sequence of great scenes that depict and portray the tragic feelings of tragic figures"—scenes which are connected by the individual character. In this sense, what Lukács means is precisely the opposite of Schmitt's claim regarding the 'tragic'. For in Lukács's view, what finally interested Shakespeare was not the historical "necessity" of the tragic situation, that is, that "the Othello-Iago-Desdemona relationship must lead to tragedy"; as Lukács sees it, Shakespeare would have thought this necessity to be merely obvious. Therefore, he would have turned his attention away from the structural necessity of tragedy (or its historical reality) to "the tragic feelings" as they are manifest in the relationships between, say, Othello, Iago, and Desdemona—namely, what they say and do to one another. "Tragedy is a necessity," Lukács demurs, "but how it takes place is not a necessity."

We can thus understand Lukács to be countering Schmitt's claim that the tragic be rooted in the ineluctability of a reality that no poet can fabricate when Lukács writes, conversely, of the way that Shakespeare changes scenes with such frequency and without the slightest regard for historical or mythical inevitability. The change of locale or setting is not 'necessary' for the tragic sense Shakespeare's work produces, any more than it is necessary for the development of character or plot. Rather, Lukács observes, Macbeth's castle in Inverness the morning after the murder, or the graveyard scene in *Hamlet*, or Lear's scenes on the heath show such scene-setting to be the "form of an irretrievable moment." Like Bradley, Lukács is trying to get at how Shakespeare's scenes move us; he asserts that Shakespeare's scene-settings elicit "feeling" by presenting the dramatic or poetic truth about history rather than the historical truth of drama and poetry.

The expression "poetic truth about history" belongs to Agnes Heller, a student of Lukács, whose book *The Time Is Out of Joint: Shakespeare as Philosopher of History* might be read as an elaboration and development of Lukács's abbreviated reflections. In her postscript to that book (included in this volume), she suggests that Shakespeare's tragedies and histories reveal not simply *what* has happened but rather that they are more interested in *how* it happened and in *that* it has happened—the dramatic truth of history rather than the historical truth of drama. Whereas, according to Heller, the historian or historiographer approximates 'what really happened' (namely, what no artist invents), Shakespeare offers history not as sheer fiction but as "revelatory truth."

By using this phrase, Heller means to place Shakespeare's histories and tragedies alongside religious truth but also to signal an important difference between them.[46] What Shakespeare's histories and tragedies share with religious revelation is, so to speak, a certain self-referential or self-authorizing quality. "Because the drama *is* the truth . . . one is confronted with the question of what exactly that truth is, not with the question of whether this is the truth." But what makes Shakespeare's "revelatory truth" different from religious revelation—and by the same token what makes Shakespeare our contemporary—is that in Shakespeare histories unfold, individuals act, "without any kind of otherworldly interference or protection." Without gods or deities to participate in the action, Shakespeare leaves us the revelation of truth about human history precisely by leaving us no possible way to explain it, justify it, or excuse it—while nevertheless keeping us fascinated by its mystery.

Thus, Shakespeare reveals the truth of history in his plays not because he reveals the structural necessity of tragic happenings, or the causal relations of plot constructions. He does not offer a transparent interpretation of motives or facts in his plays—on the contrary, for Heller the "infinite interpretability of Shakespearean drama" is connected to the way in which his plays show *that* history is full of secrets without trying to decode them, without aiming to show *what* those secrets might be.

Like Bradley, Heller views Shakespeare as interested in the "mystery" of human doings rather than in their transparency, approximate factuality, or historical interpretability. And, like Bradley, she locates the fascination of this mystery not in otherworldly principles or grand historical narratives but rather in the "internal reserves and sources of the characters and of their actions."

What do we make of Cordelia's words and deeds? Or those of Iago? Or Macbeth? Or Shylock? Or Prince Hal?

These questions are unavoidable for anyone who has encountered these figures in Shakespeare's plays. This unavoidability, Heller offers, is not simply the result of Shakespeare's poetic achievement in representing such characters; rather, it is rooted more deeply in the way we ourselves are reflected in them. In this sense, what Shakespeare's drama offers is not simply existential truths about human life through, say, the words of Lear or Brutus. Rather, his plays stage for us our own historicity. The poetic truth of Shakespeare's drama has no other ground—can have no other ground—other than its revelation of ourselves to ourselves. Furthermore, in making us recognizable to ourselves, the dramas also show us that there is no transcendental or categorical ground for this recognition. For this reason, we might conclude by resisting Heller's nomination of Shakespeare for the title 'philosopher'—although this resistance follows from a line of thought that she herself provides.

Precisely insofar as they move us—insofar as they are dramatic—the plays are not themselves philosophy. But this in no way frees us from the task of grasping why we see Shakespeare's plays as dramatic in the first place—of coming to terms with why we are moved as we are, and thus with how we must now see ourselves in Shakespeare's plays. It is the very drama of the scenes that forces the questions.

SECTION I

1   "Shakespeare"

If there is any man to conjure up in our minds that tremendous image of one "seated high on the craggy hilltop, storm, tempest, and the roaring sea at his feet, but with the radiance of the heavens about his head"[1] that man is Shakespeare. Only with the addition that below him, at the foot of his rocky throne, there murmur the masses who explain him, apologize for him, condemn him, excuse him, worship, calumniate, translate, and traduce him—and to all of whom he is deaf!

What a library of books has already been written about him, for him, against him! And I have no wish to add to it. I would rather that no one in the small circle of my readers would ever again dream of writing about him, for him, against him, excusing him or slandering him; but would rather explain him, feel him as he is, use him, and—if possible—make him alive for us in Germany. May this essay help in the task.

Shakespeare's boldest enemies have, in so many guises, mocked at him and declared that though he may be a great poet, he is not a good dramatist; and even if he is a good dramatist, he is incapable of the great classical tragedies of Sophocles, Euripides, Corneille, and Voltaire, who have taken this art to its furthest limits. And Shakespeare's boldest friends have mostly been satisfied with finding excuses and making apologies for him, always treating his beauties as compensations for his transgressions against the rules, uttering an *Absolvo te* over the accused and then idolizing his greatness the more extravagantly, the more they are obliged to shrug their shoulders at his flaws. This is still the case with his most recent editors and commentators.[2] I hope these pages will change the perspective and throw a fuller light upon his image.

But is this not too bold, too presumptuous a hope, when so many of the great have written about him? I think not. If I can demonstrate that both sides have been building on prejudice, on illusion, on nothing; if I have only to draw

a cloud from their eyes or at most adjust the image without in the lease altering anything in either eye or image, then perhaps I can ascribe it to my time
or even to chance that I should have found the place on which to position my
reader: here is the place to stand, else you will see nothing but caricature. But if
we go on winding and unwinding at the great tangle of pedantry without ever
getting any further, what a grievous destiny we shall weave!

It is from Greece that we have inherited the words *drama, tragedy, comedy*.
And as the lettered culture of the human race has, in a narrow region of the
world, made its way solely through tradition, a certain store of rules which
seemed inseparable from its teaching has naturally been carried everywhere
with it as in its womb and in its language. Since of course it is impossible to
educate a child by way of reason, but only by way of authority, impression,
and the divinity of example and of habit, so also entire nations are to an even
greater extent children in all that they learn. The kernel will not grow without
the husk, and they will never harvest the kernel without the husk, even if they
have no use for it. That is the case with Greek and northern drama.

In Greece drama developed in a way in which it could not develop in the
north. In Greece it was what it could not be in the north. Therefore in the
north it is not and cannot be what it was in Greece. Thus Sophocles' drama and
Shakespeare's drama are two things which in a certain respect have scarcely the
name in common. I believe I can demonstrate these propositions from Greece
itself and thereby decipher in no small measure the nature of northern drama
and of the greatest northern dramatist, Shakespeare. We will perceive the origins of the one by means of the other, but at the same time see it transformed,
so that it does not remain the same thing.

Greek tragedy developed as it were out of *one* scene, out of the impromptu
dithyramb, the mimed dance, the chorus. This underwent accretions, adaptations: instead of one acting figure, Aeschylus introduced two onto the stage,
invented the concept of the protagonist, and reduced the choric element.
Sophocles added the third figure, invented the stage—out of such origins, but
relatively late, Greek tragedy rose to its great heights, became a masterpiece of
the human spirit, the summit of poetry which Aristotle honours so highly, and
we, looking at Sophocles and Euripides, cannot admire deeply enough.

But at the same time we see that certain things can be explained in terms of
these origins which, if we were to look upon them as dead rules, we would be
bound to misjudge dreadfully. That simplicity of the Greek plot, that austerity
of Greek manners, that sustained, buskined quality of expression, the music,

the stage, the unity of place and time—all this lay so fundamentally and naturally, without any art or magic, in the origins of Greek tragedy that it could
come into being only in the sublimation of these characteristics. They were the
husk in which the fruit grew.

Go back to the childhood of that time: simplicity of plot really was so deeply
embedded in what was called the deeds of ancient times, republican, patriotic,
religious, heroic action, that the poet's difficulty lay in discerning parts in this
simple whole, in introducing a dramatic beginning, middle, and end, rather
than in forcing them apart, lopping them off, or in shaping a whole out of disparate events. Any reader of Aeschylus or Sophocles would see nothing incomprehensible in that. In Aeschylus' drama, what is tragedy often but an allegorical, mythological, semi-epic tableau, almost without sequence of scenes, story,
feelings? It was, as the Ancients said, nothing but chorus, with a certain amount
of story in between. Could there be the least labor or art expended on simplicity of plot in such a case? And was it any different in the most of Sophocles'
plays? His *Philoctetes, Ajax, Oedipus Coloneus*, etc. are all still very close to the
uniform nature of their origin: the dramatic tableau surrounded by the chorus.
No doubt about it! This is the genesis of the Greek stage!

Now let us see how much follows from this simple observation. Nothing less
than "the artificiality of the rule of Greek drama was—not artifice at all! It was
Nature!" Unity of plot was unity of the action before them which, according to
the circumstances of their time, country, religion, manners, could not be other
than single and simple. Unity of place—was unity of place; for the one brief
solemn act took place in one location, in the temple, the palace, as it were in
the nation's market-place. There it first admitted only mimed enactments and
narrated interpolations; then the entrances and narrated interpolations; then at
last the entrances and exits and the separate scenes were added—but of course
it was still but one scene, where the chorus bound everything together, where
in the nature of things the stage could never remain empty, and so on. And
now what child needs to have it spelt out that the natural accompaniment and
consequence of all this is unity of time? All these elements lay in the very nature
of things, so for all his skill, without them the poet could do nothing!

So it is also obvious that the art of the Greek poets took a path completely
opposite to the one which we have had ascribed to them nowadays. They did
not simplify, I think, but they complicated.³ Aeschylus made the chorus more
complex. Sophocles elaborated on Aeschylus. And if we compare Sophocles'
most cunning dramas and his masterpiece *Oedipus Rex* with Aeschylus' *Pro-*

metheus Bound or with what information we have of the ancient dithyrambs we shall perceive the astonishing art which he succeeded in bringing to them. But it was never the art of making many into one, but really the art of turning simplicity into a multiplicity, into a beautiful labyrinth of scenes. And his greatest care was still, when he had reached the most complicated point of labyrinth, to transform his spectators' perception back into the illusion of that earlier simplicity, and to unwind the tangled knot of their feelings so gently and gradually as to make them feel that they had never lost it, that previous dithyrambic feeling of oneness. That is why he separated out the scenes for them, at the same time retaining the choruses and making them the points of rest for the action. That is why, with every individual word, he did not let them lose sight of the whole, in the expectation, in the illusion of development and of completion (all these things the ingenious Euripides, when the stage had scarcely been established, promptly failed to do!). In short, Sophocles gave the action *grandeur* (which is something that has been terribly misunderstood).[4]

And anyone who reads him with clear eyes and from the point of view of Sophocles' own time will appreciate how highly Aristotle valued the genius of his art, and will realize that everything he says was virtually the opposite of what modern times have been pleased to make of it. The very fact that Aristotle moved away from Thespis and Aeschylus and based himself on the complexity of Sophocles' poetry; that he took this innovation as his starting point and located the essence of the new poetic genre there; that it became his dearest wish to develop a new Homer of the drama and compare him to his advantage with the first; that he omitted not the slightest detail that might in performance support his conception of the action of scale and grandeur—all this shows that the great philosopher too was theorizing according to the great tendency of his time, and that he is in no way to blame for the restrictive and childish follies which have turned him into the paper scaffolding of our modern stage![5] In his excellent chapter on the nature of the plot,[6] he clearly knew and recognized no other rule than the eye of the spectator, soul, illusion, and expressly stated that limitations of length, still less of kind or time or place of structure, do not admit of being determined by any other ruler. Oh, if Aristotle were alive today and saw the false, perverted use of his rules in dramas of a wholly different kind! But we had better stick to calm and dispassionate inquiry!

As everything in the world changes, so the Nature which was the true creator of Greek drama was bound to change also. Their view of the world, their customs, the state of the republics, the tradition of the heroic age, religion, even music, expression, and the degrees of illusion changed. And in the natural course of things the material for plots vanished, the opportunity for their use, the incentive for using them. True, poets could work on old material and even manner. But that did not achieve the effect. In consequence it lacked the soul. In consequence it was no longer (why should we mince our words) the thing itself. Puppet, imitation, ape, image, in which only the most blinkered devotee could find the moving spirit which once filled the statue with life. Let us turn from straight away (for the Romans were too stupid, or too clever, or too savage and immoderate to create a totally hellenising theatre) to the new Athenians[7] of Europe, and the matter will, I think, become obvious.

There is no doubt: everything that makes for this stuffed likeness of Greek theatre has scarcely been perfectly conceived and produced than in France. I do not only mean the rules of the theatre, so-called, which are laid at the good Aristotle's door: unity of time, place, action, connection between scenes, and verisimilitude of setting, and so on. What I really want to ask is whether there is anything in the world possible beyond that glib classical thing that Corneille, Racine, and Voltaire have produced, beyond that sequence of beautiful scenes, of dialogue, of lines and rhymes with their measure, their decorum, their polish? The writer of this essay not only doubts it, but all the admirers of Voltaire and the French, especially those noble Athenians themselves, will deny it outright—they have done so often enough in the past, they are still at it, and they will go on doing so: "There is nothing above it; it cannot be bettered!" And in the light of this general agreement, with that stuffed and stilted image there on the stage, they are right, and are bound to become more so, the more all the countries of Europe lose their heads to this glib smoothness and continue to ape it.

But all the time there is that oppressive, incontrovertible feeling: "This is not Greek tragedy, not in purpose, effect, kind, or nature," and the most partial admirer of the French cannot deny this, once he has experienced the Greeks. I will not even attempt to inquire whether they observe their Aristotle's rules as much as they claim, for Lessing has recently raised the most terrible doubts about the loudest pretensions. But granted all that, the drama at its very heart: neither action, nor customs, nor language, nor purpose—nothing. So what is the point of all these externals, this scrupulously preserved uniformity? Does anybody believe that a single one of the great Corneille's heroes is a Roman or a French hero? Spanish heroes! Heroes out of Seneca! Gallant heroes—dramatic fictions who outside the theatre would be called fools and who even then, at least in France, were almost as alien as they are now—that is what they are. Racine speaks the language of sensibility—and it is widely agreed that, in this respect, he is unrivalled. But even so, I would not know where sensibility ever spoke such a language as this. These are pictures of sensibility at third hand: they are never, or but rarely, the first, immediate, naked emotions, groping for words and then finding them at last. Is not Voltaire's beautiful poetic line—its mould, content, treatment of imagery, brilliance, wit, philosophy—a beautiful line indeed? Of course! The most beautiful you could imagine; and if I were a Frenchman, I would despair of writing a single line after Voltaire—but beautiful or not, it is not *theatrical* verse, appropriate to the action, language, morals, passions, purpose, of a *drama* (other than French drama); it is false, pedantic balderdash! And the ultimate aim and end of it all? Certainly not a Greek end, certainly not a tragic aim and purpose. To stage a beautiful play—as long as it is beautiful action as well—to have a number of ladies and gentlemen of elegant dress and deportment utter fine speeches and recite philosophy both sweet and useful in beautiful verse, to put them all into a story which gives an illusion of reality and holds our attention, finally to have it all performed by a cast of well-rehearsed ladies and gentlemen who go to great lengths to win our applause and approval with their declamation, the suited gifts of the sentiments, and the externalities of feeling—all this might serve most excellently as a living textbook, as an exercise in expression, deportment, and decorum, as a pattern of good, even heroic, behavior, and even as a complete academy of national wisdom and propriety in matters of living and dying (quite apart from all secondary purposes). Beautiful, instructive, educative, most excellent it may be—but it contains not a hint of the aim and purpose of the Greek theatre.

And what was this aim? According to Aristotle (and there has been enough dispute about it ever since), it is no more nor less than a certain convulsion of the heart, an agitation of the soul to a certain degree and in certain aspects— in short, a specific kind of illusion which, believe me, no French play has yet achieved, or will achieve. And consequently, whatever splendid or useful name it may bear, it is not Greek drama! It is not Sophoclean tragedy! It resembles Greek drama as an effigy might! The effigy lacks spirit, life, nature, truth—that is, all the elements that move us; that is, the tragic purpose and the achievement of that purpose—so how can it be the same thing?

This in itself proves nothing as to its merit or lack of merit, but only raises the question of difference, which I think my previous remarks have established beyond doubt. And now I leave it to the reader to decide for himself whether a copy of foreign ages, customs, and actions which is only half true, an imitation which in a certain sense was the epitome of a country's national identity? I leave it to the reader to judge (and a Frenchman will have to do his best to get round this one) whether a poetic drama which really has no purpose at all as a whole—for according to the best thinkers its greatest virtue lies only in the selection of detail—whether this can be compared with a national institution in which each minute particular has its effect and is the bearer of the richest, deepest culture. Whether finally a time was not bound to come when, with most of Corneille's most artificial plays already forgotten, we will regard Crébillon[9] and Voltaire with the same admiration with which we now look on d'Urfé's *Astrea*[10] and all the Clelias[11] and Aspasias[12] from the times of chivalry: "So clever, so wise, but what a pity it is in *Astrea* and *Clelia*." Their entire art is unnatural, extravagant, tedious! We would be fortunate if our taste for truth had already reached that stage! The entire French repertory would have been transformed into a collection of pretty lines, maxims, and sentiments—but the great Sophocles would still stand where he is now!

So let us now assume a nation which, on account of circumstances which we will not pursue, had no desire to ape ancient drama and run off with the walnut-shell, but rather wanted to create its own drama. Then, I think, our first question would still be: when, where, under what conditions, out of what materials should it do so? And it needs no proof that its creation can and will be the result of this question. If it does not develop its drama out of the chorus and the dithyramb, then it will not have any trace of choric, dithyrambic character. If its world did not offer such simplicity in its history, the spirit of its age, customs, views, language, national attitudes, traditions, and pastimes, even if they are carnival farces or puppet-plays (just as the Greeks did from the chorus)—and what they create—will be drama, as long as it achieves the true purpose of drama among this nation. Clearly, I am referring to the

> *toto divisis ab orbe Britannis*[13]

and their great Shakespeare.

That this was not Greece, neither then nor earlier, will not be denied by any *pullulus Aristoteli*,[14] and so to demand that Greek drama should develop naturally then and there (I am not speaking of mere imitation) is worse than expecting a sheep to give birth to lion-cubs. Our first and last question is solely: what is the soil like? What harvest has it been prepared for? What has been sown in it? What is its most suitable produce? And great heavens, how far we are from Greece! History, tradition, customs, religion, the spirit of the time, of the nation, of emotion, of language—how far from Greece! Whether the reader knows both periods well or but a little, he will not for a moment confuse things that have nothing in common. And if in this different time—changes for good or ill, but changed—there happened to be an age, a genius who might create a dramatic oeuvre out of this raw material as naturally, impressively, and originally as the Greeks did from theirs; and if this creation were to attain the same end, though taking very different paths; and if it were essentially a far more complexly simple and simply complex entity, that is (according to all the metaphysical definitions) a perfect whole—then what fool would compare and condemn because this latter was not the former? For its very nature, virtue, and perfection consist in the fact that it is not the same as the first; that out of the soil of the age there grew a different plant.

Shakespeare's age offered him anything but the simplicity of national customs, deeds, inclinations, and historical traditions which shaped Greek drama. And since, according to the first maxim in metaphysics, nothing will come of nothing, not only, if it were left to the philosophers, would there be no Greek drama, but, if nothing else existed besides, there would and could no longer be any drama at all. But since it is well known that genius is more than philosophy, and creation a very different thing from analysis, there came a mortal man, endowed with divine powers, who conjured out of utterly different material and with a wholly different approach the self-same effect: *fear* and *pity*! And both to a degree which the earlier treatment and material could scarcely produce. How the gods favored his venture! It was the very freshness, innovation, and difference that demonstrated the primal power of his vocation.

Shakespeare did not have a chorus to start from, but he did have puppet-plays and popular historical dramas; so out of the inferior clay of these dramas and puppet-plays he shaped the splendid creation that lives and moves before us! He found nothing like the simplicity of the Greek national character, but a multiplicity of estates, ways of life, attitudes, nations, and styles of speech, the kings and fools, fools and kings, into a splendid poetic whole! He found no such simple spirit of history, story, action: he took history as he found it, and his creative spirit combined the most various stuff into a marvelous whole; and though we cannot call it plot in the Greek sense, we could refer to it by the middle-period term 'action', or by the modern term 'event' (*événement*), 'great occurrence'—O Aristotle, if you were to appear now, what Homeric odes would you sing to the new Sophocles! You would invent a theory to fit him, such as his fellow countrymen Home[15] and Hurd,[16] Pope and Johnson have not yet created! You would rejoice to draw lines for each of your plays on plot, character, sentiments, expression, stage, as it were from the two points at the base of a triangle to meet above at the point of destination—perfection! You would say to Sophocles: "Paint the sacred panel of this altar; and thou, northern bard, paint all the sides and walls of this temple with thy immortal fresco!"

Let me continue expounding and rhapsodizing, for I am closer to Shakespeare than to the Greek. Whereas in Sophocles' drama the unity of a single action is dominant, Shakespeare aims at the entirety of an event, an occurrence. Whereas Sophocles makes a single tone predominate in his characters, Shakespeare uses all the characters, estates, walks of life he requires to produce the concerted sound of his drama. Whereas in Sophocles a single ethereal diction sings as it were in the Empyrean, Shakespeare speaks to the language of all ages, of all sorts and conditions of men; he is the interpreter of Nature in all her tongues—and such different ways can they both be the familiars of the same Divinity? And if Sophocles taught and moved and educated the Greeks, Shakespeare taught and moved and educated northern men! When I read him, it seems to me as if theatre, actors, scenery all vanish! Single leaves from the book of events, providence, the world, blowing in the storm of history. Individual impressions of nations, classes, souls, all the most various and disparate machines, all the ignorant blind instruments—which is what we ourselves are in the hand of the creator of the world—which combine to form a whole theatrical image, a grand event whose totality only the poet can survey. Who can imagine a greater poet of mankind in the northern world, and a greater poet of his age?

Step then before his stage, as before an ocean of events, where wave thunders upon wave. Scenes from nature come and go before our eyes; however disparate they seem, they are dynamically related; they create and destroy one another so that the intention of their creator, who seems to have put them together according to a crazy and disorderly plan, may be fulfilled—dark little symbols that form the silhouette of a divine theodicy. Lear, the rash, hotheaded old man, noble in his weakness as he stands before his map giving away crowns and tearing countries apart—the very first scene already bears within its seed and harvest of his fate in the dark future. Behold, soon we shall see the generous spendthrift, the hasty tyrant, the childish father even in his daughters' antechambers, pleasing, praying, begging, cursing, raving, blessing—o Heavens, and presaging madness! Then he will soon go bare-headed in the thunder and lightning, cast down to the lowest of the low, in the company of a fool, in a carry beggar's cave, almost calling down madness from above. And now see him as he is, in all the light-yoked majesty of the poor abandoned wretch; and now restored to himself, illumined by the last rays of hope only for them to be extinguished for ever! Imprisoned, dead in his arms the child and daughter who had comforted and forgiven him; dying over her body; and his faithful servant dying after the old king! O God, what vicissitudes of times, circumstances, tempests, climes, and ages! And all of it not merely a single story, a heroic political action, if you will, moving from a single beginning to a single end according to Aristotle's strictest rule[17]; but draw nearer and feel too the human spirit which integrated every person and age and character, down to the smallest secondary thing, into the picture. Two old fathers and all their very different children. The son of the one, grateful in his misfortune towards his deceived father; the other hideously ungrateful towards his affectionate father, even in his abominable good fortune. One father against his daughter, his daughters against him, their husbands, suitors, and all their accomplices in fortune and misfortune! Blind Gloucester supported by his unrecognized son, and mad Lear at the feet of his rejected daughter! And now the moment at the cross-roads of fortune, when Gloucester dies beneath his tree, and the trumpet calls, all the incidental circumstances, motives, character, and situations concentrated into the poetic work, all in a world of fiction, all developing into a whole, a whole made up of fathers, children, kings and fools, even in the most disparate scenes, in which places, times, circumstances, even, I would say, the pagan philosophy of fate and the stars which reigns throughout, all belong so essentially to the whole that I could change nothing, move nothing, nor transfer parts from other plays, or to other plays. And that is not a drama? Shakespeare is not a dramatic poet? The poet who embraces a hundred scenes of a world event in his arms, composes them with his glance, breaths into them an all-animating soul, and enraptures us, our attention, our heart, all our passions, our entire soul from beginning to end—if not more, then let father Aristotle be witness: "the scale of the living creature must allow it to be comprehended with *one* glance"[18]—and here—great Heavens! How Shakespeare feels the whole course of events in the depths of his soul and draws then to a close! A world of dramatic history, as great and as profound as Nature; but it is the creator who gives us the eye and perspective to see its greatness and profundity. √

In *Othello*, the Moor, what a world! What a whole! The living history of how the passion of this noble, unhappy man emerges, develops, erupts, and comes to its sad end. And what richness and complexity in the mechanism that goes to make *one* drama! How this Iago, this devil in human form, has to view the world in a certain way and treat everyone around him as his playthings; and how the other figures, Cassio and Rodrigo, Othello and Desdemona, with their susceptibilities as tinder to his diabolical flame, have to be grouped around him; how all are caught in his net and exploited by him, and everything hastens to this sad conclusion. As if an angel of providence were to weigh them against one another, and compose groups of souls and characters, and endow them with occasions to act in the illusion of free will, while he led them by this illusion, as if by the chain of fate, towards his controlling idea—this is how the human mind which conceived this devised, pondered, planned, and guided its course.

It should not be necessary to point out that time and place are as essential to the action as husk is to kernel, and yet they are what provoke the loudest outcry. If Shakespeare discovered the godlike art of conceiving so entire a world of the most disparate scenes as one great event, then of course it was part of the truth of his events also to idealise time and place for each scene in such a way that they too contributed to the illusion. Is there anyone in the world who is indifferent to the time and place of even trivial events in his life? And are they not particularly important in matters where the entire soul is moved, forms, and transformed? In our youth, in scenes of passion, in all the decisive actions of our lives! Is it not place and time and the fullness of external circumstances which endow the whole story with its direction, duration, and existence? And can one remove from a child, a youth, a lover, a man in the field of action, a single localizing circumstance, a single how? where? or when?, without prejudicing our whole grasp of his personality? In this respect, Shakespeare is the greatest master, simply because he is only and always the servant of Nature. When he created the events in his dramas and pondered them in his mind, he pondered times and places too. From out of all the scenes and conjunctures in the world, Shakespeare chose, as though by some law of fatality, just those which are the most powerful, the most appropriate to the feeling of the action; in which the strangest, boldest circumstances best support the illusion of truth; in which the changes of time and place over which the poet rules, proclaim most loudly: "This is not a poet, but a creator! Here is the history of the world!"

For example, when the poet was turning over in his mind as a fact of creation the terrible regicide, the tragedy called *Macbeth*—if then, dear reader, you were too timid to enter into the feeling of place and setting in any scene, then alas for Shakespeare, and for the withered page in your hand! For you will have felt nothing of its opening, with the witches on the blasted heath, nothing of the change of scene with the bloody man bringing the news of Macbeth's deeds, nothing of the king's tidings to him; you will have felt nothing of the change of scene when Macbeth is ready to listen to the witches' prophetic spirit and identifies their greeting with Duncan's previous message. You will not have seen his wife walking the castle with that fateful letter, nor how she will walk there so terribly transformed. Nor finally will you have enjoyed with the gentle king the sweet evening air where fearlessly the martlet breeds and haunts, while you, King Duncan—this lies in the workings of the invisible—are drawing near your murderous grave. The house in a bustle, making ready for guests, and Macbeth making ready for murder! Banquo's preparatory scene at night with torches and sword! The dagger, the terrible dagger in the vision! The bell—the deed has scarcely been done when there comes that knocking on places and you will find that the intention behind this creation could not have been realized other than there and in this way. The scene of Banquo's murder in the forest, the nocturnal banquet and Banquo's ghost—then again on the witches' heath (for his terrible and fateful deed is done!). Then the witches' cavern, spells, prophecies, rage, despair! The death of Macduff's children, with only their mother to shelter them, beneath the tree, and then the frightful queen sleep-walking in the castle, and the marvelous fulfillment of the prophecy—Birnam Wood drawing near—Macbeth's death at the sword of not of woman born—I would have to enumerate all the scenes, all of them, to give a local habitation to the ineffable whole, a whole of magic and regicide and destiny which is the soul of the play and breaths life into it right down to the smallest detail of time, place, and apparently wayward interlude. I would have to enumerate them so that I could summon it all before the soul as a terrible, indissoluble whole—and yet withal I would say nothing.

The individual quality of each drama, of each separate universe, pulses through place and time and composition in all the plays. Lessing compared certain aspects of *Hamlet* with that theatrical queen Semiramis.[19] How the spirit of the place fills the entire drama from beginning to end! The castle platform and the bitter cold—the watch relieved, tales told in the night, disbelief and credulity, the star, and then it appears! Is there anyone who does not sense art and nature in every word and detail! And so it proceeds. All ghostly and human guises exhausted! The cock crows and the drum rolls, the silent beckoning and the nearby hill. Speech and silence—what a setting! What a profound revelation of the truth! See how the frightened king kneels, and Hamlet strays past his father's picture in his mother's chamber! And not the other scene! Hamlet at Ophelia's grave! The touching good fellow in all his dealings with Horatio, Ophelia, Laertes, Fortinbras! The young man's playing with action, which runs through the play and almost until the end never becomes action—if for one moment you feel and look for the boards of a stage and a series of decorous versified speeches upon them, neither Shakespeare nor Sophocles nor any true poet in the world has written for you.

Oh, if only I had the words for the one main feeling prevailing in each drama, pulsing through it like a world soul. As it does in *Othello*, belonging as an essential part to the drama, as in his searching for Desdemona at night, as in their fabulous love, the sea-crossing, the tempest, as in Othello's raging passion, in Desdemona's manner of death, which has been so much derided, singing her willow-song as she undresses, while the wind knocks; as in the nature of the sin and passion itself, his entrance, his address to the candle—if only it were possible to comprehend all this in words, to express how it belongs deeply and organically to one world, one great tragic event—but it is not possible. Words cannot describe or reproduce the merest most miserable painting, so how can they render the feeling of a living world in all the scenes, circumstances, and enchantments of Nature? Peruse what you will, gentle reader, *Lear* or the *Henries*, *Caesar* or the two *Richards*, even the magical plays and the interludes; *Romeo* in particular, the sweet drama of love, a romance indeed in every detail of time and place and dream and poetry—attempt to remove something of its quality, to change it, even to simplify it for the French stage—a living world in all the authenticity of its truth transformed into this wooden nullity—a fine metamorphosis! Deprive this plant of its soil, juices, and vigor, and plant it in the air, deprive this human being of place, time, individuality—you have robbed them of breath and soul, and you have a mere image of the living creature.

For Shakespeare is Sophocles' brother, precisely where he seems to be so dissimilar, and inwardly he is wholly like him. His whole dramatic illusion is attained by means of this authenticity, truth, and historical creativity. Without it, not merely would illusion be left unachieved, but nothing of Shakespeare's drama and dramatic spirit would remain—or else I have written in vain. Hence the entire world is but the body to this great spirit. All the scenes of Nature are the limbs of this body, even as all the characters and styles of thought are the features of this spirit—and the whole might well bear the name of Spinoza's giant god: *Pan! Universum!*[20] Sophocles was true to Nature when he treated of *one* action in *one* place and at *one* time. Shakespeare could only be true to Nature when he rolled his great world events and human destinies through all the places and times—where they took place. And woe betide the frivolous Frenchman who arrives in time for Shakespeare's fifth act, expecting it will provide him with the quintessence of the play's touching sentiment. This may be true of many. French plays, where everything is versified and paraded in scenes only for immediate theatrical effect. But here, he would go home empty-handed. For the great world-event would already be over. He would witness but its last and least important consequences, men falling like flies. He would leave the theatre and scoff: Shakespeare is an affront to him, and his drama the merest foolishness.

The whole tangled question of time and place would long ago have been unraveled if some philosophical mind had only taken the trouble to ask what time and place really mean in drama.[21] If the place is the stage and the length of time that of a *divertissement au théâtre*, then the only people in the world to have observed the unity of place and the measure of time and scenes are—the French. The Greeks, with a degree of illusion higher than we can conceive, whose stage was a public institution and whose theatre was a temple of worship, never gave the unities a thought. What kind of illusion is experienced by a spectator who looks at his watch at the end of every scene to check whether such an action could take place in such a span of time, and whose chief delight it is that the poet has not cheated him out of a second, but has showed him on the stage only what would take at the same length of time in the snail's pace of his own life? What kind of creature could find this his greatest pleasure? And what kind of poet would regard this as his chiefest end, and pride himself on this nonsense of rules? "How much pretty performance I have crammed so neatly into the narrow space of this pit made of boards, called *le théatre francais*; how elegantly I have fitted it all into the prescribed length of time of a polite visit! How I have sewed and stitched, polished and patched!"—miserable master of ceremonies, a theatrical posturer, not a creator, poet, god, of the drama! The clock does not strike on tower or temple for you if you are a true dramatic poet, for you create your own space and time; and if you are capable of creating a world which can only exist in the categories of time and space, behold, your measure of space and duration is there within you, and you must conjure all your spectators to accept it, and urge it upon them—or else you are, as I have said, anything but a true dramatic poet.

Is there anyone in the world who needs to have it demonstrated that space and time are in themselves nothing, that in respect of being, action, passion, sequence of thought, and degree of attention within and without the soul, they are utterly relative? Has there never been any occasion in your life, good time-keeper of the drama, when hours turned into days and the watches of the night into years? Have you never known situations in your life when your soul dwelt sometimes outside you? Here, in your beloved's romantic chamber? There gazing upon that frozen corpse? again, in the oppression of external shame and distress—or occasions when your soul fled far beyond world and time, overleaping the places and regions of the earth, unmindful of itself, to inhabit heaven, or the soul, the heart of the one whose being you feel so deeply? And if something of this kind is possible in your slow and sluggish, vermiculate and vegetable life, where there are roots enough to hold you fast to the dead ground, and each slow length you drag along in measure enough for your snail's pace, then imagine yourself for just one moment into another, poetic world, transpose yourself into a dream. Have you never perceived how in dreams space and time vanish? What insignificant things they are, what shadows they must be in comparison with action, with the working of the soul? Have you never observed how the soul creates its own space, world, and tempo as and where it will? And if you had experienced that only once in your life, and wakened after a mere quarter of an hour, the dark remnants of your actions in the dream would cause you to swear that you had slept and dreamed and acted whole nights away, and Mahomet's dream would not for one moment seem absurd to you.[22] And is it not the first and sole duty of every genius, of every poet, above all of the dramatic poet, to carry you off into such a dream? And now think what worlds you would be throwing into disarray if you were to show the poet your pocket-watch or your drawing-room, and ask him to teach you to dream according to their prescriptions!

The poet's space and time lie in the movement of his great event, in the *ordine successivorum et simultaneorum*[23] of *his* world. How and where does he transport you? As long as he sees to it that you are transported, you are in his world. However quickly or slowly he causes the course of time to pass, it is he who makes it pass; it is he who impresses its sequence upon you: that is his measure of time. And what a master Shakespeare is in this respect too! His grand events begin slowly and ponderously in his nature, as they do in Nature itself, for it is this which he renders, but on a smaller scale. How laborious his presentation, before the springs of actions are set in motion! But once they are, how the scenes race by, how fleeting the speeches, how winged the souls, the passion, the action, and how powerful then the hastening movement, the pell-mell interjection of single words when time has run out for everyone. And finally, when the reader is entirely caught up in the illusion he has created, and is lost in the dark abyss of his world and his passion, how bold he becomes, what trains of events he commands! Lear dies after Cordelia! And Kent after Lear! It is virtually the end of his world; the Last Judgement is upon us, when everything, the Heavens included, lurches and collapses, and the mountains fall! The measure of time is no more. Not for our merry clock-watcher, of course, who turns up unscathed for the fifth act to measure by his time-piece how many died and how long it took. But Great Heavens, if that is supposed to be criticism, theatre, illusion—so much the worse for criticism, theatre, illusion! What do all these empty words mean?

At this point the heart of my inquiry might begin: what art, what creator's skills did Shakespeare employ to turn some base romance or tale or fabulous history into such a living poetic whole? What laws of historical, philosophical, or dramatic art are revealed in all his doings, in all the secrets of his craft? What an inquiry! How much it could contribute to our reading his philosophy of the human soul, our drama! But I am not a member of all our academies of history and philosophy and the fine arts, where in any case they turn their minds to anything but such a question. Even Shakespeare's own countrymen do not consider it. What historical errors his commentators have so often castigated him for, what beautiful historical passages have been faulted—for example in that bulky edition by Warburton![24] And has it occurred to the author of the most recent essay on him[25] to raise my fundamental question: "how did Shakespeare turn tales and romances into poetic drama?"? Hardly. Just as it scarcely occurred to the Aristotle of this British Sophocles, Lord Home.[26]

So just a nod in the direction of the usual classifications of his plays. Not long ago a writer who certainly had a deep feeling for his Shakespeare had the bright idea of making that fishmonger of a courtier with his grey beard and wrinkled face, his eyes purging thick amber and his plentiful lack of wit together with weak hams, of making the childish Polonius, I say, into his Aristotle, and suggesting that the string of . . . als and . . . cals he splutters out should be taken seriously as the basis of classification for all of Shakespeare's plays. I doubt it.[27] True, it is Shakespeare's mischievous habit to put into the mouths of children and fools all those empty commonplaces, moral sentiments, and classifications which, when applied to a hundred instances, are appropriate to all and to none. And a new Stobaeus or *Florilegium* or *cornucopia* of Shakespeare's wisdom, such as the English already possess and we Germans, praise be, are supposed to have had of late,[28] would give the greatest pleasure precisely to figures like Polonius and Lancelot, the fools and harlequins, poor Dickon and bombastic king of knights,[29] because all the sane and sensible human beings in Shakespeare do not have any more to say than the moment requires. But even here I still have my doubts. It is probable that in this passage Polonius is intended to be just a great baby who takes clouds to be camels and camels to be bass-viols and in his youth once enacted Julius Caesar and was accounted a good actor and was killed by Brutus and knows very well

Why Day is Day, Night Night and Time is Time[30]

—spinning a top of theatrical words here too. But who would want to build a theory upon that? And what virtue lies in the distinctions Tragedy, Comedy, History, Pastoral, Tragical-Historical or Historical-Pastoral, Pastoral-Comical or Comical-Historical-Pastoral? And were we to shuffle those . . . cals a hundred times, what insight would we have in the end? Not one single play would be a Greek tragedy, Comedy or Pastoral, nor should it be. Every play is History in the widest sense, which of course from time to time shades off in varying degrees into tragedy, comedy, etc., but the colors are so infinitely nuanced that in the last resort each play remains and cannot but remain—what it is: History! The heroic drama of the nation's destiny conjuring the illusion of the Middle Ages or (with the exception of a few plays which are really entertainments and interludes) a great and entire enactment of a world event, of a human destiny.

Sadder and more important is the thought that even this great creator of history and the world soul grows older himself, that the words and customs and categories of the age fall into the sere and yellow leaf, and that we ourselves are already so remote from these great rules of the days of chivalry that even Garrick,[31] who has revived Shakespeare and been the guardian angel of his grave, has had to change, cut, and mutilate his works so much. And soon perhaps, as everything gets blurred and tends in different directions, even his drama will become incapable of living performance, and will become the fragment of a Colossus, an Egyptian pyramid which everyone gazes at in amazement and no one understands. Happy am I that, though time is running out, I still live at a time when it is possible for me to understand him; and when you, my friend,[32] who feel and recognize yourself in reading his dramas, and whom

I have embraced more than once before his sacred image, can still dream the sweet dream worthy of your powers, that one day you will raise a monument to him here in our degenerate country, drawn from our age of chivalry and written in our language. I envy you that dream. May your noble German powers not flag until the garland hangs aloft. And should you too in later times perceive how the ground shakes beneath your feet, and the rabble round about stand still and gape or jeer, and the everlasting pyramids cannot re-awaken the spirit of ancient Egypt—your work will stand. And a faithful successor will seek out your grave and write with pious hand the words that have summed up the lives of almost all the worthies in the world:

Voluit! quiescit! [33]

2   From *Wilhelm Meister's Apprenticeship*

. . . "You all know Shakespeare's incomparable Hamlet: our public reading of it at the Castle yielded every one of us the greatest satisfaction. On that occasion, we proposed to act the piece; and I, not knowing what I undertook, engaged to play the Prince's part. This I conceived that I was studying, while I began to get by heart the strongest passages, the soliloquies, and those scenes in which force of soul, vehemence and elevation of feeling have the freest scope; where the agitated heart is allowed to display itself with touching expressiveness.

"I farther conceived that I was penetrating quite into the spirit of the character, while I endeavoured as it were to take upon myself the load of deep melancholy under which my prototype was labouring, and in this humour to pursue him through the strange labyrinths of his caprices and his singularities. Thus learning, thus practising, I doubted not but I should by and by become one person with my hero.

"But the farther I advanced, the more difficult did it become for me to form any image of the whole, in its general bearings; till at last it seemed as if impossible. I next went through the entire piece, without interruption; but here too I found much that I could not away with. At one time the characters, at another time the manner of displaying them, seemed inconsistent; and I almost despaired of finding any general tint, in which I might present my whole part with all its shadings and variations. In such devious paths I toiled, and wandered long in vain; till at length a hope arose that I might reach my aim in quite a new way.

"I set about investigating every trace of Hamlet's character, as it had shown itself before his father's death: I endeavoured to distinguish what in it was independent of this mournful event; independent of the terrible events that followed; and what most probably the young man would have been, had no such thing occurred.

"Soft, and from a noble stem, this royal flower had sprung up under the immediate influences of majesty: the idea of moral rectitude with that of princely elevation, the feeling of the good and dignified with the consciousness of high birth, had in him been unfolded simultaneously. He was a prince, by birth a prince; and he wished to reign, only that good men might be good without obstruction. Pleasing in form, polished by nature, courteous from the heart, he was meant to be the pattern of youth and the joy of the world.

"Without any prominent passion, his love for Ophelia was a still presentiment of sweet wants. His zeal in knightly accomplishments was not entirely his own; it needed to be quickened and inflamed by praise bestowed on others for excelling in them. Pure in sentiment, he knew the honourable-minded, and could prize the rest which an upright spirit tastes on the bosom of a friend. To a certain degree, he had learned to discern and value the good and the beautiful in arts and sciences; the mean, the vulgar was offensive to him; and if hatred could take root in his tender soul, it was only so far as to make him properly despise the false and changeful insects of a court, and play with them in easy scorn. He was calm in his temper, artless in his conduct; neither pleased with idleness, nor too violently eager for employment. The routine of a university he seemed to continue when at court. He possessed more mirth of humour than of heart; he was a good companion, pliant, courteous, discreet, and able to forget and forgive injury; yet never able to unite himself with those who overstept the limits of the right, the good, and the becoming . . ."

. . . Loving Shakespeare as our friend did, he failed not to lead round the conversation to the merits of that dramatist. Expressing, as he entertained, the liveliest hopes of the new epoch which these exquisite productions must form in Germany he ere long introduced his Hamlet, who had busied him so much of late.

Serlo declared that he would long ago have played the piece, had this been possible, and that he himself would willingly engage to act Polonius. He added, with a smile: "An Ophelia, too, will certainly turn up, if we had but a Prince."

Wilhelm did not notice that Aurelia seemed a little hurt at her brother's sarcasm. Our friend was in his proper vein, becoming copious and didactic, expounding how he would have Hamlet played. He circumstantially delivered to his hearers the opinions we before saw him busied with; taking all the trouble possible to make his notion of the matter acceptable, sceptical as Serlo showed himself regarding it.

"Well, then," said the latter, finally, "suppose we grant you all this, what will you explain by it?"

"Much, everything," said Wilhelm. "Conceive a prince such as I have painted him, and that his father suddenly dies. Ambition and the love of rule are not the passions that inspire him. As a king's son he would have been contented; but now he is first constrained to consider the difference which separates a sovereign from a subject. The crown was not hereditary; yet a longer possession of it by his father would have strengthened the pretensions of an only son, and secured his hopes of the succession. In place of this, he now beholds himself excluded by his uncle, in spite of specious promises, most probably forever. He is now poor in goods and favour, and a stranger in the scene which from youth he had looked upon as his inheritance. His temper here assumes its first mournful tinge. He feels that now he is not more, that he is less, than a private nobleman; he offers himself as the servant of every one; he is not courteous and condescending, he is needy and degraded.

"His past condition he remembers as a vanished dream. It is in vain that his uncle strives to cheer him, to present his situation in another point of view. The feeling of his nothingness will not leave him.

"The second stroke that came upon him wounded deeper, bowed still more. It was the marriage of his mother. The faithful tender son had yet a mother, when his father passed away. He hoped, in the company of his surviving noble-minded parent, to reverence the heroic form of the departed; but his mother too he loses, and it is something worse than death that robs him of her. The trustful image, which a good child loves to form of its parents, is gone. With the dead there is no help; on the living no hold. She also is a woman, and her name is Frailty, like that of all her sex.

"Now first does he feel himself completely bent and orphaned; and no happiness of life can repay what he has lost. Not reflective or sorrowful by nature, reflection and sorrow have become for him a heavy obligation. It is thus that we see him first enter on the scene. I do not think that I have mixed aught foreign with the piece, or overcharged a single feature of it."

Serlo looked at his sister, and said, "Did I give thee a false picture of our friend? He begins well; he has still many things to tell us, many to persuade us of." Wilhelm asseverated loudly, that he meant not to persuade, but to convince; he begged for another moment's patience.

"Figure to yourselves this youth," cried he, "this son of princes: conceive him vividly, bring his state before your eyes, and then observe him when he learns that his father's spirit walks; stand by him in the terrors of the night, when the venerable ghost itself appears before him. A horrid shudder passes over him; he

Johann Wolfgang von Goethe

speaks to the mysterious form; he sees it beckon him; he follows it, and hears. The fearful accusation of his uncle rings in his ears; the summons to revenge, and the piercing repeated prayer, Remember me!

"And when the ghost has vanished, who is it that stands before us? A young hero panting for vengeance? A prince by birth, rejoicing to be called to punish the usurper of his crown? No! trouble and astonishment take hold of his solitary young man; he grows bitter against smiling villains, swears that he will not forget the spirit, and concludes with the significant ejaculation:

> The time is out of joint: O cursed spite,
> That ever I was born to set it right! (*Ihave tochanged* ?)

"In these words, I imagine, will be found the key to Hamlet's whole procedure. To me it is clear that Shakespeare meant, in the present case, to represent the effects of a great action laid upon a soul unfit for the performance of it. In this view the whole piece seems to me to be composed. There is an oak-tree planted in a costly jar, which should have borne only pleasant flowers in its bosom; the roots expand, the jar is shivered.

"A lovely, pure, noble and most moral nature, without the strength of nerve which forms a hero, sinks beneath a burden which it cannot bear and must not cast away. All duties are holy for him; the present is too hard. Impossibilities have been required of him; not in themselves impossibilities, but such for him. He winds, and turns, and torments himself; he advances and recoils; at ever put in mind, ever puts himself in mind; at last does all but lose his purpose from his thoughts; yet still without recovering his peace of mind . . ."

. . . One evening a dispute arose among our friends about the novel and the drama, and which of them deserved the preference. Serlo said it was a fruitless and misunderstood debate; both might be superior in their kinds, only each must keep within the limits proper to it.

"About their limits and their kinds," said Wilhelm, "I confess myself not altogether clear."

"Who *is* so?" said the other; "and yet perhaps it were worth while to come a little closer to the business."

They conversed together long upon the matter; and in fine, the following was nearly the result of their discussion:

"In the novel as well as in the drama, it is human nature and human action that we see. The difference between these sorts of fiction lies not merely in their outward form; not merely in the circumstance that the personages of the one

42

are made to speak, while those of the other have commonly their history narrated. Unfortunately many dramas are but novels, which proceed by dialogue; and it would not be impossible to write a drama in the shape of letters.

"But in the novel, it is chiefly *sentiments* and *events* that are exhibited; in the drama, it is characters and deeds. The novel must go slowly forward; and the sentiments of the hero, by some means or another, must restrain the tendency of the whole to unfold itself and to conclude. The drama on the other hand, must hasten, and the character of the hero must press forward to the end; it does not restrain, but is restrained. The novel-hero must be suffering, at least he must not in a high degree be active; in the dramatic one, we look for activity and deeds. Grandison, Clarissa, Pamela, the Vicar of Wakefield, Tom Jones himself, are, if not suffering, at least retarding personages; and the incidents are all in some sort modelled by their sentiments. In the drama the hero models nothing by himself; all things withstand him, and he clears and casts away the hindrances from off his path, or else sinks under them."

Our friends were also of opinion, that in the novel some degree of scope may be allowed to Chance; but that it must always be led and guided by the sentiments of the personages; on the other hand, that Fate, which, by means of outward unconnected circumstances, carries forward men, without their own concurrence, to an unforeseen catastrophe, can have place only in the drama; that Chance may produce pathetic situations, but never tragic ones; Fate, on the other hand, ought always to be terrible; and is in the highest sense tragic, when it brings into a ruinous concatenation the guilty man, and the guiltless that was unconcerned with him.

These considerations led them back to the play of Hamlet, and the peculiarities of its composition. The hero in this case, it was observed, is endowed more properly with sentiments than with a character; it is events alone that push him on; and accordingly the piece has in some measure the expansion of a novel. But as it is Fate that draws the plan; as the story issues from a deed of terror, and the hero is continually driven forward to a deed of terror, the work is tragic in the highest sense, and admits of no other than a tragic end.

3 · From "The Spirit of Christianity and Its Fate"

With Abraham, the true progenitor of the Jews, the history of this people begins, i.e., his spirit is the unity, the soul, regulating the entire fate of his posterity. This spirit appears in a different guise after every one of its battles against
different forces or after becoming sullied by adopting an alien nature as a result
of succumbing to might or seduction. Thus it appears in a different form either
as arms and conflict or else as submission to the fetters of the stronger; this latter form is called "fate."

Of the course taken by the development of the human race before Abraham,
of this important period in which men strove by various routes to revert from
barbarism, which followed the loss of the state of nature, to the unity which
had been broken, of this course only a few dim traces have been preserved to
us. The impression made on men's hearts by the flood in the time of Noah
must have been a deep distraction and it must have caused the most prodi-
gious disbelief in nature. Formerly friendly or tranquil, nature now abandoned
the equipoise of her elements, now requited the faith the human race had in
her with the most destructive, invincible, irresistible hostility; in her fury she
spared nothing; she made none of the distinctions which love might have made
but poured savage devastation over everything.

Certain phenomena, reactions to the impression derived from this general
manslaughter by hostile elements, have been indicated to us by history. If man
was to hold out against the outbursts of a nature now hostile, nature had to be
mastered; and since the whole can be divided only into idea and reality, so also
the supreme unity of mastery lies either in something thought or in something
real. It was in a thought-product that Noah built the distracted world together
again; his thought-produced ideal he turned into a [real] Being[1] and then set
everything else over against it, so that in this opposition realities were reduced
to thoughts, i.e., to something mastered. This Being promised him to confine

within their limits the elements which were his servants, so that no flood was ever again to destroy mankind. Among living things, things capable of being mastered in this way,[2] men were subjected to the law, to the command so to restrain themselves as not to kill one another; to overstep these restraints was to fall under the power of this Being and so to become lifeless. For being mastered in this way man was recompensed by being given mastery over animals; but while this single rendering of life—the killing of plants and animals—was sanctioned and while enmities [between man and nature] which need made inevitable were turned into a legal mastery, life was yet so far respected that men were prohibited from eating the blood of animals because in it lay the life, the soul, of the animals (Gen. ix:4).[3]

Per contra (if I may be allowed here to link with the Mosaic chronicles the corresponding exposition which Josephus—*Antiquities of the Jews* i.4—gives of Nimrod's history), Nimrod placed the unity in *man* and installed him as the being who was to make the other realties into thoughts, i.e., to kill and master them. He endeavored so far to master nature that it could no longer be dangerous to men. He put himself in a state of defense against it, "a rash man and one boasting in the strength of his arm. In the event of God's having a mind to overwhelm the world with a flood again, he threatened to neglect no means and no power to make an adequate resistance to Him. For he had resolved to build a tower which was to be far higher than the waves and streams could ever rise and in this way to avenge the downfall of his forefathers" (according to another tale, Eupolemus in Eusebius,[4] the tower was to have been built by the very survivors of the flood). "He persuaded men that they had acquired all good things for themselves by their own courage and strength; and in this way he altered everything and in a short time founded a despotic tyranny." He united men after they had become mistrustful, estranged from one another and ready to scatter. But the unity he gave them was not a reversion to a cheerful social life in which they trusted nature and one another; he kept them together indeed, but by force. He defended himself against water by walls; he was a hunter and a king. In this battle against need, therefore, the elements, animals, and men had to endure the law of the stronger, though the law of a living being.

Against the hostile power of [nature] Noah saved himself by subjecting both it and himself to something more powerful; Nimrod, by taming it himself. Both made a peace of *necessity* with the foe and thus perpetuated the hostility. Neither was reconciled with it, unlike a more beautiful[5] pair, Deucalion and Pyrrha, who, after the flood in their time, invited men once again to friendship with the world, to nature, made them forget their need and hostility in joy and pleasure, made a peace of *love*, were the progenitors of more beautiful peoples, and made their age the mother of a newborn natural life which maintained its bloom of youth.

Abraham born in Chaldaea, had in youth already left a fatherland in his father's company. Now, in the plains of Mesopotamia, he tore himself free altogether from his family as well, in order to be wholly self-subsistent, independent man, to be an overlord himself. He did this without having been injured or disowned, without the grief which after a wrong or an outrage signifies love's enduring need, when love, injured indeed but not lost, goes in quest of a new fatherland in order to flourish and enjoy itself there. The first act which made Abraham the progenitor of a nation is a disseverance which snaps the bonds of communal life and love. The entirety of the relationships in which he had hitherto lived with men and nature, these beautiful relationships of his youth (Josh. xxiv:2),[6] he spurned.

Cadmus, Danaus, etc., had forsaken their fatherland too, but they forsook it in battle; they went in question of a soil where they would be free and they sought it that they might love. Abraham wanted *not* to love, wanted to be free by not loving. Those others, in order to live in pure, beautiful, unions, as was no longer given to them in their own land, carried these gods forth with them. Abraham wanted to be free from these very relationships, while the others by their gentle arts and manners won over the less civilized aborigines and intermingled with them to form a happy and gregarious people.

The same spirit which had carried Abraham away from his kin led him through his encounters with foreign peoples during the rest of his life; this was the spirit of self-maintenance in strict opposition to everything—the product of his thought raised to be the unity dominant over the nature which he regarded as infinite and hostile (for the only relationship possible between hostile entities is mastery of one by the other). With his herds Abraham wandered hither and thither without bringing parts of it any nearer to him by cultivating and improving them. Had he done so, he would have become attached to them and might have adopted them as parts of *his* world. The land was simply given over to his cattle for grazing. The water slept in deep wells without living movement; digging for it was laborious; it was dearly bought or struggled for, an extorted property, a necessary requirement for him and his cattle. The groves which often gave him coolness and shade he soon left again; in them he had the theophanies, appearances of his perfect Object on High, but he did not tarry with them in the love which would have made them worthy of the Divinity and participant in Him. He was a stranger on earth, a stranger to the soil and to men alike . . .

. . . He shrank from relating himself to an equal on a footing of grateful feelings. Even his son he forbade to marry any Canaanitish woman but made him take a wife from his kinsfolk, and they lived at a great distance from him.

The whole world Abraham regarded as simply his opposite; if he did not take it to be a nullity, he looked on it as sustained by the God who was alien to it. Nothing in nature was supposed to have any part in God; everything was simply under God's mastery. Abraham, as the opposite of the whole world could have had no higher mode of being than that of the other term in the opposition, and thus he likewise was supported by God. Moreover, it was through God alone that Abraham came into a mediated relation with the world, the only kind of link with the world possible for him. His Ideal subjugated the world to him, gave him as much of the world as he needed, and put him in security against the rest. Love alone was beyond his power; even the one love he had, his love for his son, even his hope of posterity—the one mode of extending his being, the one mode of immortality he knew and hoped for—could depress him, trouble his all-exclusive heart and disquiet it to such an extent that even this love he once wished to destroy; and his heart was quieted only through the certainty of the feeling that this love was not so strong as to render him unable to slay his beloved son with his own hand.

Mastery was the only possible relationship in which Abraham could stand the infinite world opposed to him; but he was unable himself to make this mastery actual, and it therefore remained ceded to his Ideal . . .

. . . The great tragedy of the Jewish people is no Greek tragedy; it can rouse neither terror nor pity, for both of these arise only out of the fate which follows from the inevitable slip of a beautiful character; it can arouse horror alone. The fate of the Jewish people is the fate of Macbeth who stepped out of nature itself, clung to alien Beings, and so in their service had to trample and slay everything holy in human nature, had at last to be forsaken by his gods (since these were objects and he their slave) and be dashed to pieces on his faith itself.

. . . The command "Thou shalt not kill" [Matt. v:21–22] is a maxim which is recognized as valid for the will of every rational being and which can be valid as a principle of a universal legislation. Against such a command Jesus sets the

47

higher genius of reconcilability (a modification of love) which not only does not act counter to this law but makes it wholly superfluous; it has in itself a so much richer, more living, fullness that so poor a thing as a law is nothing for it at all. In reconcilability the law loses its form, the concept is displaced by life; but what reconcilability thereby loses in respect of the universality which grips all particulars together in the concept is only a seeming loss and a genuine infinite gain on account of the wealth of living relations with the individuals (perhaps few) with whom it comes into connection /.

... Over against the positivity of the Jews, Jesus set man; over against the laws and their obligatoriness he set the virtues, and in these the immortality of "positive" man is overcome ...

... Man confronts himself; his character and his deeds become the man himself. He has barriers only where he erects them himself, and his virtues are determinacies which he fixes himself. This possibility of making a clear-cut opposition [between virtue and vice] is freedom, is the "or" in "virtue or vice." In the opposition of law to nature, or the universal to the particular, both opposites are posited, are actual; the one is not unless the other is. In the moral freedom which consists in the opposition of virtue to vice, the attainment of one is the exclusion of the other; and, hence, if one is actual, the other is only possible.

The opposition of duty to inclination has found its unification in the modifications of love, i.e., in the virtues. Since law was opposed to love, not in its content but in its form, it could be taken up into love, though in this process it lost its shape. To a trespass, however, law is opposed in content; trespass precludes it, and yet it *is*. Trespass is a destruction of nature and since nature is one, there is as much destruction in what destroys as in what is destroyed. If what is one is opposed, then a unification of the opposites is available only in the concept [not in reality]. A law has been made; if the thing opposed to it has been destroyed, there still remains the concept, the law; but it then expresses only the deficiency, only a gap, because its content has in reality been annulled; and it is then called a penal law. This form of law (and the law's content) is the direct opposite of life because it signalizes the destruction of life. But it seems all the more difficult to think how the law and this form, as penal justice can be superseded. In the previous supersession of law by the virtues, it was only the form of law, not its content, which had vanished; here, however, the content would be superseded along with the form, since the content is punishment.

Punishment lies directly in the offended law. The trespasser has forfeited the same right which his trespass has injured in another. The trespasser has put himself outside the concept which is the content of the law. The law merely states that he must lose the rights comprised in the law; but, because the law is directly only a thought, it is only the concept of the trespasser which loses the right; and in order that this loss may be actualized, i.e., in order that the trespasser may really lose what his concept has lost, the law must be linked with life and clothed with might. Now if the law persists in its awful majesty, there is no escaping it, and there is no canceling the fact that the punishment of the trespass is deserved. The law cannot forgo the punishment, cannot be merciful, or it would cancel itself. The law has been broken by the trespasser; its content no longer exists for him; he has canceled it. But the form of the law, universality, pursues him and clings to his trespass; his deed becomes universal, and the right which he has canceled is also canceled for him. Thus, the law remains, and the punishment, his desert, remains. But the living being whose might has been united with the law, the executor who deprives the trespasser in reality of the right which he has lost in the concept, i.e., the judge, is not abstract justice, but a living being, and justice is only his special characteristic. Punishment is inevitably deserved; that is inescapable. But the execution of justice is not inevitable, because as a characteristic of a living being it may vanish and another characteristic may come on the scene instead. Justice thus becomes something contingent; there may be a contraction between it as universal, as thought, and it as real, i.e., in a living being. An avenger can forgive, can forgo his revenge, and a judge can give up acting as a judge, i.e., can pardon. But this does not satisfy justice, for justice is unbending; and, so long as laws are supreme, so long as there is no escape from them, so long must the individual be sacrificed to the universal, i.e., be put to death. For this reason, it is also contradictory to contemplate satisfying the law by punishing one man as a representative of many like criminals, since, in so far as the others are looked on as suffering punishment in him, he is their universal, their concept; and the law, as ordering or punishing, is only law by being opposed to a particular. The condition of the law's universality lies in the fact that either men in acting, or else their actions, are particulars; and the actions are particulars in so far as they are considered in their bearing on universality, on the laws, i.e., considered as conforming to them or contravening them. From this point of view, their relation to the law, their specific character, can suffer no alteration; they are realities, they are what they are; what has happened cannot be undone; punishment follows the deed, and that connection is indissoluble. If there is no way to make an action undone, if its reality is eternal, then no reconciliation is possible, not even through suffering punishment. To be sure, the law is satisfied when the trespasser is punished, since thus, the contradiction between its declared fiat and the reality of the trespasser is annulled, and along with it the exception which the trespasser wished to make to the universality of the law. Only the trespasser is not reconciled with the law, whether the law is in his eyes something alien, or whether it is present in him subjectively as a bad conscience. The alien power which the trespasser has created and armed against himself, this hostile being, ceases to work on him once it has punished him. When in its turn it has done to him just what he did himself, it then lets go but it still withdraws to a threatening attitude; it has not lost its shape or been made friendly. In the bad conscience (the consciousness of a bad action, of one's self as a bad man) punishment, once suffered, alters nothing. For the trespasser always sees himself as a trespasser; over his action as a reality he has no power, and this his reality is in contradiction with his consciousness of the law.

And yet the man cannot bear this disquiet[7]; from the terrifying reality of evil and the immutability of the law he can fly to grace alone. The oppression and grief of a bad conscience may drive him once more to a dishonesty, i.e., it may drive him to try running away from himself and therefore from the law and justice; he throws himself into the bosom of the administrator of abstract justice in order to experience his goodness, in the hope that he will close an eye and look on him as other than he is. It is not that he denies his transgression, but he has the dishonest wish that his transgression may be denied by goodness itself, and he finds consolation in the thought, in the untrue idea, which another being may frame of him. Thus, at this level no return is possible to unity of consciousness by a pure route; except in dishonest entreaty there can be no cancellation of punishment, of the threatening law and the bad conscience. There can be no other cancellation so long as punishment has to be regarded solely as something absolute, so long as it is unconditional, or so long as it has no aspect from which both it and what conditions it can be seen to be subordinate to a higher sphere. Law and punishment cannot be reconciled, but they can be transcended if fate can be reconciled.

Punishment is the effect of a transgressed law from which the trespasser has torn himself free but on which he still depends; he cannot escape from the law or from punishment or from what he has done. Since the characteristic of the law is universality, the trespasser has ~~smashed the matter of the law, but~~ its form ~~universality~~ remains. The law, whose master he believed he had become, remains, but in its content it now appears in opposition to him because it has the shape of the deed which contradicts what previously was the law, while the content of the deed now has the shape of universality and is law.

This perversion of the law, the fact that it becomes the contrary of what it was before, is punishment. Because the man has cut himself loose from the law, he still remains in subjection to it. And since the law, as a universal, remains, so too does the deed, since it is the particular. ✓

Punishment represented as fate is of a quite different kind. In fate, punishment is a hostile power, an individual thing, in which universal and particular are united in the sense that in it there is cleavage and command and its execution; there is such a cleavage, however, when law is in question, because the law is only a rule, something thought, and needs an opposite, a reality, from which it acquires its force. In the hostile power of fate, universal is not severed from particular in the way in which the law, as a universal, is opposed to man or his inclinations as the particular. Fate is just the enemy, and man stands over against it as a power fighting against it. Law, on the contrary, as universal, is lord of the particular and has subdued this man to obedience. The trespass of the man regarded as in the toils of fate is therefore not a rebellion of the subject against his ruler, the slave's flight from his master, liberation from subservience, not a revivification out of a dead situation, for the man is alive, and before he acts there is no cleavage, no opposition, much less a mastery. Only through a departure from that united life which is neither regulated by law nor at variance with law, only through the killing of life, is something alien produced. Destruction of life is not the nullification of life, but its diremption, and the destruction consists in its transformation into an enemy. It is immortal, and, if slain, it appears as its terrifying ghost which vindicates every branch of life and lets loose its Eumenides. The illusion of trespass, its belief that it destroys the other's life and thinks itself enlarged thereby, is dissipated by the fact that the disembodied spirit of the injured life comes on the scene against the trespass, just as Banquo who came as a friend to Macbeth was not blotted out when he was murdered but immediately thereafter took his seat, not as a guest at the feast, but as an evil spirit. The trespasser intended to have to do with another's life, but he has only destroyed his own, for life is not different from life, since life dwells in the single Godhead. In his arrogance he has destroyed indeed, but only the friendliness of life; he has perverted life into an enemy. It is the deed

G. W. F. Hegel

itself which has created a law whose domination now comes on the scene; this law is the unification, in the concept, of the equality between the injured, apparently alien, life and the trespasser's own forfeited life. It is now for the first time that the injured life appears as a hostile power against the trespasser and maltreats him as he has maltreated the other. Hence, punishment as fate is the equal reaction of the trespasser's own deed, of a power which he himself has armed, of an enemy made an enemy by himself.

A reconciliation with fate seems still more difficult to conceive than one with the penal law, since a reconciliation with fate seems to require a cancellation of annihilation. But fate, so far as reconcilability is concerned, has this advantage of the penal law, that it occurs within the orbit of life, while a crime falling under law and punishment occurs on the contrary in the orbit of insurmountable oppositions and absolutely real events. In the latter orbit it is inconceivable that there should be any possibility of canceling punishment or banishing the consciousness of being really evil, because the law is a power to which life is subject, above which there is nothing, not even the Deity, since God is only the power which the highest thought has, is only the administrator of the law. A real event can only be forgotten, i.e., it can be conceived in idea and then can fade away in another weakness [in oblivion], though thereby its being would nonetheless still be posited as abiding. In the case of punishment as fate, however, the law is later than life and is outranked by it. There, the law is only the lack of life, defective life appearing as a power. And life can heal its wounds again; this severed hostile life can return into itself again and annul the bungling achievement of a trespass, can annul the law and punishment. When the trespasser feels the disruption of his own life (suffers punishment) or knows himself (in his bad conscience) as disrupted, then the working of his fate commences and this feeling of a life disrupted must become a longing for what has been lost. The deficiency is recognized as part of himself, as what was to have been in him and is not. This lack is not a not-being but is life known and felt as not-being.

To have felt this fate as possible is to fear it; and this is a feeling quite different from the fear of punishment. The former is fear of a separation, an awe of *one's self*; fear of punishment is fear of something alien, for even if the law is known as one's own, still in the fear of punishment the punishment is something alien unless the fear is conceived as fear of being unworthy. In punishment, however, there is added to the feeling of unworthiness the reality of a misfortune. The loss of a wellbeing which one's concept [or essence] has lost

52

and which therefore one no longer deserves. Hence punishment presupposes an alien being who is lord of this reality [i.e., who inflicts the pain of punishment], and fear of punishment is fear of him. In fate, on the other hand, the hostile power is the power of life made hostile; hence, fear of fate is not the fear of an *alien* being. Moreover, punishment betters nothing, for it is only suffering, a feeling of impotence in face of a lord with whom the trespasser has and wants nothing in common. Its only effect is forwardness, obstinacy in opposition to an enemy by whom it would be a disgrace to be subdued, for that would be the man's self-surrender. In fate, however, the man recognizes his own life, and his supplication to it is not supplication to a lord but a reversion and an approach to himself.

The fate in which the man senses what he has lost creates a longing for the lost life. This longing, if we are to speak of bettering and being bettered, may in itself be called a bettering, because, since it is a sense of the loss of life it recognizes what has been lost as life, as what was once its friend, and this recognition is already itself an enjoyment of life. And the man animated by this longing may be conscientious in the sense that, in the contradiction between the consciousness of his guilt and the renewed sensing of life, he may still hold himself back from returning to the latter; he may prolong his bad conscience and feeling of grief and stimulate it every moment; and thus he avoids being frivolous with life, because he postpones reunion with it, postpones greeting it as a friend again, until his longing for reunion springs from the deepest recesses of his soul. In sacrifices and penances criminals have made afflictions for themselves; as pilgrims in hair shirts and walking every step barefoot in the hot sand, they have prolonged and multiplied their afflictions and their consciousness of being evil; what they have lost, this gap in their life, they have felt in their very bones, and yet in this experience, though they sense their life as something hostile, they yet sense it wholly as life; and this has made it possible to resume it again. Opposition is the possibility of reunification, and the extent to which in affliction life is felt as an opposite is also the extent of the possibility of resuming it again. It is in the fact that even the enemy is felt as life that there lies the possibility of reconciling fate. This reconciliation is thus neither the destruction or subjection of something alien, nor a contradiction between consciousness of one's self and the hoped-for difference in another's idea of one's self, nor a contradiction between desert in the eyes of the law and the actualization of the same, or between man as concept and man as reality. This sensing of life, a sensing which finds itself again, is love, and in love fate is reconciled. Thus considered, the trespasser's deed is no fragment; the action which issues from life, from the whole, also reveals the whole. But the trespass which is transgression of a law *is* only a fragment, since there is outside it from the start the law which does not belong to it. The trespass which issues from life reveals the whole, but as divided, and the hostile parts can coalesce again into the whole. Justice is satisfied, since the trespasser has sensed as injured in himself the same life that he has injured. The pricks of conscience have become blunt, since the deed's evil spirit has been chased away. There is no longer anything hostile in the man, and the deed remains at most as a soulless carcass lying in the charnel-house of actualities, in memories.

But fate has a more extended domain than punishment has. It is aroused even by guilt without crime, and hence it is implicitly stricter than punishment. Its strictness often seems to pass over into the most crying injustice when it makes its appearance, more terrible than ever, over against the most exalted form of guilt, the guilt of innocence.[8] I mean that, since laws are purely conceptual unifications of opposites, these concepts are far from exhausting the many-sidedness of life. Punishment exercises its domination only in so far as there is a consciousnesses of life at the point where a disunion has been reunified *conceptually*; but over the relations of life which have not been dissolved, over the sides of life which are given as *vitally* united. Over the domains of the virtues, it exercises no power. Fate, on the other hand, is incorruptible, and unbounded like life itself. It knows no given ties, no differences of standpoint or position, no precinct of virtue. Where life is injured, be it ever so rightly, i.e., even if no dissatisfaction is felt, there fate appears, and one may therefore say "never has innocence suffered; every suffering is guilt." But the honor of a pure soul is all the greater the more consciously it has done injury to life in order to maintain the supreme values, while a trespass is all the blacker the more consciously an impure soul has injured life.

A fate appears to arise only through another's deed; but this is only the occasion of the fate. What really produces it is the manner of receiving and reacting against the other's deed. If someone suffers an unjust attack, he can arm and defend himself and his right, or he may do the reverse. It is with his reaction, be it battle or submissive grief, that his guilt, his fate, begins. In neither case does he suffer punishment; but he suffers no wrong either. In battle he clings to his right and defends it. Even in submission he does not sacrifice his right; his grief is the contradiction between recognizing his right and lacking the force actually to hold onto it; he does not struggle for it, and his fate is his lack of will. If a man fights for what is in danger, he has not lost what he is struggling for; but by facing danger he has subjected himself to fate, for he enters on the battlefield of might against might and ventures to oppose his adversary. Courage, however, is greater than grieving submission, for even though it succumbs, it has first recognized this possibility [of failure] and so has consciously made itself responsible for it; grieving passively, on the contrary, clings to its loss and fails to oppose it with all its strength. Yet the suffering of courage is also a just fate, because the man of courage engages with the sphere of might and right. Hence the struggle for right, like passive suffering, is an unnatural situation in which there lies the contradiction between the concept of right and its actuality. For even in the struggle for right there is a contradiction; the right is something thought, a universal, while in the aggressor it is also a thought, though a different one; and hence there would here be two universals which would cancel each other out and yet they persist. Similarly, the combatants are opposed as real entities, different living beings; life is in conflict with life, which once again is a self-contradiction. By the self-defense of the injured party, the aggressor is likewise attacked and thereby is granted the right of self-defense; both are right, both are at war; and this gives both the right of self-defense. Thus, either they leave to power and strength the decision as to the side on which right lies, and then, since right and reality have nothing in common with one another, they confuse the two and make the former dependent on the latter; or else, they throw themselves on the mercy of a judge, i.e., their enmity leads them to surrender themselves unarmed and dead. They renounce their own mastery of actuality, they renounce might, and let something alien, a law on the judge's lips pass sentence on them. Hence, they submit to a treatment against which both parties had protested, for they had gainsaid the injury to their right, had set themselves against treatment by another.[9]

The truth of both opposites, courage and passivity, is so unified in beauty of soul that the life in the former remains though opposition falls away, while the loss of right in the latter remains, but the grief disappears. There thus arises a transcendence of right without suffering, a living free elevation above the loss of right and above struggle. The man who lets go what another approaches with hostility, who ceases to call his what the other assails, escapes grief for loss, escapes handling by the other or by the judge, escapes the necessity of engaging with the other. If any side of him is touched he withdraws himself therefrom and simply lets go into the other's hands a thing which in the moment of the attack he has alienated. To renounce his relationships[10] in this way is to abstract from himself, but this process has no fixed limits. (The more vital the relations are, out of which, once they are sullied, a noble nature must withdraw himself, since he could not remain in them without himself becoming contaminated, the greater of his misfortune. But this misfortune is neither just nor unjust; it only becomes his fate because his disdain of those relations is his own will, his free choice. Every grief which thus results to him is so far just and is now his unhappy fate, a fate which he himself has consciously wrought; and it is his distinction to suffer justly, because he is raised so above these rights that he *willed* to have them for enemies. Moreover, since this fate is rooted in himself, he can endure it, face it, because his griefs are not a pure passivity, the predominance of an alien being, but are produced by himself.) To save himself the man kills himself; to avoid seeing his own being in another's power; he no longer calls it his own, and so he annihilates himself in wishing to maintain himself, since anything in another's power would no longer be the man himself, and there is nothing in him which could not be attacked and sacrificed.[11]

Unhappiness may become so great that his fate, the self-destruction, drives him so far toward the reunification of life that he must withdraw into the void altogether. But, by himself setting an absolutely total fate against himself, the man has *eo ipso* lifted himself above fate entirely. Life has become untrue to him, not he to life. He has fled from life but done no injury to it. He may long for it as for an absent friend, but it cannot pursue him like an enemy. On no side is he vulnerable; like a sensitive plant he withdraws into himself when touched. Rather than make life his enemy, rather than rouse a fate against himself, he flies from life. Hence Jesus [Luke xiv:26] requires his friends to forsake father, mother, and everything in order to avoid entry into a league with the profane world and so into the sphere where a fate becomes possible. Again [Matt. v:40 and 29–30]: "If a man takes thy coat give him thy cloak also; if a member offend thee, cut it off."

4

"Dramatic Poetry,"
from *Aesthetics: Lectures on Fine Art*

Because drama has been developed into the most perfect totality of content and form, it must be regarded as the highest stage of poetry and of art generally. For in contrast to the other perceptible materials, stone, wood, colour, and notes, speech is alone the element worthy of the expression of spirit; and of the particular kinds of the art of speech dramatic poetry is the one which unites the objectivity of epic with the subjective character of lyric. It displays a complete action as actually taking place before our eyes; the action originates in the minds of the characters who bring it about, but at the same time its outcome is decided by the really substantive nature of the aims, individuals, and collisions involved. But this conciliation of epic with the inner life of the person who is acting in front of us does not permit drama to describe, as epic does, the *external* aspect of the locality and the environment, as well as of what happens and is done, and it therefore demands a complete scenic production in order to give real life to the whole work of art. Lastly, the action itself in the entirety of its mental and physical actuality is susceptible of two opposed modes of treatment, tragic and comic, and the predominant principle of these provides us with a distinction in kind as a third chief aspect of dramatic poetry . . .

Difference Between Ancient and Modern Dramatic Poetry

The same principle which gave us the basis for the division of dramatic art into tragedy and comedy provides us with the essential turning-points in the history of their development. For the lines of this development can only consist in setting out and elaborating the chief features implicit in the nature of dramatic action, where in tragedy the whole treatment and execution presents what is *substantial* and fundamental in the characters and their aims and conflicts, while in comedy the central thing is the character's *inner* life and his *private* personality.

We are not concerned here to provide a complete history of art and therefore we may start by setting aside those beginnings of dramatic art which we encounter in the East. However far Eastern poetry advanced in epic and some sorts of lyric, the whole Eastern outlook inhibits *ab initio* an adequate development of dramatic art. The reason is that truly *tragic* action necessarily presupposes either a live conception of *individual* freedom and independence or at least an individual's determination and willingness to accept freely and on his own account the responsibility for his own act and its consequences; and for the emergence of *comedy* there must have asserted itself in a still higher degree the free right of the subjective personality and its self-assured dominion. In the East these conditions are not fulfilled. Mohammedan poetry, in particular, with its grandiose sublimity is throughout far away from any attempt at dramatic expression, because in such poetry, although the independence of the individual may be vigorously asserted, the One fundamental power still more persistently dominates its every creature and decides its lot irreversibly. Dramatic art demands the vindication of (a) a particular element in an individual's action, and (b) a personality probing its own depths, and it follows from what I have said that neither of these demands can be met in Mohammedan poetry. Indeed the individual's subjection to the will of God remains, precisely in Mohammedanism, all the more abstract the more abstractly universal is the One power which dominates the whole and which in the last resort inhibits anything particular. Consequently we find the beginnings of drama only in China and India; yet even here, to judge from the few samples so far known to us, there is no question of the accomplishment of a free individual action but merely of giving life to events and feelings in specific situations presented successively on the stage.

Therefore the real beginning of dramatic poetry must be sought in Greece where the principle of free individuality makes the perfection of the classical form of art possible for the first time. Yet within this form of art the individual can enter in connection with action only so far as is directly required by the free vitalization of the *substantive* content of human aims. Therefore what principally counts in Greek drama, whether tragedy or comedy, is the universal and essential element in the aim which the characters are realizing: in tragedy, the moral justification of the agent's consciousness in respect of a specific action, the vindication of the act in and by itself; and, in comedy, at least in the old comedy, it is also the general public interests that are emphasized, statesmen and their way of steering the state, war and peace, the people and its moral situation, philosophy and its corruption, and so forth. Therefore neither the various descriptions of the human heart and personal character nor particular complications and intrigues can find their place completely in Greek drama, nor does the interest turn on the fates of individuals. Sympathy is claimed above all not for these particular and personal matters but simply for the battle between the essential powers that rule human life and between the gods that dominate the human heart, and for this battle's outcome. The *tragic* heroes come on the scene as the individual representatives of these powers in much the same way as the figures of *comedy* expose the general corruption into which the fundamental tendencies of public life have been actually perverted contemporaneously with the comedy.

In modern, or romantic, poetry, on the other hand, the principal topic is provided by an individual's passion, which is satisfied in the pursuit of a purely subjective end, and, in general, by the fate of a single individual and his character in special circumstances.

Accordingly the poetic interest here lies in the greatness of the characters who by their imagination or disposition and aptitude display the full wealth of their heart, and their elevation over their situations and actions, as a real possibility[1] (even if this be often impaired and destroyed solely by circumstances and complications), but at the same time they find a reconciliation in the very greatness of their nature. Therefore in this mode of treatment our interest is directed, so far as the particular matter at issue in an action is concerned, not on its moral justification and necessity but on the individual person and his affairs. This being so, a *leitmotiv* is thus provided by love, ambition, etc.; indeed, even crime is not excluded, though this easily becomes a rock difficult to circumnavigate. For after all if a criminal, especially one like the hero in Müllner's[2] *Guilt*, is weak and through and through base, he is only a disgusting sight. Here above all, therefore, we must demand formal greatness of character and a personality powerful enough to sustain everything negative and, without denying its acts or being inwardly wrecked, to accept its fate.—Nevertheless the substantive and fundamental ends, country, family, crown, and empire, are not to be held aloof at all, even if what matters to the individual character is not the substantial nature of these ends but his own individuality; but in that case they form on the whole the specific ground on which the individual stands with his own subjective character and where he gets into a conflict, instead of providing him with the proper ultimate object of his willing and acting.

Then, further, alongside this subjective element there may come on the scene a spread of particular details concerning both the inner life and also the external circumstances and relations within which the action proceeds. Therefore we find legitimately in place here, in distinction from the simple conflicts in Greek tragedy, a variety and wealth of dramatis personae, extraordinary and always newly involved complications, labyrinths of intrigue, accidental occurrences, in short all those features which, no longer fettered by the impressive and substantive character of an essential subject-matter, are indicative of what is typical in the romantic, as distinct from the classical, form of art.

Nevertheless despite this apparently unbounded mass of particulars, even here, if the whole play is to remain dramatic and poetic, the specific character of the collision which has to be fought out must be visibly emphasized, and, on the other hand, especially in tragedy, the authority of a higher world-governor, whether Providence or fate, must be made obvious in the course and outcome of the particular action.

The Concrete Development of Dramatic Poetry and Its Genres

The essential differences of conception and poetic execution [in drama] have now been considered. Along with them are the different *genres* of dramatic art and they acquire their truly real perfection only when they are developed at this or that stage [in history]. Therefore, in conclusion, our consideration must be directed to this concrete manner of their evolution.

If for the reason given above we exclude oriental beginnings, the first main sphere confronting us at once is the dramatic poetry of the Greeks because that is the stage at which tragedy proper, and comedy too, had their highest intrinsic worth. It was in that poetry that for the first time there was a clear consciousness of what the real essence of tragedy and comedy is. After these opposed ways of looking at human action had been firmly separated and strictly distinguished from one another, tragedy and comedy developed organically, and first one, and then the other, attained the summit of perfection. Still later, Roman dramatic art gives us only a pale reflection of the Greek achievement, and here the Romans did not achieve even that measure of success which later came to them in their similar efforts in epic and lyric.—In order to touch briefly on only the points of greatest importance, I will limit a more detailed consideration of these stages to tragedy as viewed by Aeschylus and Sophocles and comedy by Aristophanes.

I have said of *tragedy* already that the basic form determining its organization and structure is to be found in emphasis on the substantial aspect of aims and their objects, as well as of individuals, their conflicts, and their fates.

The general background of a tragic action is provided in a tragedy, as it was in epic, by that world-situation which I have previously called the 'heroic' age. In that age the universal ethical powers have not been explicitly fixed as either the law of the land or as moral precepts and duties. Consequently, only in heroic times can these powers enter in original freshness as the gods who either oppose one another in their own activities or appear themselves as the living heart of free human individuals. But if the ethical order is to be exhibited from the outset as the substantive foundation and general background out of which the actions of individuals grow and develop into a conflict and then are tugged back out of it into unity again, we are confronted by two different forms of the ethical order in action.

First, the naïve consciousness which wills the substantial order as a *whole,* i.e. as an undivided identity of its different aspects. This consciousness therefore remains blameless and neutral, in undisturbed peace with itself and others. But this is a purely universal consciousness, undifferentiated in its worship, faith, and fortune. It therefore cannot attain to any specific action.[3] On the contrary, it has a sort of horror of the schism implicit there. Although, inactive itself, it reverences as higher that spiritual courage which, having selected its aim, proceeds to decide and act, it is still incapable of embarking on any such course. It knows that it is but the terrain or spectator of action. Therefore, there is nothing left for it to do with the agents, whom it venerates as higher than itself, and with the energy of their decisions and struggles, but to oppose to them the object of its own wisdom, i.e. the substantive ideality[4] of the ethical powers.

The *second* aspect is the individual 'pathos' which drives the dramatis personae, acting with an ethical justification, into opposition with others and thereby brings them into a conflict. The individuals animated by this 'pathos' are not what we call 'characters' in the modern sense of the word, but neither are they mere abstractions. They occupy a vital central position between both, because they are firm figures who simply are what they are, without any inner conflict, without any hesitating recognition of someone else's 'pathos', and therefore (the opposite of our contemporary 'irony') lofty, absolutely determinate individuals, although this determinacy of theirs is based on and is representative of a particular ethical power. Since it is only the *opposition* of such individuals, justified in their action, which constitutes the essence of tragedy, it can come into view only on the territory of actual *human* life. For it

61

is only in that life that a particular quality can be the substance of an individual in the sense that he puts himself with his entire being and interests into such a quality and makes it an overmastering passion. On the other hand, in the case of the *blessed gods* the undifferenced divine nature is the essential thing, and, if opposition arises, there is in the last resort no seriousness about it and, as I have already pointed out in dealing with the Homeric epic, it is ultimately dissolved again ironically.[5]

Each of these two aspects is as important as the other for the whole drama. Both of them—the one and undivided consciousness of the Divine [or of the ethical powers], and the action which, resolving on ethical ends and achieving them, involves battle but comes on the scene with divine force and as a divine deed—provide the principal elements which in its works of art Greek tragedy displays as harmonized, i.e. in the chorus and the heroic agents.

In recent times the significance of the Greek *chorus* has been much discussed, and in the course of this discussion a question has been raised about whether it can or should be introduced into modern tragedy too. People have felt the need for such a substantial groundwork and yet at the same time have been unable to introduce or insert it because they have not understood or grasped deeply enough the nature of what is genuinely tragic or the necessity of the chorus in the Greek conception of tragedy. The chorus has indeed been understood to some extent by those who say that its business is tranquil reflection on the whole thing at issue while the dramatis personae remain caught in their own particular aims and situations and have now gained in the chorus and its meditations a criterion of the worth of their characters and actions, just as the public has found in the chorus an objective representative of its own judgement on what is going on in front of it in the work of art.

Upholders of this view have hit on part of the truth, because in fact the chorus confronts us as a higher moral consciousness, aware of the substantial issues, warning against false conflicts, and weighing the outcome. Nevertheless the chorus is not at all a moralist, disengaged like a spectator, a person reflecting on the thing purely from outside, in himself uninteresting and tedious, and introduced simply for the sake of his reflections. On the contrary, the chorus is the actual substance of the moral life and action of the heroes themselves; in contrast to these individuals it is the people as the fruitful soil out of which they grow (just as flowers and towering trees do from their own native soil) and by the existent character of which they are conditioned. Consequently the chorus is essentially appropriate in an age where moral complications cannot

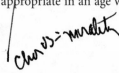

yet be met by specific valid and just laws and firm religious dogmas, but where the ethical order appears only in its direct and living actuality and remains only the equilibrium of a stable life secure against the fearful collisions to which the energies of individuals in their opposing actions must lead. But what the chorus gives us is the consciousness that such a secure refuge is actually present. Therefore the chorus does not in fact encroach on the action; it does not actively exercise any right against the warring heroes but pronounces judgement purely contemplatively; it warns and sympathizes, or it appeals to divine law and those inner powers which imagination portrays to itself objectively as the group of the gods who hold sway. In so expressing itself it is lyrical, as we saw; for it does nothing and has no events to relate epically. But what it says preserves at the same time the epic character of substantial universality and it does therefore move in one mode of lyric which may, in distinction from the proper form of odes, sometimes approach the paean and the dithyramb.

This position of the chorus in Greek tragedy needs essential emphasis. Just as the Greek theatre itself has its external terrain, its scene, and its surroundings, so the chorus, the people, is as it were the scene of the spirit; it may be compared, in architecture, with a temple surrounding the image of the gods, for here it is an environment for the heroes in the action. In our case, however, statues stand under the open sky without such a background, and modern tragedy does not need one either, because its actions do not rest on this substantial basis but on the individual's will and character as well as on the apparently external accidents of occurrences and circumstances.

This all implies that it is an utterly false view to regard the chorus as something casually dragged in and a mere relic of the time when Greek drama originated. No doubt its external origin is to be traced to the fact that at festivals of Dionysus the chief thing, in art at any rate, was choral song, until subsequently, as a break, a narrator came on the scene, and his message was finally transformed and elevated into the actual figures of a dramatic action. But in the age of tragedy's full bloom the chorus was not retained at all merely in honour of this feature of religious festivals and Dionysus worship; on the contrary it was developed ever more beautifully and in a more measured way simply because it belongs essentially to the dramatic action itself and is so necessary to it that the decay of tragedy is especially manifested in the deterioration of the choruses which no longer remain an integral part of the whole but sink down into being an unnecessary ornament. On the other hand, the chorus is plainly unsuitable for romantic tragedy which in any case did not originate in choral songs. On the contrary, the subject-matter here is of such a kind that any introduction of choruses in the Greek sense must inevitably have misfired. For even the oldest so-called mystery-plays, moralities, and other farces from which romantic drama arose, do not present any action in the original Greek sense or any emergence from that consciousness which is unaware of division in life or the Divine. Neither does the chorus fit in with chivalry or absolute monarchy, for there the people have to obey or become partisans involved in action only in the interests of their fortune or misfortune. In general it cannot find its proper place where it is individual passions, aims, and characters that are at issue or where the play of intrigue is being pursued.

The second chief feature, contrasted with the chorus, consists of the *individuals* who act and come continually into conflict. In Greek tragedy, as I have said more than once, the occasion for collisions is produced by the moral justification of a specific act, and not at all by an evil will, a crime, or infamy, or by mere misfortune, blindness, and the like. For evil in the abstract has no truth in itself and is of no interest. But, on the other hand, it must not look as if moral traits of character have been assigned to individuals merely by [the dramatist's] *intention,* for on the contrary their justification must be shown to lie in them *essentially.* Criminal types, like those of today, good-for-nothings, or even so-called 'morally noble' criminals with their empty chatter about fate, we therefore do not find in Greek tragedy any more than a decision or a deed resting on purely private interest and personal character, on thirst for power, lust, honour, or other passions, the right of which can be rooted only in an individual's private inclination and personality. But an individual's decision, justified by the object he aims at, is carried out in a one-sided and particular way, and therefore in specific circumstances, which already carry in themselves the real possibility of conflicts, he injures another and equally moral sphere of the human will. To this sphere another person clings as his own actual 'pathos' and in carrying out his aim opposes and reacts against the former individual. In this way the collision of equally justified powers and individuals is completely set afoot.

The range of the subject-matter here may be variously particularized but its essence is not very extensive. The chief conflict treated most beautifully by Sophocles, with Aeschylus as his predecessor, is that between the state, i.e. ethical life in its *spiritual* universality, and the family, i.e. *natural* ethical life. These are the clearest powers that are presented in tragedy, because the full reality of ethical existence consists in harmony between these two spheres and in absence of discord between what an agent has actually to do in one and what he has to do in the other. In this connection I need refer only to Aeschylus' *Seven Against Thebes* and, still more appositely, Sophocles' *Antigone*. Antigone honours the bond of kinship, the gods of the underworld, while Creon honours Zeus alone, the dominating power over public life and social welfare. In [Euripides'] *Iphigenia in Aulis,* in Aeschylus' *Agamemnon, Choephori,* and *Eumenides,* and in Sophocles' *Electra* we find a similar conflict. Agamemnon, as King and commander of the army, sacrifices his daughter in the interest of the Greeks and the Trojan expedition; thereby he snaps the bond of love for his daughter and his wife. This bond Clytemnestra, his wife and Iphigenia's mother, retains in the depths of her heart, and in revenge she prepares a shameful death for her home-coming husband. Orestes, her son and the King's son, honours his mother but he has to defend the right of his father, the King, and he slays the womb that bore him.

This is a subject valid for every epoch and therefore this presentation of it, despite all national differences, continues to excite our lively human and artistic sympathy.

A second main type of collision is less concrete. The Greek tragedians are fond of portraying it especially in the fate of Oedipus. The most perfect example of this has been left to us by Sophocles in his *Oedipus Tyrannus* and *Oedipus Coloneus.* What is at issue here is the right of the wide awake consciousness, the justification of what the man has self-consciously willed and knowingly done, as contrasted with what he was fated by the gods to do and actually did unconsciously and without having willed it. Oedipus has killed his father; he has married his mother and begotten children in this incestuous alliance; and yet he has been involved in these most evil crimes without either knowing or willing them. The right of our deeper consciousness today would consist in recognizing that since he had neither intended nor known these crimes himself, they were not to be regarded as his own deeds. But the Greek, with his plasticity of consciousness, takes responsibility for what he has done as an individual and does not cut his purely subjective self-consciousness apart from what is objectively the case.

Lastly, there are other collisions depending partly on special circumstances and partly on the general relation between an individual's action and the Greek μοῖρα [fate]. For our purpose, these are of less importance.

But in considering all these tragic conflicts we must above all reject the false idea that they have anything to do with guilt or innocence. The tragic heroes are just as much innocent as guilty. On the presupposition that a man is only guilty if alternatives are open to him and he decides arbitrarily on what he does, the Greek plastic figures are innocent: they act out of this character of theirs, on *this* 'pathos', because this character, this 'pathos' is precisely what they are: their act is not preceded by either hesitation or choice. It is just the strength of the great characters that they do not choose but throughout, from start to finish, *are* what they will and accomplish. They are what they are, and never anything else, and this is their greatness. For weakness in action consists only in a cleavage between the individual and his object, in which case character, will, and aim do not appear as having grown into an absolute unity; and since no fixed aim is alive in the individual's soul as the substance of his own individuality, as the 'pathos' and power animating his whole will, he may swither irresolutely from this to that and let caprice decide. From this swithering the Greek plastic figures are exempt; for them the bond between the subject and what he wills as his object remains indissoluble. What drives them to act is precisely an ethically justified 'pathos' which they assert against one another with the eloquence of their 'pathos' not in sentimental and personal rhetoric or in the sophistries of passion, but in solid and cultivated objective language. (Sophocles above everyone else was a master in the depth, measure, and plastic and living beauty of language of this kind.) At the same time, however, their 'pathos' is pregnant with collisions and it leads them to injurious and guilty acts. But they do not claim to be innocent of these at all. On the contrary, what they did, and actually had to do, is their glory. No worse insult could be given to such a hero than to say that he had acted innocently. It is the honour of these great characters to be culpable. They do not want to arouse sympathy or pity, for what arouses pity is not anything substantive, but subjective grief, the subjective depth of personality. But their firm and strong character is one with its essential 'pathos', and what excites our admiration is this indestructible harmony and not the pity and emotion that Euripides alone has slipped into expressing.

The tragic complication leads finally to no other result or denouement but this: the two sides that are in conflict with one another preserve the justification which both have, but what each upholds is one-sided, and this one-sidedness is stripped away and the inner, undisturbed harmony returns in the attitude of the chorus which clearly assigns equal honour to all the gods. The true development of the action consists solely in the cancellation of conflicts *as conflicts,* in the reconciliation of the powers animating action which struggled to destroy one another in their mutual conflict. Only in that case does finality lie not in misfortune and suffering but in the satisfaction of the spirit, because only with such a conclusion can the necessity of what happens to the individuals appear as absolute rationality, and only then can our hearts be morally at peace: shattered by the fate of the heroes but reconciled fundamentally. Only by adherence to this view can Greek tragedy be understood.

Therefore we should not interpret such a conclusion as a purely moral outcome where evil is punished and virtue rewarded, i.e. "when vice vomits, virtue sits at table." Here there is no question at all of an introverted personality's subjective reflection and its good and evil, but, when the collision was complete, of the vision of an affirmative reconciliation and the equal validity of both the powers that were in conflict. Neither is the necessity of the outcome a blind fate, a purely irrational and unintelligible destiny which many people call 'classical', but a rational one, although the rationality here does not appear as a self-conscious Providence whose divine end and aim becomes manifest to itself and others in the world and individuals. On the contrary, the rationality consists in the fact that the power supreme over individual gods and men cannot allow persistence either to one-sided powers that make themselves independent and thereby overstep the limits of their authority or to the conflicts that follow in consequence. Fate drives individuality back within its limits and destroys it if these are crossed. But an irrational compulsion and innocent suffering would inevitably produce in the soul of the spectator mere indignation instead of moral peace and satisfaction.

In another way, therefore, a tragic reconciliation is nevertheless different from an epic one. If we look at Achilles and Odysseus, for example, they reach their goal, and this is proper; but they are not steadily favored by fortune; on the contrary, they have to taste the bitter wine of a sense of finitude and to fight their way through difficulty, loss, and sacrifice. For Truth demands that in the course of life and the objective sweep of events the nullity of the finite shall come into appearance too. The wrath of Achilles is appeased, he obtains from Agamemnon what he had been injured by losing, he wreaks his revenge on Hector, the funeral celebrations for Patroclus are completed, and Achilles is recognized as the most glorious of men. But his wrath and its appeasement has cost him his dearest friend, the noble Patroclus; in order to avenge his loss on Hector, he finds himself compelled to desist from his wrath and plunge once more into the battle against the Trojans, and when he is recognized as the most glorious of men he has at the same time a sense of his early death. Similarly, Odysseus does in the end arrive at Ithaca, the goal of his wishes, but asleep and alone after long years of delay and toil, after losing all his companions and all the booty from Troy. Thus both have paid their debt to finitude, and Nemesis has entered into its rights by the downfall of Troy and the fate of the Greek heroes. But Nemesis is simply the ancient justice which degrades what has risen too high only in order to restore by misfortune the mere equilibrium of good and ill fortune, and it touches and affects the realm of finitude without any further moral judgement. This is epic justice in the field of events, the comprehensive reconciliation which consists in mere equalization. The more profound tragic reconciliation, on the other hand, depends on the advance of specific ethical substantive powers out of their opposition to their true harmony. But the ways in which this harmony can be brought about are very different, and I will therefore bring to your notice only the chief features at issue in this connection.

First, it needs special emphasis that if the one-sidedness of a 'pathos' is the real ground of the collisions, this can only mean that it is carried out into actually living action, and the one-sided 'pathos' has become the one and only 'pathos' of a specific individual. Now if the one-sidedness is to be cancelled, it is the individual, since he has acted solely as this *one* 'pathos', who must be got rid of and sacrificed. For the individual is only this *one* life and, if this is not to prevail on its own account as this *one*, then the individual is shattered.

This sort of development is most complete when the individuals who are at variance appear each of them in their concrete existence as a totality,[7] that in themselves they are in the power of what they are fighting, and therefore they violate what, if they were true to their own nature, they should be honouring. For example, Antigone lives under the political authority of Creon [the present King]; she is herself the daughter of a King [Oedipus] and the fiancée of Haemon [Creon's son], so that she ought to pay obedience to the royal command. But Creon too, as father and husband, should have respected the sacred tie of blood and not ordered anything against its pious observance. So there is immanent in both Antigone and Creon something that in their own way they attack, so that they are gripped and shattered by something intrinsic to their own actual being. Antigone suffers death before enjoying the bridal dance, but Creon too is punished by the voluntary deaths of his son and his wife, incurred, the one on account of Antigone's fate, the other because of Haemon's death. Of all the masterpieces of the classical and the modern world—and I know nearly all of them and you should and can[8]—the *Antigone* seems to me to be the most magnificent and satisfying work of art of this kind.

But the tragic denouement need not every time require the downfall of the participating individuals in order to obliterate the one-sidedness of both sides and their equal meed of honour. We all know that the *Eumenides* of Aeschylus does not end with the death of Orestes or the discomfiture of the Eumenides. (These were the Furies, the avengers of a mother's blood, and the violation of family piety, against Apollo who means to maintain the dignity and veneration of the King and the head of the family, and who provoked Orestes to kill his mother.) On the contrary, Orestes is excused punishment and both the gods are honoured. But at the same time we see clearly in this decisive conclusion what their gods meant to the Greeks when they brought them before their eyes in a combat between one another as particular individuals. To the contemporary Athenians they were only elements which were bound together into the entire harmony of ethical life. The votes of the Areopagus were equal; it is Athene, the goddess representing the whole substance of living Athenian life, who inserts the white stone which liberates Orestes, but she promises altars and worship to the Eumenides and Apollo equally.

Secondly, in contrast to this objective reconciliation, the assuaging of conflict may be of a subjective kind when the individual agent gives up the one-sidedness of his aim. But in this desertion of a substantive 'pathos' of his own he would appear as lacking in character, and this contradicts the solidity of the Greek plastic figures. In this case, therefore, the individual can only put himself at the mercy of a higher power and its advice and command, so that while he persists on his own account in his 'pathos', his obstinate will is broken by a god. In such a case the knots cannot be untied but, as in the *Philoctetes*, for example, are cut by a *deus ex machina*.

Finally, more beautiful than this rather external sort of denouement is an inner reconciliation which, because of its subjective character, already borders on our modern treatment. The most perfect classical example of this that we have before us is the eternally marvellous *Oedipus Coloneus*. Oedipus has murdered his father, taken the Theban throne, and mounted the marriage-bed with his mother. These unconsciously committed crimes do not make him unhappy; but of old he had solved a riddle and now he forcibly extracts [from the oracle] a knowledge of his own dark fate and acquires the dreadful realization that it has been accomplished in himself. With this solution of the riddle in his own person he has lost his happiness as Adam did when he came to the knowledge of good and evil [Gen. iii]. The seer now, he blinds himself, resigns the throne, exiles himself from Thebes, just as Adam and Eve were driven from Paradise,

69

G. W. F. Hegel

and wanders away a helpless old man. In Colonus, sore afflicted, instead of
listening to his son's request that he might return, he invokes on him his own
Furies [or curse]; he expunges all his own inner discord and is purified within.
Then a god himself calls him [i.e. to death]; his blind eyes are transfigured and
clear; his bones become a salvation and safeguard of the state that received him
as friend and guest. This transfiguration in death is for us, as for him, a visible
reconciliation within his own self and personality. Attempts have been made to
find a Christian tone here: the vision of a sinner whom God pardons and a fate
endured in life but compensated with bliss in death. But the Christian religious
reconciliation is a transfiguration of the soul which, bathed in the spring
of eternal salvation, is lifted above its deeds and existence in the real world,
because it makes the heart itself into the grave of the heart (yes, the spirit can
do this), pays the imputations of earthly guilt with its own earthly individuality
and now holds itself secure against those imputations in the certainty of its
own eternal and purely spiritual bliss. On the other hand, the transfiguration of
Oedipus always still remains the Greek transfer of consciousness from the strife
of ethical powers, and the violations involved, into the unity and harmony of
the entire ethical order itself.

What is further implied in this reconciliation is *subjective* satisfaction, and
this enables us to make the transition to the sphere of comedy, the opposite of
tragedy.

What is comical, as we saw, is a personality or subject who makes his own
actions contradictory and so brings them to nothing, while remaining tranquil
and self-assured in the process. Therefore comedy has for its basis and starting-
point what tragedy may end with, namely an absolutely reconciled and cheerful
heart. Even if its possessor destroys by the means he uses whatever he wills and
so comes to grief in himself because by his own efforts he has accomplished the
very opposite of what he aimed at, he still has not lost his peace of mind on that
account. But, on the other hand, this subjective self-assurance is only possible
if the aims, and so with them the characters in question, either have no real
substance in themselves or, if they have, then their essentiality has been made
an aim and been pursued in a shape really opposed to it fundamentally and
therefore in a shape without substance; and the result is that it is always only
what is inherently null and indifferent that comes to grief, and the individual
remains firm on his feet and undisturbed.

On the whole this is also the character of the old Greek comedy as it has
been preserved for us in the plays of Aristophanes. In this matter we must

70

be very careful to distinguish whether the dramatis personae are comical themselves or only in the eyes of the audience. The former case alone can be counted as really comical, and here Aristophanes was a master. On these lines, an individual is only portrayed as laughable when it is obvious that he is not serious at all about the seriousness of his aim and will, so that this seriousness always carries with it, in the eyes of the individual himself, its own destruction, because from beginning to end he cannot devote himself to any higher and universally valid interest which would bring him into a conflict of substance [i.e. with another such interest]. Even if he really does so devote himself, he can only exhibit a character which, owing to what it directly and presently is, has already annihilated what it apparently wanted to accomplish, and we can see at once that the substantial interest has never had a real hold on him. The comical therefore plays its part more often in people with lower views, tied to the real world and the present, i.e. among men who are what they are once and for all, who cannot be or will anything different, and, though incapable of any genuine 'pathos', have not the least doubt about what they are and what they are doing. But at the same time they reveal themselves as having something higher in them because they are not seriously tied to the finite world with which they are engaged but are raised above it and remain firm in themselves and secure in face of failure and loss. It is to this absolute freedom of spirit which is utterly consoled in advance in every human undertaking, to this world of private serenity, that Aristophanes conducts us. If you have not read him, you can scarcely realize how men can take things so easily.

The interests within which this kind of comedy moves need not be drawn at all from spheres opposed to morality, religion, and art; on the contrary, the old Greek comedy keeps precisely within this objective and substantive sphere, but it is by subjective caprice, vulgar folly, and absurdity that individuals bring to nought actions which had a higher aim. And here Aristophanes had available to him rich and happy material partly in the Greek gods and partly in the Athenians. For making the gods into human individuals has itself produced a contrast with the loftiness of their significance owing to their being so represented and particularized, particularized and humanized right down to detail, and their form can be portrayed as an empty pride in a subjective personality thus inappropriately given to them. But what Aristophanes especially loves is to expose to the ridicule of his fellow-citizens in the most comical and yet profound way the follies of the masses, the insanity of their orators and statesmen, the absurdity of the [Peloponnesian] war, and above all, most mercilessly, the new direction that Euripides had taken in tragedy. The persons in whom he embodies the objects of his magnificent ridicule are made into fools from the start by his inexhaustible humour, so that we can see at once that we are to get nothing but ineptitude from them. Take, for example, Strepsiades, who wants to go to the philosophers to learn how to be rid of his debts, or Socrates, who offers to teach Strepsiades and his son[9]; or Dionysus, who is made to descend into the underworld in order to bring a true tragedian up from there[10]; or Cleon,[11] the women,[12] and the Greeks who want to draw the goddess of peace from the well[13]; and so forth. The keynote resounding in all these portrayals is the self-confidence of all these figures, and it is all the more imperturbable the more incapable they obviously are of accomplishing their undertaking. The fools are such naïve fools, and even the more sensible of them also have such an air of contradiction with what they are devoted to, that they never lose this naïve personal self-assurance, no matter how things go. It is the smiling blessedness of the Olympian gods, their unimpaired equanimity which comes home in men and can put up with anything. In all this Aristophanes is obviously not a cold or malignant scoffer. On the contrary he is a man of most gifted mind, the best of citizens to whom the welfare of Athens was always a serious matter and who proved to be a true patriot throughout. Therefore, as I have said earlier, what is portrayed in his comedies is not the complete dissolution of religion and morality but both the all-pervasive corruption which plumes itself on keeping step with the fundamental powers, and also the shape of things and the appearance of individuals, which are a mask concealing the fact that real truth and substance are no longer there and can be simply and openly handed over to the unfeigned play of subjective caprice. Aristophanes presents to us the absolute contradiction between (a) the true essence of religion and political and ethical life, and (b) the subjective attitude of citizens and individuals who should give actuality to that essence. But in this very triumph of the subjective attitude, whatever its insight, there is implicit one of the greatest symptoms of Greek corruption, and thus these pictures of a naïve fundamental '*all is well with me*' are the final great outcome of the poetry of this gifted, civilized, and ingenious Greek people.

—We turn now at once to the dramatic art of the modern world, and here too I will only bring out in general some of the main differences of importance in relation to tragedy, drama, and comedy.

At its plastic height in Greece, tragedy remains one-sided by making the validity of the substance and necessity of ethical life its essential basis and by leaving undeveloped the individuality of the dramatis personae and the depths of their personal life. Comedy on its side brings to view in a converse mode of plasticity, and to perfection, the subjective personality in the free expatiation of its absurdity and its absurdity's dissolution.

Modern tragedy adopts into its own sphere from the start the principle of subjectivity. Therefore it takes for its proper subject matter and contents the subjective inner life of the character who is not, as in classical tragedy, a purely individual embodiment of ethical powers, and, keeping to this same type, it makes actions come into collision with one another as the chance of external circumstances dictates, and makes similar accidents decide, or seem to decide, the outcome. Here there are the following chief points to discuss:

(a) the nature of the various aims which the characters have and which are to be attained;

(b) the tragic characters themselves and the collisions to which they are subjected;

(c) the difference from Greek tragedy in respect of the sort of denouement and the tragic reconciliation.

However far the centre of romantic tragedy is from the individual's sufferings and passions (in the strict sense of that word),[14] nevertheless in human action a basis of specific ends drawn from the concrete spheres of family, state, church, etc. is never missing. For, by acting, man, as man, enters the sphere of the real world and its particular concerns. But since now it is not the substantial element in these spheres which engrosses the interest of individuals, their aims are broadly and variously particularized and in such detail that what is truly substantial can often glimmer through them in only a very dim way; and, apart from this, these aims acquire an altogether different form. For example, in the religious sphere, the dominating subject-matter is no longer the particular ethical powers made by imagination into individual gods and displayed either in their own person or as the 'pathos' of human heroes, but instead the story of Christ, the saints, etc. In the political sphere what is brought before us in all sorts of different ways is especially the monarchy, the power of vassals, the strife between dynasties or between members of one and the same royal family. Indeed, furthermore, civil and private rights and other relationships are dealt with and, similarly, even aspects of family life arise which were not yet compatible with Greek drama. For since the principle of subjectivity itself has gained its right in the [religious, political, and social] spheres mentioned above, it follows that new features appear even in them which modern man is entitled to make the aim and guide of his action.

On the other hand, it is the right of personality as such which is firmly established as the sole subject-matter, and love, personal honour, etc. are taken as ends so exclusive that the other relationships either can only appear as the external ground on which these modern interests are played out or else stand on their own account in conflict against the demands of the individual's subjective heart. The situation is more profound when the individual character, in order to achieve his goal, does not shrink from wrong and crime, even if he has not envisaged himself as unjust and criminal in choosing his end.

But instead of having this particular and personal character the ends chosen may be extensive, universal, and comprehensive in scope, or, again, they may be adopted and pursued as having substance in themselves. (a) As an example of the former case I will only refer to Goethe's *Faust*, the one absolutely philosophical tragedy. Here on the one side, dissatisfaction with learning and, on the other, the freshness of life and enjoyment in the world, in general the tragic quest for harmony between the Absolute in its essence and appearance and the individual's knowledge and will. All this provides a breadth of subject-matter which no other dramatist has ventured to compass in one and the same work. A similar example is Schiller's [*Robbers* where] Karl Moor is enraged by the entire civil order and the whole situation of the world and mankind in his day, and his *rebellion* against it has this universal significance. Wallenstein likewise adopts a great universal aim, the unity and peace of Germany. He failed in his aim partly because his forces, collected artificially and held together by purely external links, broke up and scattered just when things became serious for him, and partly because he revolted against the authority of the Emperor, a power on which he and his undertaking were bound to be shipwrecked. Universal ends, like those pursued by Karl Moor and Wallenstein, cannot be accomplished by a single individual by making others his obedient instruments; on the contrary, such ends prevail by their own force, sometimes with the will of the many, sometimes against it and without their knowledge. (b) As examples of the adoption of ends in virtue of their substantial character, I will mention only some tragedies of Calderón in which the rights and duties involved in love, honour, etc. are used by the dramatis personae as a sort of code of laws rigid and inflexible in themselves. Something similar occurs frequently in Schiller's characters, although their point of view is quite different; anyway this is true in the sense that these individuals adopt and fight for their aims by regarding them at the same time as universal and absolute human rights. So, for example, in *Intrigue and Love* Major Ferdinand means to defend natural rights against fashionable conventions and, above all, the Marquis Posa [in *Don Carlos*] demands freedom of thought as an inalienable possession of mankind.

But in modern tragedy it is generally the case that individuals do not act for the sake of the *substantial* nature of their end, nor is it that nature which proves to be their motive in their passion; on the contrary, what presses for satisfaction is the *subjectivity* of their heart and mind and the privacy of their own character. For consider the examples just cited: in the case of the Spanish dramas, what the heroes of love and honour aim at is in itself of such a subjective kind that the rights and duties involved in it can coincide immediately with what their own heart wishes. And, in Schiller's youthful works, bragging about nature, human rights, and the reform of mankind is little more than the extravagance of a subjective enthusiasm; when in his later years Schiller tried to vindicate a more mature 'pathos', this happened simply because he had it in mind to restore in modern dramatic art the principle of Greek tragedy.

In order to exhibit in more detail the difference in this respect between Greek and modern tragedy, I will direct attention only to Shakespeare's *Hamlet*. His character is rooted in a collision similar to that treated by Aeschylus in the *Choephori* and Sophocles in the *Electra*. For in Hamlet's case too his father, the King, is murdered and his mother has married the murderer. But whereas in the Greek poets the King's death does have an ethical justification, in Shakespeare it is simply and solely an atrocious crime and Hamlet's mother is guiltless of it. Consequently the son has to wreak his revenge only on the fratricide King in whom he sees nothing really worthy of respect. Therefore the collision turns strictly here not on a son's pursuing an ethically justified revenge and being forced in the process to violate the ethical order, but on Hamlet's personal character. His noble soul is not made for this kind of energetic activity; and, full of disgust with the world and life, what with decision, proof, arrangements for carrying out his resolve, and being bandied from pillar to post, he eventually perishes owing to his own hesitation and a complication of external circumstances.

If we turn now, in the second place, to that aspect which is of more outstanding importance in modern tragedy, to the characters, namely, and their conflict, the first thing that we can take as a starting-point is, in brief summary, the following:

The heroes of Greek classical tragedy are confronted by circumstances in which, after firmly identifying themselves with the one ethical 'pathos' which alone corresponds to their own already established nature, they necessarily come into conflict with the opposite but equally justified ethical power. The romantic dramatis personae, on the other hand, are from the beginning in the midst of a wide field of more or less accidental circumstances and conditions within which it is possible to act either in this way or in that. Consequently the conflict, for which the external circumstances do of course provide the occasion, lies essentially in the character to which the individuals adhere in their passion, not because of any substantial justification but because they are what they are once and for all. The Greek heroes too do act in their individual capacity, but, as I have said, when Greek tragedy is at its height their individuality is itself of necessity an inherently ethical 'pathos', whereas in modern tragedy it remains a matter of chance whether the individual's character is gripped by something intrinsically justified or whether he is led into crime and wrong, and in either case he makes his decision according to his own wishes and needs, or owing to external influences, etc. It is true, therefore, that character and an ethical end may coincide, but since aims, passions, and the subjective inner life are all particular [and not universal], this coincidence is not the essential foundation and objective condition of the depth and beauty of a [modern] tragedy.

Few generalizations can be made about further differences in [modern] characterization because this sphere is wide open to variations of every kind. I will therefore touch on only the following chief aspects.

A first contrast which strikes the eye quickly enough is that between (a) the individuals who come on the scene as living and concrete people, and (b) an abstract and therefore formal characterization. As an example of the latter we can cite especially the tragic figures in French and Italian drama. They originate from an imitation of classical models and may count more or less as mere personifications of specific passions—love, honour, fame, ambition, tyranny, etc. They relate the motives of their actions as well as the degree and kind of their feelings with great declamatory splendour and much rhetorical skill, but this way of explaining themselves reminds us more of Seneca's failures than of the Greek dramatic masterpieces. Spanish tragedy too borders on this abstract characterization; but in this case the passion of love, in conflict with honour, friendship, royal authority, etc., is itself of such an abstractly subjective kind, and the rights and duties involved are so sharply emphasized, that a fuller individualization of the characters is impossible, since in this as it were subjective substantiality[15] this passion is supposed to be prominent as the real interest of the piece. Nevertheless the Spanish figures often have a solidity, even

76

if there is little in it, and a sort of brittle personality which the French ones lack; at the same time, in contrast to the cold simplicity of the action's development in French tragedy, the Spanish, even in tragedy, can make up for a deficiency in variations of character by an acutely invented wealth of interesting situations and complications.

But in the portrayal of concretely human individuals and characters it is especially the English who are distinguished masters and above them all Shakespeare stands at an almost unapproachable height. For even if some purely single passion, like ambition in Macbeth or jealousy in Othello, becomes the entire 'pathos' of his tragic heroes, still such an abstraction does not devour their more far-reaching individuality at all, because despite this determinant they still always remain complete men. Indeed the more Shakespeare proceeds to portray on the infinite breadth of his 'world-stage'[16] the extremes of evil and folly, all the more, as I have remarked earlier, does he precisely plunge his figures who dwell on these extremes into their restrictedness; of course he equips them with a wealth of poetry but he actually gives them spirit and imagination, and, by the picture in which they can contemplate and see themselves objectively like a work of art, he makes them free artists of their own selves, and thereby, with his strongly marked and faithful characterization, can interest us not only in criminals but even in the most downright and vulgar clouts and fools. The way that his tragic characters reveal themselves is of a similar kind: individual, real, directly living, extremely varied, and yet, where this emerges necessarily, of a sublimity and striking power of expression, of a depth of feeling and gift for invention in images and similes produced on the spur of the moment, of a rhetoric, not pedantic but issuing from the actual feeling and outpouring of the character—take all this into account, this combination of directly present life and inner greatness of soul, and you will scarcely find any other modern dramatist who can be compared with Shakespeare. Goethe in his youth did try to achieve a similar truth to nature and an individuality of personality but without achieving the inner force and height of passion [of Shakespeare's characters], and Schiller again has fallen into a violence which has no really solid kernel in its expansive storming.

A second difference in modern characters consists in their being either firm or inwardly hesitant and discordant. The weakness of irresolution, the swithering of reflection, perplexity about the reasons that are to guide decision—all this does occur here and there in the tragedies of Euripides, but he already abandons polished plasticity of character and action and goes over to subjective emotion.

In modern tragedy such dithering figures generally appear by being themselves in the grip of a twofold passion which drives them from one decision or one deed to another simultaneously. This vacillation I have mentioned already in another context,[17] and here I will only add that, even if the tragic action must depend on a collision, to put this discord into one and the same individual must always involve much awkwardness. For mental distraction into opposed interests has its source partly in a vagueness and stupidity of mind, partly in weakness and immaturity. We have some figures of this sort even in Goethe's youthful[18] productions: Weislingen [in *Götz*], for example, Fernando in *Stella*, and Clavigo [in *Clavigo*] above all. These are men in two minds who cannot acquire a finished and therefore firm individuality. It is quite different if two opposed spheres of life or two opposite duties, etc., seem equally sacrosanct to a character already assured in himself and yet sees himself compelled to align himself with one to the exclusion of the other. In that case the vacillation is only a transitional phase and is not the nerve of the man's character itself.

Again, a different kind consists of the tragic case where someone is led astray by passion against his better judgement into opposite aims (like Joan in Schiller's *Maid of Orleans*), and now must perish unless he can rescue himself from this discord both within and in his external actions. Yet, if the lever of the tragedy is this personal tragedy of inner discord, there is about it something now sad and painful, now aggravating, and the poet does better to avoid it instead of looking for it and pre-eminently developing it.

But what is worst of all is to exhibit such indecision and vacillation of character, and of the whole man, as a sort of perverse and sophistical dialectic and then to make it the main theme of the entire drama, so that truth is supposed to consist precisely in showing that no character is inwardly firm and self-assured. The one-sided aims of particular passions and characters should certainly not come to be realized without a struggle, and in everyday life when the force of circumstances reacts against them, and other individuals oppose them, they are not spared the experience of their finitude and instability. But this outcome, which alone forms an appropriate conclusion, must not be inserted by a sort of dialectical machinery into the individual's own character, for otherwise the person as *this* personality is only an empty indeterminate form instead of growing in a living way along with determinate aims and a defined character.

It is something different again if a change in the whole man's inner condition appears itself to be a logical consequence of precisely his own peculiarities, so that what develops and emerges is something that was implicit in his character from the start. For example, in *King Lear*, Lear's original folly is intensified into madness in his old age, just as Gloucester's mental blindness is changed into actual physical blindness and only then are his eyes opened to the true difference in the love of his sons.

It is precisely Shakespeare who gives us, in contrast to this portrayal of vacillating characters inwardly divided against themselves, the finest examples of firm and consistent characters who come to ruin simply because of this decisive adherence to themselves and their aims. Without ethical justification, but upheld solely by the formal inevitability of their personality, they allow themselves to be lured to their deed by external circumstances, or they plunge blindly on and persevere by the strength of their will, even if now what they do they accomplish only from the necessity of maintaining themselves against others or because they *have* reached once and for all the point that they have reached. The passion, implicitly in keeping with the man's character, had not broken out hitherto, but now it arises and is fully developed—this progress and history of a great soul, its inner development, the picture of its self-destructive struggle against circumstances, events, and their consequences—all this is the main theme in many of Shakespeare's most interesting tragedies.

The last important point—the one we now have still to discuss—concerns the tragic denouement to which the modern characters are driven as well as the sort of tragic reconciliation with which this is compatible. In Greek tragedy it is eternal justice which, as the absolute power of fate, saves and maintains the harmony of the substance of the ethical order against the particular powers which were becoming independent and therefore colliding, and because of the inner rationality of its sway we are satisfied when we see individuals coming to ruin. If a similar justice appears in modern tragedy, then, owing to the non-universal nature of aims and characters, it is colder, more like criminal justice, owing to the greater reflectiveness of the wrong and crime into which individuals are forced when they are intent on accomplishing their ends. For example, Macbeth, Lear's elder daughters and their husbands, Richard III, the President in [Schiller's] *Intrigue and Love*, deserve for their atrocities nothing better than what happens to them. This sort of denouement is usually so presented that the individuals are shipwrecked on a power confronting them which they had deliberately defied in the pursuit of their own private ends. So, for example, Wallenstein is wrecked by the stability of the Emperor's power, but even old Piccolomini, who in [secretly] upholding the established order has become a traitor to his friend and misused the form of friendship, is punished by the death of his son who was sacrificed to the end that his father really wanted to achieve.[19] Götz von Berlichingen too attacks an existent and firmly established political order and therefore perishes, just as Weislingen and Adelheid[20] meet an unfortunate end owing to wrong and disloyalty, although they are on the side of this legal order and its power. This subjectivity of character immediately implies the demand that the individuals must have shown themselves inwardly reconciled to their own particular fate. This satisfaction may be religious when the heart knows that it is assured of a higher and indestructible bliss in exchange for the destruction of its mundane individuality, or alternatively it may be of a more abstract and mundane kind when the strength and equanimity of the character persists, even to destruction, without breaking, and so preserves its subjective freedom, in the face of all circumstances and misfortunes, with energy unjeopardized; or, finally, it may be more concrete owing to a recognition that its fate, however bitter, is merely the one appropriate to its action.

But on the other hand the tragic denouement is also displayed as purely the effect of unfortunate circumstances and external accidents which might have turned out otherwise and produced a happy ending. In this case the sole spectacle offered to us is that the modern individual with the non-universal nature of his character, his circumstances, and the complications in which he is involved, is necessarily surrendered to the fragility of all that is mundane and must endure the fate of finitude. But this mere affliction is empty, and, in particular, we are confronted by a purely horrible external necessity when we see fine minds, noble in themselves, perishing in such a battle against the misfortune of entirely external circumstances. Such a history may touch us acutely, and yet it seems only dreadful and we feel a pressing demand for a necessary correspondence between the external circumstances and what the inner nature of those fine characters really is. It is only from this point of view that we can feel ourselves reconciled in e.g. the fate of Hamlet or Juliet. Looked at from the outside, Hamlet's death seems to be brought about accidentally owing to the fight with Laertes and the exchange of rapiers. But death lay from the beginning in the background of Hamlet's mind. The sands of time do not content him. In his melancholy and weakness, his worry, his disgust at all the affairs of life, we sense from the start that in all his terrible surroundings he is a lost man, almost consumed already by inner disgust before death comes to him from outside. The same is the case in *Romeo and Juliet*. The soil on which these tender blooms were planted is foreign to them, and we are left with nothing but to bewail the tragic transience of so beautiful a love which is shattered by the crazy calculations of a noble and well-meaning cleverness, just as a tender rose in the vale of this transitory world is withered by rude storms and tempests. But the woe that we feel is only a grievous reconciliation, an unhappy bliss in misfortune.

Since the poets present to us the mere downfall of individuals, they can equally well give such a turn to equally accidental complications that, however little other circumstances may also seem to produce this result, a happy outcome for the situation and the characters can be produced, and this is something which may be of interest to us. A happy denouement has at least as much justification as an unhappy one, and when it is a matter of considering this difference alone, I must admit that for my part a happy denouement is to be preferred. And why not? To prefer misfortune, just because it is misfortune, instead of a happy resolution, has no other basis but a certain superior sentimentality which indulges in grief and suffering and finds more interest in them than in the painless situations that it regards as commonplace. Thus if the interests at issue are in themselves of such a kind that it is really not worthwhile for an individual to sacrifice himself for them, since without self-sacrifice he can renounce them or come to an agreement with others about them, then the conclusion need not be tragic. For the tragedy of conflicts and their resolution must in general prevail only where this is necessary for justifying them in virtue of some higher outlook. But if there is no such inevitability, mere suffering and misfortune are not justified by anything.

This is the natural reason for plays and dramas that are midway between tragedy and comedy. I have already indicated the strictly poetical element in this kind of dramatic poetry. But in Germany touching features of civil life and family circles have been all the rage or there has been preoccupation with chivalry to which an impetus has been given since the time of Goethe's *Götz*, but what has been celebrated above all in this field and most frequently is the triumph of the subjectively moral outlook. The usual topics here are money and property, class-differences, unfortunate love-affairs, mental wickedness in trifling matters and narrow social circles, and the like, and, in general, with what we see elsewhere every day, only with this difference that in these moralizing plays virtue and duty win the day and vice is put to shame and punished or is moved to repentance, so that the reconciliation is supposed to lie in this moral conclusion where both vice and virtue get their due. Thus the chief interest is made to lie in the individual's own personal disposition and the goodness or evil of his heart. But the more the abstract moral disposition is made the kingpin, the less can it be a passionate concentration on something, on a really substantial end, that the individual is tied to, while in the last resort even a definite character cannot hold out and accomplish its aim. For once everything is shuffled into the moral disposition and the heart, there is no support any longer, given this subjectivity and strength of moral reflection, for a character otherwise firm or at least for his personal ends. The heart can break, and its dispositions may alter. Such touching plays as Kotzebue's *Menschenhass und Reue* [*Misanthropy and Repentance*] and many of the moral trespasses in Iffland's dramas, taken strictly, have a result which is really neither good nor bad. The chief theme usually ends in forgiveness and the promise of reform and then there appears every possibility of inner conversion and the repudiation of the old self. Here there is of course the lofty nature and the greatness of the spirit. But if the young wastrel, like most of Kotzebue's characters and like Iffland's too here and there, is a blackguard, a rascal, and now promises to reform, then in the case of such a fellow who is worthless from the start, conversion is only hypocrisy, or so superficial that it has not gripped his heart, and an end has been made of the thing in only an external way for a moment, but at bottom it can only lead to false starts when the thing is only played over and over again from the beginning.

Finally, in modern comedy especially there is an essentially important difference on which I have touched already in connection with Greek comedy, namely whether the folly and one-sidedness of the dramatis personae appears laughable to the audience only or to themselves as well, whether therefore the characters in the comedy can be mocked solely by the audience or by themselves also. Aristophanes, the comic author par excellence, made the latter alternative the fundamental principle of his plays. But in the new comedy in Greece and later in Plautus and Terence the opposite tendency was developed, and this has acquired such universal prominence in modern comedy that a multitude of our comic productions verges more or less on what is purely prosaically laughable and even on what is bitter and repugnant. This is the attitude especially of Molière, for example, in his more subtle comedies which are not meant to be farces. There is a reason for prose here, namely that the characters are deadly serious in their aims. They pursue them therefore with all the fervour of this seriousness and when at the end they are deceived or have their aim frustrated by themselves, they cannot join in the laughter freely and with satisfaction but, duped, are the butt of the laughter of others, often mixed as it is with malice.

So, for example, Molière's *Tartuffe, le faux dévot*, is unmasked as a downright villain, and this is not funny at all but a very serious matter; and the duping of the deceived Orgon leads to such painful misfortune that it can be assuaged only by a deus ex machina, i.e. when the police officer at the end says to him [2. 1905–9]:

> *Remettez-vous, monsieur, d'une alarme si chaude,*
> *Nous vivons sous un prince, ennemi de la fraude,*
> *Un prince dont les yeux se font jour dans les cœurs,*
> *Et que ne peut tromper tout l'art des imposteurs.*[21]

There is nothing really comical either about the odious *idée fixe* of such rigid characters as Molière's miser,[22] whose absolutely serious involvement in his narrow passion inhibits any liberation of his mind from this restriction.
    Next, as a substitute for this kind of thing, mastery in this field has the best opportunity for its cleverness by displaying its subtly developed skill in the precise portrayal of characters or the carrying out of a well-considered intrigue. The intrigue generally arises from the fact that an individual tries to achieve his aims by deceiving other people. He seems to share their interests and to further them, but this false furtherance actually produces the contradiction of falling into his own trap and so coming to grief himself. Next, on the other hand, the opposite means are commonly employed, i.e. the individual puts a false face on himself in order to put others into a similar perplexity: this coming and going makes possible in the most ingenious way endless tergiversation and complicated involvement in all sorts of situation. In inventing such intrigues and their complications the Spanish are the finest masters and have given us in this sphere much that is attractive and excellent. The subject-matter here *La Celestine?* is provided by interests such as love, honour, etc. In tragedy these lead to the most profound collisions, but in comedy (for example, the pride which will not confess a love that has been long felt and at the end is just for this reason betrayed) they are clearly without substance from the start and are annulled comically. Finally, the characters who contrive and conduct such intrigues in modern comedy are usually, like the slaves in Roman comedy, servants or chambermaids who have no respect for the aims of their masters, but further them or frustrate them as their own advantage dictates and only give us the laughable spectacle of masters being really the servants, or the servants masters, or at least they provide an occasion for other comic situations which they contrive by external means or by their own arrangements. We ourselves, as

spectators, are in the secret and we can always feel assured in the face of all the cunning and every betrayal, often very seriously pursued against the most estimable fathers, uncles, etc., and now we can laugh over every contradiction implicit or obvious in such trickeries.

In this way modern comedy displays to the spectators (partly in character-sketches, partly in comical complications of situations and circumstances) private interests and characters involved in them with their casual obliquities, absurdities, unusual behaviour, and follies. But such a frank joviality as pervades the comedies of Aristophanes as a constant reconciliation does not animate this kind of modern comedy at all. Indeed these comedies of intrigue may be actually repulsive when downright evil, the cunning of servants, the deceitfulness of sons and wards, gains the victory over honest masters, fathers, and trustees when these older people have themselves not been actuated by bad prejudice or eccentricities which would have made them laughable in their helpless folly and put them at the mercy of the projects of other people.

Nevertheless, in contrast to this on the whole prosaic way of treating comedy, the modern world has developed a type of comedy which is truly comical and truly poetic. Here once again the keynote is good humour, assured and careless gaiety despite all failure and misfortune, exuberance and the audacity of a fundamentally happy craziness, folly, and idiosyncrasy in general. Consequently there is presented here once more (in a deeper wealth and inwardness of humour), whether in wider or narrower circles of society, in a subject-matter whether important or trivial, what Aristophanes achieved to perfection in his field in Greece. As a brilliant example of this sort of thing I will name Shakespeare once again, in conclusion, but without going into detail.

Now, with the development of the kinds of comedy we have reached the real end of our philosophical inquiry. We began with symbolic art where personality struggles to find itself as form and content and to become objective to itself. We proceeded to the plastic art of Greece where the Divine, now conscious of itself, is presented to us in living individuals. We ended with the romantic art of emotion and deep feeling where absolute subjective personality moves free in itself and in the spiritual world. Satisfied in itself, it no longer unites itself with anything objective and particularized and it brings the negative side of this dissolution into consciousness in the humour of comedy. Yet on this peak comedy leads at the same time to the dissolution of art altogether. All art aims at the identity, produced by the spirit, in which eternal things, God, and absolute truth are revealed in real appearance and shape to our contemplation, to our hearts and minds. But if comedy presents this unity only as its self-destruction because the Absolute, which wants to realize itself, sees its self-actualization destroyed by interests that have now become explicitly free in the real world and are directed only on what is accidental and subjective, then the presence and agency of the Absolute no longer appears positively unified with the characters and aims of the real world but asserts itself only in the negative form of cancelling everything not correspondent with it, and subjective personality alone shows itself self-confident and self-assured at the same time in this dissolution.

Now at the end we have arranged every essential category of the beautiful and every essential form of art into a philosophical garland, and weaving it is one of the worthiest tasks that philosophy is capable of completing. For in art we have to do, not with any agreeable or useful child's play, but with the liberation of the spirit from the content and forms of finitude, with the presence and reconciliation of the Absolute in what is apparent and visible, with an unfolding of the truth which is not exhausted in natural history but revealed in world-history. Art itself is the most beautiful side of that history and it is the best compensation for hard work in the world and the bitter labour for knowledge. For this reason my treatment of the subject could not consist in a mere criticism of works of art or an instruction for producing them. My one aim has been to seize in thought and to prove the fundamental nature of the beautiful and art, and to follow it through all the stages it has gone through in the course of its realization. I hope that in this chief point my exposition has satisfied you. And now when the link forged between us generally and in relation to our common aim has been broken, it is my final wish that the higher and indestructible bond of the Idea of beauty and truth may link us and keep us firmly united now and for ever.

5   "The Substance of Shakespearean Tragedy,"
from *Shakespearean Tragedy*

The question we are to consider in this lecture may be stated in a variety of ways. We may put it thus: What is the substance of a Shakespearean tragedy, taken in abstraction both from its form and from the differences in point of substance between one tragedy and another? Or thus: What is the nature of the tragic aspect of life as represented by Shakespeare? What is the general fact shown now in this tragedy and now in that? And we are putting the same question when we ask: What is Shakespeare's tragic conception, or conception of tragedy?

These expressions, it should be observed, do not imply that Shakespeare himself ever asked or answered such a question; that he set himself to reflect on the tragic aspects of life, that he framed a tragic conception, and still less that, like Aristotle or Corneille, he had a theory of the kind of poetry called tragedy. These things are all possible; how far any one of them is probable we need not discuss; but none of them is presupposed by the question we are going to consider. This question implies only that, as a matter of fact, Shakespeare in writing tragedy did represent a certain aspect of life in a certain way, and that through examination of his writings we ought to be able, to some extent, to describe this aspect and way in terms addressed to the understanding. Such a description, so far as it is true and adequate, may, after these explanations, be called indifferently an account of the substance of Shakespearean tragedy, or an account of Shakespeare's conception of tragedy or view of the tragic fact.

Two further warnings may be required. In the first place, we must remember that the tragic aspect of life is only one aspect. We cannot arrive at Shakespeare's whole dramatic way of looking at the world from his tragedies alone, as we can arrive at Milton's way of regarding things, or at Wordsworth's or at Shelley's, by examining almost any one of their important works. Speaking very broadly, one may say that these poets at their best always look at things in one light; but *Hamlet* and *Henry IV* and *Cymbeline* reflect things from quite distinct positions, and Shakespeare's whole dramatic view is not to be identified with any one of these reflections. And, in the second place, I may repeat that in these lectures, at any rate for the most part, we are to be content with his *dramatic view*, and are not to ask whether it corresponded exactly with his opinions or creed outside his poetry—the opinions or creed of the being whom we sometimes oddly call "Shakespeare the man." It does not seem likely that outside his poetry he was a very simple-minded Catholic or Protestant or Atheist, as some have maintained; but we cannot be sure, as with those other poets we can, that in his works he expressed his deepest and most cherished convictions on ultimate questions, or even that he had any. And in his dramatic conceptions there is enough to occupy us.

1

In approaching our subject it will be best, without attempting to shorten the path by referring to famous theories of the drama, to start directly from the facts, and to collect from them gradually an idea of Shakespearean Tragedy. And first, to begin from the outside, such a tragedy brings before us a considerable number of persons (many more than the persons in a Greek play, unless the members of the Chorus are reckoned among them); but it is pre-eminently the story of one person, the 'hero',[1] or at most of two, the 'hero' and 'heroine'. Moreover, it is only in the love-tragedies, *Romeo and Juliet* and *Antony and Cleopatra*, that the heroine is as much the centre of the action as the hero. The rest, including *Macbeth*, are single stars. So that, having noticed the peculiarity of these two dramas, we may henceforth, for the sake of brevity, ignore it, and may speak of the tragic story as being concerned primarily with one person.

The story, next, leads up to, and includes, the *death* of the hero. On the one hand (whatever may be true of tragedy elsewhere), no play at the end of which the hero remains alive is, in the full Shakespearean sense, a tragedy; and we no longer class *Troilus and Cressida* or *Cymbeline* as such, as did the editors of the Folio. On the other hand, the story depicts also the troubled part of the hero's life which precedes and leads up to his death; and an instantaneous death occurring by 'accident' in the midst of prosperity would not suffice for it. It is, in fact, essentially a tale of suffering and calamity conducting to death.

The suffering and calamity are, moreover, exceptional. They befall a conspicuous person. They are themselves of some striking kind. They are also, as a rule, unexpected, and contrasted with previous happiness or glory. A tale, for example, of a man slowly worn to death by disease, poverty, little cares, sordid vices, petty persecutions, however piteous or dreadful it might be, would not be tragic in the Shakespearean sense.

Such exceptional suffering and calamity, then, affecting the hero, and—we must now add—generally extending far and wide beyond him, so as to make the whole scene a scene of woe, are an essential ingredient in tragedy and a chief source of the tragic emotions, and especially of pity. But the proportions of this ingredient, and the direction taken by tragic pity, will naturally vary greatly. Pity, for example, has a much larger part in *King Lear* than in *Macbeth*, and is directed in the one case chiefly to the hero, in the other chiefly to minor characters.

Let us now pause for a moment on the ideas we have so far reached. They would more than suffice to describe the whole tragic fact as it presented itself to the mediaeval mind. To the mediaeval mind a tragedy meant a narrative rather than a play, and its notion of the matter of this narrative may readily be gathered from Dante or, still better, from Chaucer. Chaucer's *Monk's Tale* is a series of what he calls 'tragedies'; and this means in fact a series of tales *de Casibus Illustrium Virorum*—stories of the Falls of Illustrious Men, such as Lucifer, Adam, Hercules and Nebuchadnezzar. And the Monk ends the tale of Croesus thus:

> Anhanged was Cresus, the proudè kyng;
> His roial tronè myghte hym nat availle.
> Tragédie is noon oother maner thyng,
> Ne kan in syngyng criè ne biwaille
> But for that Fortune alwey wole assaile
> With unwar strook the regnès that been proude;
> For whan men trusteth hire, thanne wol she faille,
> And covere hire brighte facè with a clowde.

A total reverse of fortune, coming unawares upon a man who "stood in high degree," happy and apparently secure—such was the tragic fact to the mediaeval mind. It appealed strongly to common human sympathy and pity; it startled also another feeling, that of fear. It frightened men and awed them. It made them feel that man is blind and helpless, the plaything of an inscrutable power, called by the name of Fortune or some other name—a power which appears to smile on him for a little, and then on a sudden strikes him down in his pride.

Shakespeare's idea of the tragic fact is larger than this idea and goes beyond it; but it includes it, and it is worth while to observe the identity of the two in a certain point which is often ignored. Tragedy with Shakespeare is concerned always with persons of 'high degree'; often with kings or princes; if not, with leaders in the state like Coriolanus, Brutus, Antony; at the least, as in *Romeo and Juliet*, with members of great houses, whose quarrels are of public moment. There is a decided difference here between *Othello* and our three other tragedies, but it is not a difference of kind. Othello himself is no mere private person; he is the General of the Republic. At the beginning we see him in the Council-Chamber of the Senate. The consciousness of his high position never leaves him. At the end, when he is determined to live no longer, he is as anxious as Hamlet not to be misjudged by the great world, and his last speech begins,

> Soft you; a word or two before you go.
> I have done the state some service, and they know it.[2]

And this characteristic of Shakespeare's tragedies, though not the most vital, is neither external nor unimportant. The saying that every death-bed is the scene of the fifth act of a tragedy has its meaning, but it would not be true if the word 'tragedy' bore its dramatic sense. The pangs of despised love and the anguish of remorse, we say, are the same in a peasant and a prince; but, not to insist that they cannot be so when the prince is really a prince, the story of the prince, the triumvir, or the general, has a greatness and dignity of its own. His fate affects the welfare of a whole nation or empire; and when he falls suddenly from the height of earthly greatness to the dust, his fall produces a sense of contrast, of the powerlessness of man, and of the omnipotence—perhaps the caprice—of Fortune or Fate, which no tale of private life can possibly rival. Such feelings are constantly evoked by Shakespeare's tragedies—again in varying degrees. Perhaps they are the very strongest of the emotions awakened by the early tragedy of *Richard II*, where they receive a concentrated expression in Richard's famous speech about the antic

> Death, who sits in the hollow crown
> That rounds the mortal temples of a king,

grinning at his pomp, watching till his vanity and his fancied security have wholly encased him round, and then coming and boring with a little pin through his castle wall. And these feelings, though their predominance is subdued in the mightiest tragedies, remain powerful there. In the figure of the maddened Lear we see

> A sight most pitiful in the meanest wretch,
> Past speaking of in a king;

and if we would realise the truth in this matter we cannot do better than compare with the effect of *King Lear* the effect of Tourgénief's parallel and remarkable tale of peasant life, *A King Lear of the Steppes*.

2

A Shakespearean tragedy as so far considered may be called a story of exceptional calamity leading to the death of a man in high estate. But it is clearly much more than this, and we have now to regard it from another side. No amount of calamity which merely befell a man, descending from the clouds like lightning, or stealing from the darkness like pestilence, could alone provide the substance of its story. Job was the greatest of all the children of the east, and his afflictions were well-nigh more than he could bear; but even if we imagined them wearing him to death, that would not make his story tragic. Nor yet would it become so, in the Shakespearean sense, if the fire, and the great wind from the wilderness, and the torments of his flesh were conceived as sent by a supernatural power, whether just or malignant. The calamities of tragedy do not simply happen, nor are they sent; they proceed mainly from actions, and those the actions of men.

We see a number of human beings placed in certain circumstances; and we see, arising from the co-operation of their characters in these circumstances, certain actions. These actions beget others, and these others beget others again, until this series of inter-connected deeds leads by an apparently inevitable sequence to a catastrophe. The effect of such a series on our imagination is to make us regard the sufferings which accompany it, and the catastrophe in which it ends, not only or chiefly as something which happens to the persons concerned, but equally as something which is caused by them. This at least may be said of the principal persons, and, among them, of the hero, who always contributes in some measure to the disaster in which he perishes.

This second aspect of tragedy evidently differs greatly from the first. Men, from this point of view, appear to us primarily as agents, "themselves the authors of their proper woe"; and our fear and pity, though they will not cease or diminish, will be modified accordingly. We are now to consider this second aspect, remembering that it too is only one aspect, and additional to the first, not a substitute for it.

The 'story' or 'action' of a Shakespearean tragedy does not consist, of course, solely of human actions or deeds; but the deeds are the predominant factor. And these deeds are, for the most part, actions in the full sense of the word; not things done 'tween asleep and wake,' but acts or omissions thoroughly expressive of the doer—characteristic deeds. The centre of the tragedy, therefore, may be said with equal truth to lie in action issuing from character, or in character issuing in action.

Shakespeare's main interest lay here. To say that it lay in *mere* character, or was a psychological interest, would be a great mistake, for he was dramatic to the tips of his fingers. It is possible to find places where he has given a certain indulgence to his love of poetry, and even to his turn for general reflections; but it would be very difficult, and in his later tragedies perhaps impossible, to detect passages where he has allowed such freedom to the interest in character apart from action. But for the opposite extreme, for the abstraction of mere 'plot' (which is a very different thing from the tragic 'action'), for the kind of interest which predominates in a novel like *The Woman in White*, it is clear that he cared even less. I do not mean that this interest is absent from his dramas; but it is subordinate to others, and is so interwoven with them that we are rarely conscious of it apart, and rarely feel in any great strength the half-intellectual, half-nervous excitement of following an ingenious complication. What we do feel strongly, as a tragedy advances to its close, is that the calamities and catastrophe follow inevitably from the deeds of men, and that the main source of these deeds is character. The dictum that, with Shakespeare, "character is destiny" is no doubt an exaggeration, and one that may mislead (for many of his tragic personages, if they had not met with peculiar circumstances, would have escaped a tragic end, and might even have lived fairly untroubled lives); but it is the exaggeration of a vital truth.

This truth, with some of its qualifications, will appear more clearly if we now go on to ask what elements are to be found in the 'story' or 'action', occasionally or frequently, beside the characteristic deeds, and the sufferings and circumstances, of the persons. I will refer to three of these additional factors.

(a) Shakespeare, occasionally and for reasons which need not be discussed here, represents abnormal conditions of mind; insanity, for example, somnambulism, hallucinations. And deeds issuing from these are certainly not what we called deeds in the fullest sense, deeds expressive of character. No; but these abnormal conditions are never introduced as the origin of deeds of any dramatic moment. Lady Macbeth's sleep-walking has no influence whatever on the events that follow it. Macbeth did not murder Duncan because he saw a dagger in the air: he saw the dagger because he was about to murder Duncan. Lear's insanity is not the cause of a tragic conflict any more than Ophelia's; it is, like Ophelia's, the result of a conflict; and in both cases the effect is mainly pathetic. If Lear were really mad when he divided his kingdom, if Hamlet were really mad at any time in the story, they would cease to be tragic characters.

(b) Shakespeare also introduces the supernatural into some of his tragedies; he introduces ghosts, and witches who have supernatural knowledge. This supernatural element certainly cannot in most cases, if in any, be explained away as an illusion in the mind of one of the characters. And further, it does contribute to the action, and is in more than one instance an indispensable part of it: so that to describe human character, with circumstances, as always the *sole* motive force in this action would be a serious error. But the supernatural is always placed in the closest relation with character. It gives a confirmation and a distinct form to inward movements already present and exerting an influence; to the sense of failure in Brutus, to the stifled workings of conscience in Richard, to the half-formed thought or the horrified memory of guilt in Macbeth, to suspicion in Hamlet. Moreover, its influence is never of a compulsive kind. It forms no more than an element, however important, in the problem which the hero has to face; and we are never allowed to feel that it has removed his capacity or responsibility for dealing with this problem. So far indeed are we from feeling this, that many readers run to the opposite extreme, and openly or privately regard the supernatural as having nothing to do with the real interest of the play.

(c) Shakespeare, lastly, in most of his tragedies allows to 'chance' or 'accident' an appreciable influence at some point in the action. Chance or accident here will be found, I think, to mean any occurrence (not supernatural, of course) which enters the dramatic sequence neither from the agency of a character, nor from the obvious surrounding circumstances.[3] It may be called an accident, in this sense, that Romeo never got the Friar's message about the potion, and that Juliet did not awake from her long sleep a minute sooner; an accident that Edgar arrived at the prison just too late to save Cordelia's life; an accident that Desdemona dropped her handkerchief at the most fatal of moments; an accident that the pirate ship attacked Hamlet's ship, so that he was able to return forthwith to Denmark. Now this operation of accident is a fact, and a prominent fact, of human life. To exclude it *wholly* from tragedy, therefore, would be, we may say, to fail in truth. And, besides, it is not merely a fact. That men may start a course of events but can neither calculate nor control it, is a *tragic* fact. The dramatist may use accident so as to make us feel this; and there are also other dramatic uses to which it may be put. Shakespeare accordingly admits it. On the other hand, any *large* admission of chance into the tragic sequence[4] would certainly weaken, and might destroy, the sense of the causal connection of character, deed, and catastrophe. And Shakespeare really uses it very sparingly. We seldom find ourselves exclaiming, "What an unlucky accident!" I believe most readers would have to search painfully for instances. It is, further, frequently easy to see the dramatic intention of an accident; and some things which look like accidents have really a connection with character, and are therefore not in the full sense accidents. Finally, I believe it will be found that almost all the prominent accidents occur when the action is well advanced and the impression of the causal sequence is too firmly fixed to be impaired.

Thus it appears that these three elements in the 'action' are subordinate, while the dominant factor consists in deeds which issue from character. So that, by way of summary, we may now alter our first statement, "A tragedy is a story of exceptional calamity leading to the death of a man in high estate," and we may say instead (what in its turn is one-sided, though less so), that the story is one of human actions producing exceptional calamity and ending in the death of such a man.[5]

Before we leave the 'action', however, there is another question that may usefully be asked. Can we define this 'action' further by describing it as a conflict?

The frequent use of this idea in discussions on tragedy is ultimately due, I suppose, to the influence of Hegel's theory on the subject, certainly the most important theory since Aristotle's. But Hegel's view of the tragic conflict is not only unfamiliar to English readers and difficult to expound shortly, but it had its origin in reflections on Greek tragedy and, as Hegel was well aware, applies only imperfectly to the works of Shakespeare.[6] I shall, therefore, confine myself to the idea of conflict in its more general form. In this form it is obviously suitable to Shakespearean tragedy; but it is vague, and I will try to make it more precise by putting the question, Who are the combatants in this conflict?

Not seldom the conflict may quite naturally be conceived as lying between two persons, of whom the hero is one; or, more fully, as lying between two parties or groups, in one of which the hero is the leading figure. Or if we prefer to speak (as we may quite well do if we know what we are about) of the passions, tendencies, ideas, principles, forces, which animate these persons or groups, we may say that two of such passions or ideas, regarded as animating two persons

or groups, are the combatants. The love of Romeo and Juliet is in conflict with
the hatred of their houses, represented by various other characters. The cause
of Brutus and Cassius struggles with that of Julius, Octavius and Antony. In
Richard II the King stands on one side, Bolingbroke and his party on the other.
In *Macbeth* the hero and heroine are opposed to the representatives of Duncan.
In all these cases the great majority of the dramatis personae fall without difficulty into antagonistic groups, and the conflict between these groups ends with
the defeat of the hero.

Yet one cannot help feeling that in at least one of these cases, *Macbeth*, there
is something a little external in this way of looking at the action. And when we
come to some other plays this feeling increases. No doubt most of the characters in *Hamlet, King Lear, Othello*, or *Antony and Cleopatra* can be arranged in
opposed groups[7]; and no doubt there is a conflict; and yet it seems misleading
to describe this conflict as one *between these groups*. It cannot be simply this.
For though Hamlet and the King are mortal foes, yet that which engrosses our
interest and dwells in our memory at least as much as the conflict between
them, is the conflict *within* one of them. And so it is, though not in the same
degree, with *Antony and Cleopatra* and even with *Othello*; and, in fact, in a certain measure, it is so with nearly all the tragedies. There is an outward conflict
of persons and groups, there is also a conflict of forces in the hero's soul; and
even in *Julius Caesar* and *Macbeth* the interest of the former can hardly be said
to exceed that of the latter.

The truth is, that the type of tragedy in which the hero opposes to a hostile
force an undivided soul, is not the Shakespearean type. The souls of those who
contend with the hero may be thus undivided; they generally are; but, as a rule,
the hero, though he pursues his fated way, is, at least at some point in the action, and sometimes at many, torn by an inward struggle; and it is frequently
at such points that Shakespeare shows his most extraordinary power. If further
we compare the earlier tragedies with the later, we find that it is in the latter,
the maturest works, that this inward struggle is most emphasised. In the last of
them, *Coriolanus*, its interest completely eclipses towards the close of the play
that of the outward conflict. *Romeo and Juliet, Richard III, Richard II*, where the
hero contends with an outward force, but comparatively little with himself, are
all early plays.

If we are to include the outer and the inner struggle in a conception more
definite than that of conflict in general, we must employ some such phrase as
'spiritual force'. This will mean whatever forces act in the human spirit, whether

94

good or evil, whether personal passion or impersonal principle; doubts, desires, scruples, ideas—whatever can animate, shake, possess, and drive a man's soul. In a Shakespearean tragedy some such forces are shown in conflict. They are shown acting in men and generating strife between them. They are also shown, less universally, but quite as characteristically, generating disturbance and even conflict in the soul of the hero. Treasonous ambition in Macbeth collides with loyalty and patriotism in Macduff and Malcolm: here is the outward conflict. But these powers or principles equally collide in the soul of Macbeth himself: here is the inner. And neither by itself could make the tragedy.[8]

We shall see later the importance of this idea. Here we need only observe that the notion of tragedy as a conflict emphasises the fact that action is the centre of the story, while the concentration of interest, in the greater plays, on the inward struggle emphasises the fact that this action is essentially the expression of character.

3

Let us turn now from the 'action' to the central figure in it; and, ignoring the characteristics which distinguish the heroes from one another, let us ask whether they have any common qualities which appear to be essential to the tragic effect.

One they certainly have. They are exceptional beings. We have seen already that the hero, with Shakespeare, is a person of high degree or of public importance, and that his actions or sufferings are of an unusual kind. But this is not all. His nature also is exceptional, and generally raises him in some respect much above the average level of humanity. This does not mean that he is an eccentric or a paragon. Shakespeare never drew monstrosities of virtue; some of his heroes are far from being 'good'; and if he drew eccentrics he gave them a subordinate position in the plot. His tragic characters are made of the stuff we find within ourselves and within the persons who surround them. But, by an intensification of the life which they share with others, they are raised above them; and the greatest are raised so far that, if we fully realise all that is implied in their words and actions, we become conscious that in real life we have known scarcely any one resembling them. Some, like Hamlet and Cleopatra, have genius. Others, like Othello, Lear, Macbeth, Coriolanus, are built on the grand scale; and desire, passion, or will attains in them a terrible force. In almost all we observe a marked one-sidedness, a predisposition in some particular direction; a total incapacity, in certain circumstances, of resisting the force which draws in this direction; a fatal tendency to identify the whole being with one interest, object, passion, or habit of mind. This, it would seem, is, for Shakespeare, the fundamental tragic trait. It is present in his early heroes, Romeo and Richard II, infatuated men, who otherwise rise comparatively little above the ordinary level. It is a fatal gift, but it carries with it a touch of greatness; and when there is joined to it nobility of mind, or genius, or immense force, we realise the full power and reach of the soul, and the conflict in which it engages acquires that magnitude which stirs not only sympathy and pity, but admiration, terror, and awe.

The easiest way to bring home to oneself the nature of the tragic character is to compare it with a character of another kind. Dramas like *Cymbeline* and the *Winter's Tale*, which might seem destined to end tragically, but actually end otherwise, owe their happy ending largely to the fact that the principal characters fail to reach tragic dimensions. And, conversely, if these persons were put in the place of the tragic heroes, the dramas in which they appeared would cease to be tragedies. Posthumus would never have acted as Othello did; Othello, on his side, would have met Iachimo's challenge with something more than words. If, like Posthumus, he had remained convinced of his wife's infidelity, he would not have repented her execution; if, like Leontes, he had come to believe that by an unjust accusation he had caused her death, he would never have lived on, like Leontes. In the same way the villain Iachimo has no touch of tragic greatness. But Iago comes nearer to it, and if Iago had slandered Imogen and had supposed his slanders to have led to her death, he certainly would not have turned melancholy and wished to die. One reason why the end of the *Merchant of Venice* fails to satisfy us is that Shylock is a tragic character, and that we cannot believe in his accepting his defeat and the conditions imposed on him. This was a case where Shakespeare's imagination ran away with him, so that he drew a figure with which the destined pleasant ending would not harmonise.

In the circumstances where we see the hero placed, his tragic trait, which is also his greatness, is fatal to him. To meet these circumstances something is required which a smaller man might have given, but which the hero cannot give. He errs, by action or omission; and his error, joining with other causes, brings on him ruin. This is always so with Shakespeare. As we have seen, the idea of the tragic hero as a being destroyed simply and solely by external forces is quite alien to him; and not less so is the idea of the hero as contributing to his destruction only by acts in which we see no flaw. But the fatal imperfection or error, which is never absent, is of different kinds and degrees. At one extreme stands the excess and precipitancy of Romeo, which scarcely, if at all, diminish our regard for him; at the other the murderous ambition of Richard III. In most cases the tragic error involves no conscious breach of right; in some (e.g. that of Brutus or Othello) it is accompanied by a full conviction of right. In Hamlet there is a painful consciousness that duty is being neglected; in Antony a clear knowledge that the worse of two courses is being pursued; but Richard and Macbeth are the only heroes who do what they themselves recognise to be villainous. It is important to observe that Shakespeare does admit such heroes,[9] and also that he appears to feel, and exerts himself to meet, the difficulty that arises from their admission. The difficulty is that the spectator must desire their defeat and even their destruction; and yet this desire, and the satisfaction of it, are not tragic feelings. Shakespeare gives to Richard therefore a power which excites astonishment, and a courage which extorts admiration. He gives to Macbeth a similar, though less extraordinary, greatness, and adds to it a conscience so terrifying in its warnings and so maddening in its reproaches that the spectacle of inward torment compels a horrified sympathy and awe which balance, at the least, the desire for the hero's ruin.

The tragic hero with Shakespeare, then, need not be 'good', though generally he is 'good' and therefore at once wins sympathy in his error. But it is necessary that he should have so much of greatness that in his error and fall we may be vividly conscious of the possibilities of human nature.[10] Hence, in the first place, a Shakespearean tragedy is never, like some miscalled tragedies, depressing. No one ever closes the book with the feeling that man is a poor mean creature. He may be wretched and he may be awful, but he is not small. His lot may be heart-rending and mysterious, but it is not contemptible. The most confirmed of cynics ceases to be a cynic while he reads these plays. And with this greatness of the tragic hero (which is not always confined to him) is connected, secondly, what I venture to describe as the centre of the tragic impression. This central feeling is the impression of waste. With Shakespeare, at any rate, the pity and fear which are stirred by the tragic story seem to unite with, and even to merge in, a profound sense of sadness and mystery, which is due to this impression of waste. "What a piece of work is man," we cry; "so much more beautiful and so much more terrible than we knew! Why should he be so if this beauty and greatness only tortures itself and throws itself away?" We seem to have before us a type of the mystery of the whole world, the tragic fact which extends far beyond the limits of tragedy. Everywhere, from the crushed rocks beneath our feet to the soul of man, we see power, intelligence, life and glory, which astound us and seem to call for our worship. And everywhere we see them perishing, devouring one another and destroying themselves, often with dreadful pain, as though they came into being for no other end. Tragedy is the typical form of this mystery, because that greatness of soul which it exhibits oppressed, conflicting and destroyed, is the highest existence in our view. It forces the mystery upon us, and it makes us realise so vividly the worth of that which is wasted that we cannot possibly seek comfort in the reflection that all is vanity.

4

In this tragic world, then, where individuals, however great they may be and however decisive their actions may appear, are so evidently not the ultimate power, what is this power? What account can we give of it which will correspond with the imaginative impressions we receive? This will be our final question.

The variety of the answers given to this question shows how difficult it is. And the difficulty has many sources. Most people, even among those who know Shakespeare well and come into real contact with his mind, are inclined to isolate and exaggerate some one aspect of the tragic fact. Some are so much influenced by their own habitual beliefs that they import them more or less into their interpretation of every author who is 'sympathetic' to them. And even where neither of these causes of error appears to operate, another is present from which it is probably impossible wholly to escape. What I mean is this. Any answer we give to the question proposed ought to correspond with, or to represent in terms of the understanding, our imaginative and emotional experience in reading the tragedies. We have, of course, to do our best by study and effort to make this experience true to Shakespeare; but, that done to the best of our ability, the experience is the matter to be interpreted, and the test by which the interpretation must be tried. But it is extremely hard to make out exactly what this experience is, because, in the very effort to make it out, our reflecting mind, full of everyday ideas, is always tending to transform it by the application of these ideas, and so to elicit a result which, instead of representing the fact, conventionalises it. And the consequence is not only mistaken theories; it is that many a man will declare that he feels in reading a tragedy what he never really felt, while he fails to recognise what he actually did feel. It is not likely that we shall escape all these dangers in our effort to find an answer to the question regarding the tragic world and the ultimate power in it.

It will be agreed, however, first, that this question must not be answered in 'religious' language. For although this or that dramatis persona may speak of gods or of God, of evil spirits or of Satan, of heaven and of hell, and although the poet may show us ghosts from another world, these ideas do not materially influence his representation of life, nor are they used to throw light on the mystery of its tragedy. The Elizabethan drama was almost wholly secular; and while Shakespeare was writing he practically confined his view to the world of non-theological observation and thought, so that he represents it substantially in one and the same way whether the period of the story is pre-Christian or Christian.[11] He looked at this 'secular' world most intently and seriously; and he painted it, we cannot but conclude, with entire fidelity, without the wish to enforce an opinion of his own, and, in essentials, without regard to anyone's hopes, fears, or beliefs. His greatness is largely due to this fidelity in a mind of extraordinary power; and if, as a private person, he had a religious faith, his tragic view can hardly have been in contradiction with this faith, but must have been included in it, and supplemented, not abolished, by additional ideas.

Two statements, next, may at once be made regarding the tragic fact as he represents it: one, that it is and remains to us something piteous, fearful and mysterious; the other, that the representation of it does not leave us crushed, rebellious or desperate. These statements will be accepted, I believe, by any reader who is in touch with Shakespeare's mind and can observe his own. Indeed such a reader is rather likely to complain that they are painfully obvious. But if they are true as well as obvious, something follows from them in regard to our present question.

From the first it follows that the ultimate power in the tragic world is not adequately described as a law or order which we can see to be just and benevolent—as, in that sense, a 'moral order': for in that case the spectacle of suffering and waste could not seem to us so fearful and mysterious as it does. And from the second it follows that this ultimate power is not adequately described as a fate, whether malicious and cruel, or blind and indifferent to human happiness and goodness: for in that case the spectacle would leave us desperate or rebellious. Yet one or other of these two ideas will be found to govern most accounts of Shakespeare's tragic view or world. These accounts isolate and exaggerate single aspects, either the aspect of action or that of suffering; either the close and unbroken connection of character, will, deed and catastrophe, which, taken alone, shows the individual simply as sinning against, or failing to conform to, the moral order and drawing his just doom on his own head; or else that pressure of outward forces, that sway of accident, and those blind and agonised struggles, which, taken alone, show him as the mere victim of some power which cares neither for his sins nor for his pain. Such views contradict one another, and no third view can unite them; but the several aspects from whose isolation and exaggeration they spring are both present in the fact, and a view which would be true to the fact and to the whole of our imaginative experience must in some way combine these aspects.

Let us begin, then, with the idea of fatality and glance at some of the impressions which give rise to it, without asking at present whether this idea is their natural or fitting expression. There can be no doubt that they do arise and that they ought to arise. If we do not feel at times that the hero is, in some sense, a doomed man; that he and others drift struggling to destruction like helpless creatures borne on an irresistible flood towards a cataract; that, faulty as they may be, their fault is far from being the sole or sufficient cause of all they suffer; and that the power from which they cannot escape is relentless and immovable, we have failed to receive an essential part of the full tragic effect.

The sources of these impressions are various, and I will refer only to a few. One of them is put into words by Shakespeare himself when he makes the player-king in *Hamlet* say:

> Our thoughts are ours, their ends none of our own;

'their ends' are the issues or outcomes of our thoughts, and these, says the speaker, are not our own. The tragic world is a world of action, and action is the translation of thought into reality. We see men and women confidently attempting it. They strike into the existing order of things in pursuance of their ideas. But what they achieve is not what they intended; it is terribly unlike it. They understand nothing, we say to ourselves, of the world on which they operate. They fight blindly in the dark, and the power that works through them makes them the instrument of a design which is not theirs. They act freely, and yet their action binds them hand and foot. And it makes no difference whether they meant well or ill. No one could mean better than Brutus, but he contrives misery for his country and death for himself. No one could mean worse than Iago, and he too is caught in the web he spins for others. Hamlet, recoiling from the rough duty of revenge, is pushed into blood-guiltiness he never dreamed of, and forced at last on the revenge he could not will. His adversary's murders, and no less his adversary's remorse, bring about the opposite of what they sought. Lear follows an old man's whim, half generous, half selfish; and in a moment it looses all the powers of darkness upon him. Othello agonises over an empty fiction, and, meaning to execute solemn justice, butchers innocence and strangles love. They understand themselves no better than the world about them. Coriolanus thinks that his heart is iron, and it melts like snow before a fire. Lady Macbeth, who thought she could dash out her own child's brains, finds herself hounded to death by the smell of a stranger's blood. Her husband thinks that to gain a crown he would jump the life to come, and finds that the crown has brought him all the horrors of that life. Everywhere, in this tragic world, man's thought, translated into act, is transformed into the opposite of itself. His act, the movement of a few ounces of matter in a moment of time, becomes a monstrous flood which spreads over a kingdom. And whatsoever he dreams of doing, he achieves that which he least dreamed of, his own destruction.

All this makes us feel the blindness and helplessness of man. Yet by itself it would hardly suggest the idea of fate, because it shows man as in some degree, however slight, the cause of his own undoing. But other impressions come to aid it. It is aided by everything which makes us feel that a man is, as we say, terribly unlucky; and of this there is, even in Shakespeare, not a little. Here come in some of the accidents already considered, Juliet's waking from her trance a minute too late, Desdemona's loss of her handkerchief at the only moment when the loss would have mattered, that insignificant delay which cost Cordelia's life. Again, men act, no doubt, in accordance with their characters; but what is it that brings them just the one problem which is fatal to them and would be easy to another, and sometimes brings it to them just when they are least fitted to face it? How is it that Othello comes to be the companion of the one man in the world who is at once able enough, brave enough, and vile enough to ensnare him? By what strange fatality does it happen that Lear has such daughters and Cordelia such sisters? Even character itself contributes to these feelings of fatality. How could men escape, we cry, such vehement propensities as drive Romeo, Antony, Coriolanus, to their doom? And why is it that a man's virtues help to destroy him, and that his weakness or defect is so intertwined with everything that is admirable in him that we can hardly separate them even in imagination?

If we find in Shakespeare's tragedies the source of impressions like these, it is important, on the other hand, to notice what we do *not* find there. We find practically no trace of fatalism in its more primitive, crude and obvious forms. Nothing, again, makes us think of the actions and sufferings of the persons as somehow arbitrarily fixed beforehand without regard to their feelings, thoughts and resolutions. Nor, I believe, are the facts ever so presented that it seems to us as if the supreme power, whatever it may be, had a special spite against a family or an individual. Neither, lastly, do we receive the impression (which, it must be observed, is not purely fatalistic) that a family, owing to some hideous crime or impiety in early days, is doomed in later days to continue a career of portentous calamities and sins. Shakespeare, indeed, does not appear to have taken much interest in heredity, or to have attached much importance to it.

What, then, is this 'fate' which the impressions already considered lead us to describe as the ultimate power in the tragic world? It appears to be a mytho-logical expression for the whole system or order, of which the individual char-acters form an inconsiderable and feeble part; which seems to determine, far more than they, their native dispositions and their circumstances, and, through these, their action; which is so vast and complex that they can scarcely at all un-derstand it or control its workings; and which has a nature so definite and fixed that whatever changes take place in it produce other changes inevitably and without regard to men's desires and regrets. And whether this system or order is best called by the name of fate or no,[12] it can hardly be denied that it does ap-pear as the ultimate power in the tragic world, and that it has such characteris-tics as these. But the name 'fate' may be intended to imply something more—to imply that this order is a blank necessity, totally regardless alike of human weal and of the difference between good and evil or right and wrong. And such an implication many readers would at once reject. They would maintain, on the contrary, that this order shows characteristics of quite another kind from those which made us give it the name of fate, characteristics which certainly should not induce us to forget those others, but which would lead us to describe it as a moral order and its necessity as a moral necessity.

5

Let us turn, then, to this idea. It brings into the light those aspects of the tragic fact which the idea of fate throws into the shade. And the argument which leads to it in its simplest form may be stated briefly thus: "Whatever may be said of accidents, circumstances and the like, human action is, after all, presented to us as the central fact in tragedy, and also as the main cause of the catastrophe. That necessity which so much impresses us is, after all, chiefly the necessary connection of actions and consequences. For these actions we, without even raising a question on the subject, hold the agents responsible; and the tragedy would disappear for us if we did not. The critical action is, in greater or less degree, wrong or bad. The catastrophe is, in the main, the return of this action on the head of the agent. It is an example of justice; and that order which, present alike within the agents and outside them, infallibly brings it about, is therefore just. The rigour of its justice is terrible, no doubt, for a tragedy is a terrible story; but, in spite of fear and pity, we acquiesce, because our sense of justice is satisfied."

Now, if this view is to hold good, the 'justice' of which it speaks must be at once distinguished from what is called 'poetic justice'. 'Poetic justice' means that prosperity and adversity are distributed in proportion to the merits of the agents. Such 'poetic justice' is in flagrant contradiction with the facts of life, and it is absent from Shakespeare's tragic picture of life; indeed, this very absence is a ground of constant complaint on the part of Dr. Johnson. "The doer must suffer." [Greek, *Drasanti pathein*]—this we find in Shakespeare. We also find that villainy never remains victorious and prosperous at the last. But an assignment of amounts of happiness and misery, an assignment even of life and death, in proportion to merit, we do not find. No one who thinks of Desdemona and Cordelia; or who remembers that one end awaits Richard III and Brutus, Macbeth and Hamlet; or who asks himself which suffered most, Othello or Iago; will ever accuse Shakespeare of representing the ultimate power as 'poetically' just.

And we must go further. I venture to say that it is a mistake to use at all these terms of justice and merit or desert. And this for two reasons. In the first place, essential as it is to recognise the connection between act and consequence, and natural as it may seem in some cases (e.g. Macbeth's) to say that the doer only gets what he deserves, yet in very many cases to say this would be quite unnatural. We might not object to the statement that Lear deserved to suffer for his folly, selfishness and tyranny; but to assert that he deserved to suffer what he did suffer is to do violence not merely to language but to any healthy moral sense. It is, moreover, to obscure the tragic fact that the consequences of action cannot be limited to that which would appear to us to follow 'justly' from them. And, this being so, when we call the order of the tragic world just, we are either using the word in some vague and unexplained sense, or we are going beyond what is shown us of this order, and are appealing to faith.

But, in the second place, the ideas of justice and desert are, it seems to me, in *all* cases—even those of Richard III and of Macbeth and Lady Macbeth—untrue to our imaginative experience. When we are immersed in a tragedy, we feel towards dispositions, actions, and persons such emotions as attraction and re-

pulsion, pity, wonder, fear, horror, perhaps hatred; but we do not *judge*. This is
a point of view which emerges only when, in reading a play, we slip, by our own
fault or the dramatist's, from the tragic position, or when, in thinking about
the play afterwards, we fall back on our everyday legal and moral notions. But
tragedy does not belong, any more than religion belongs, to the sphere of these
notions; neither does the imaginative attitude in presence of it. While we are
in its world we watch what is, seeing that so it happened and must have happened, feeling that it is piteous, dreadful, awful, mysterious, but neither passing
sentence on the agents, nor asking whether the behaviour of the ultimate power
towards them is just. And, therefore, the use of such language in attempts to render our imaginative experience in terms of the understanding is, to say the least,
full of danger.[13]

Let us attempt then to re-state the idea that the ultimate power in the tragic
world is a moral order. Let us put aside the ideas of justice and merit, and speak
simply of good and evil. Let us understand by these words, primarily, moral
good and evil, but also everything else in human beings which we take to be excellent or the reverse. Let us understand the statement that the ultimate power
or order is 'moral' to mean that it does not show itself indifferent to good and
evil, or equally favourable or unfavourable to both, but shows itself akin to
good and alien from evil. And, understanding the statement thus, let us ask
what grounds it has in the tragic fact as presented by Shakespeare.

Here, as in dealing with the grounds on which the idea of fate rests, I choose
only two or three out of many. And the most important is this. In Shakespearean tragedy the main source of the convulsion which produces suffering and
death is never good: good contributes to this convulsion only from its tragic
implication with its opposite in one and the same character. The main source,
on the contrary, is in every case evil; and, what is more (though this seems to
have been little noticed), it is in almost every case evil in the fullest sense, not
mere imperfection but plain moral evil. The love of Romeo and Juliet conducts
them to death only because of the senseless hatred of their houses. Guilty ambition, seconded by diabolic malice and issuing in murder, opens the action in
Macbeth. Iago is the main source of the convulsion in *Othello*; Goneril, Regan
and Edmund in *King Lear*. Even when this plain moral evil is not the obviously
prime source within the play, it lies behind it: the situation with which Hamlet
has to deal has been formed by adultery and murder. *Julius Caesar* is the only
tragedy in which one is even tempted to find an exception to this rule. And
the inference is obvious. If it is chiefly evil that violently disturbs the order of

the world, this order cannot be friendly to evil or indifferent between evil and good, any more than a body which is convulsed by poison is friendly to it or indifferent to the distinction between poison and food.✓

Again, if we confine our attention to the hero, and to those cases where the gross and palpable evil is not in him but elsewhere, we find that the comparatively innocent hero still shows some marked imperfection or defect—irresolution, precipitancy, pride, credulousness, excessive simplicity, excessive susceptibility to sexual emotions, and the like. These defects or imperfections are certainly, in the wide sense of the word, evil, and they contribute decisively to the conflict and catastrophe. And the inference is again obvious. The ultimate power which shows itself disturbed by this evil and reacts against it, must have a nature alien to it. Indeed its reaction is so vehement and 'relentless' that it would seem to be bent on nothing short of good in perfection, and to be ruthless in its demand for it.

To this must be added another fact, or another aspect of the same fact. Evil exhibits itself everywhere as something negative, barren, weakening, destructive, a principle of death. It isolates, disunites, and tends to annihilate not only its opposite but itself. That which keeps the evil man[14] prosperous, makes him succeed, even permits him to exist, is the good in him (I do not mean only the obviously 'moral' good). When the evil in him masters the good and has its way, it destroys other people through him, but it also destroys *him*. At the close of the struggle he has vanished, and has left behind him nothing that can stand. What remains is a family, a city, a country, exhausted, pale and feeble, but alive through the principle of good which animates it; and, within it, individuals who, if they have not the brilliance or greatness of the tragic character, still have won our respect and confidence. And the inference would seem clear. If existence in an order depends on good, and if the presence of evil is hostile to such existence, the inner being or soul of this order must be akin to good.

These are aspects of the tragic world at least as clearly marked as those which, taken alone, suggest the idea of fate. And the idea which they in their turn, when taken alone, may suggest, is that of an order which does not indeed award 'poetic justice', but which reacts through the necessity of its own 'moral' nature both against attacks made upon it and against failure to conform to it. Tragedy, on this view, is the exhibition of that convulsive reaction; and the fact that the spectacle does not leave us rebellious or desperate is due to a more or less distinct perception that the tragic suffering and death arise from collision, not with a fate or blank power, but with a moral power, a power akin to all that

105

we admire and revere in the characters themselves. This perception produces something like a feeling of acquiescence in the catastrophe, though it neither leads us to pass judgment on the characters nor diminishes the pity, the fear, and the sense of waste, which their struggle, suffering and fall evoke. And, finally, this view seems quite able to do justice to those aspects of the tragic fact which give rise to the idea of fate. They would appear as various expressions of the fact that the moral order acts not capriciously or like a human being, but from the necessity of its nature, or, if we prefer the phrase, by general laws—a necessity or law which of course knows no exception and is as 'ruthless' as fate.

It is impossible to deny to this view a large measure of truth. And yet without some amendment it can hardly satisfy. For it does not include the whole of the facts, and therefore does not wholly correspond with the impressions they produce. Let it be granted that the system or order which shows itself omnipotent against individuals is, in the sense explained, moral. Still—at any rate for the eye of sight—the evil against which it asserts itself, and the persons whom this evil inhabits, are not really something outside the order, so that they can attack it or fail to conform to it; they are within it and a part of it. It itself produces them—produces Iago as well as Desdemona, Iago's cruelty as well as Iago's courage. It is not poisoned, it poisons itself. Doubtless it shows by its violent reaction that the poison *is* poison, and that its health lies in good. But one significant fact cannot remove another, and the spectacle we witness scarcely warrants the assertion that the order is responsible for the good in Desdemona, but Iago for the evil in Iago. If we make this assertion we make it on grounds other than the facts as presented in Shakespeare's tragedies.

Nor does the idea of a moral order asserting itself against attack or want of conformity answer in full to our feelings regarding the tragic character. We do not think of Hamlet merely as failing to meet its demand, of Antony as merely sinning against it, or even of Macbeth as simply attacking it. What we feel corresponds quite as much to the idea that they are *its* parts, expressions, products; that in their defect or evil *it* is untrue to its soul of goodness, and falls into conflict and collision with itself; that, in making them suffer and waste themselves, *it* suffers and wastes itself; and that when, to save its life and regain peace from this intestinal struggle, it casts them out, it has lost a part of its own substance—a part more dangerous and unquiet, but far more valuable and nearer to its heart, than that which remains—a Fortinbras, a Malcolm, an Octavius. There is no tragedy in its expulsion of evil: the tragedy is that this involves the waste of good.

Thus we are left at last with an idea showing two sides or aspects which we can neither separate nor reconcile. The whole or order against which the individual part shows itself powerless seems to be animated by a passion for perfection: we cannot otherwise explain its behaviour towards evil. Yet it appears to engender this evil within itself, and in its effort to overcome and expel it it is agonised with pain, and driven to mutilate its own substance and to lose not only evil but priceless good. That this idea, though very different from the idea of a blank fate, is no solution of the riddle of life is obvious; but why should we expect it to be such a solution? Shakespeare was not attempting to justify the ways of God to men, or to show the universe as a Divine Comedy. He was writing tragedy, and tragedy would not be tragedy if it were not a painful mystery. Nor can he be said even to point distinctly, like some writers of tragedy, in any direction where a solution might lie. We find a few references to gods or God, to the influence of the stars, to another life: some of them certainly, all of them perhaps, merely dramatic—appropriate to the person from whose lips they fall. A ghost comes from Purgatory to impart a secret out of the reach of its hearer—who presently meditates on the question whether the sleep of death is dreamless. Accidents once or twice remind us strangely of the words, "There's a divinity that shapes our ends." More important are other impressions. Sometimes from the very furnace of affliction a conviction seems borne to us that somehow, if we could see it, this agony counts as nothing against the heroism and love which appear in it and thrill our hearts. Sometimes we are driven to cry out that these mighty or heavenly spirits who perish are too great for the little space in which they move, and that they vanish not into nothingness but into freedom. Sometimes from these sources and from others comes a presentiment, formless but haunting and even profound, that all the fury of conflict, with its waste and woe, is less than half the truth, even an illusion, "such stuff as dreams are made on." But these faint and scattered intimations that the tragic world, being but a fragment of a whole beyond our vision, must needs be a contradiction and no ultimate truth, avail nothing to interpret the mystery. We remain confronted with the inexplicable fact, or the no less inexplicable appearance, of a world travailing for perfection, but bringing to birth, together with glorious good, an evil which it is able to overcome only by self-torture and self-waste. And this fact or appearance is tragedy.[15]

6   From *The Origin of German Tragic Drama*

mourning play

"Trauerspiel and Tragedy"[1]

Fate leads to death. Death is not punishment but atonement, as expression of the subjection of the guilty life to the law of natural life. That guilt which has often been the focal point of theory of the tragic has its home and fate in the drama of fate. This guilt, which according to the ancient statutes falls upon men from without through misfortune, is taken over by a hero in the course of the tragic action and absorbed into himself. By reflecting it in his consciousness of himself, he escapes its demonic jurisdiction. If "consciousness of the dialectic of their fate" was looked for in tragic heroes, and "mystic rationalism" was found in tragic reflections,[2] then what is meant here is perhaps the new, the tragic guilt of the hero—although the context leaves it open to doubt, and makes the words extremely problematical. A paradox, like every manifestation of the tragic order, this guilt consists only in the proud consciousness of guilt, in which the tragic hero escapes his enslavement as an "innocent," by demonic guilt. What Lukács says is true of the tragic hero, and of him alone: "From an external point of view there is no guilt and can be none; each sees the guilt of the other as a chance ensnarement, as something which the slightest difference, even in a puff of wind, might have made turn out differently. But in the assumption of guilt, man assents to everything that has befallen him ... Exalted men ... let go of nothing, once it has been a part of their lives; tragedy is therefore their prerogative."[3] This is a variation of Hegel's famous statement: "It is a point of honour with such great characters that they are guilty." This is always the guilt of those who are guilty by their own actions which, by malicious accident, throws the guiltless into the abyss of general guilt.[4] In tragic poetry the ancient curse which has been passed down from generation to generation, becomes the inner, self-discovered possession of the tragic character. And it is thus extinguished. In the drama of fate, on the other hand, it is worked out; and so a distinction between the tragedy and the *Trauerspiel* illuminates the remark that the tragedy usually moves "to and fro," like some restless spirit, between the persons of the bloody tragedies.[5] "The subject of fate cannot be determined."[6] The *Trauerspiel* therefore has no individual hero, only constellations of heroes. The majority of the main characters found in so many baroque dramas—Leo and Balbus in *Leo Armenius*, Catharina and Chach Abas in *Catherina von Georgien*, Cardenio and Celinde in the drama of the name, Nero and Agrippina, Masinissa and Sophisbe in Lohenstein's drama—are not tragic characters, but are suited to the mournful play.

Destiny is not only divided among the characters, it is equally present among the objects. "It is characteristic of the tragedy of fate not only that a curse or guilt is inherited within whole families, but also that this is associated with . . . a fatal stage property."[7] For once human life has sunk into the merely creaturely, even the life of apparently dead objects secures power over it. The effectiveness of the object where guilt has been incurred is a sign of the approach of death. The passionate stirrings of creaturely life in man—in a word, passion itself—bring the fatal property into the action. It is nothing other than the seismographic needle, which registers its vibrations. In the drama of the fate of the nature of man, which is expressed in blind passion, and the nature of things, which is expressed in blind fate, are both equally subject to the law of fate. The more adequate the instrument which registers it, the more clearly this law can be seen. It is not therefore a matter of no importance whether, as in so many German tragedies of fate, some trivial stage-property bears down on the victim in a series of unworthy twists of the plot, or whether, as in the work of Calderón,[8] ancient motifs come to light on such occasions. The full truth of A. W. Schlegel's remark that he knew of "no dramatist who was equally skilled in giving a poetic quality to theatrical effect,"[9] becomes clear in this context. Calderón was a master in this art, because theatrical effect is an essential, inner constituent of his most characteristic form, the drama of fate. And the mysterious externality of this dramatist does not consist so much in the way the stage-property constantly comes to the fore in the twists of the drama of fate, but in the precision with which the passions themselves take on the nature of stage-properties. In a drama of jealousy the dagger becomes identical with the passions which guide it because in the work of Calderón jealousy is as sharp and as functional as a dagger. His whole mastery lies in the extreme exactitude with which, in a play like the Herod-drama, the passion is distinguished from the psychological motive to action which the modern reader looks for in it.

This has been observed, but only as an object of criticism. "The natural thing would have been to motivate the death of Maryann by Herod's jealousy. Indeed this particular solution was quite compellingly obvious, and the purposefulness with which Calderón worked against it, in order to give the 'tragedy of fate' its appropriate conclusion, is plain to see."[10] For Herod does not kill his wife out of jealousy; rather it is *through* jealousy that she loses her life. Through jealousy Herod is subject to fate, and in its sphere fate makes the same use of jealousy, the dangerously inflamed nature of man, as it does of the dagger to bring about disaster and to serve as a sign of disaster. And chance, in the sense of the breaking down of the action into fragmented elements or things, corresponds entirely to the meaning of stage-property. The stage-property is therefore the criterion by which the genuine romantic drama of fate is distinguished from the ancient tragedy which renounces any order of fate.

The tragedy of fate is implicit in the *Trauerspiel*. Only the introduction of the stage-property lies between it and the German baroque drama. Its exclusion is a sign of the genuine influence of antiquity, or a genuine Renaissance trait. For there is hardly any more pronounced distinction between modern and ancient drama than the absence of the latter from the profane world of things. And the same is true of the classical period of the baroque in Germany. But if tragedy is completely released from the world of things, the world towers oppressively over the horizon of the *Trauerspiel*. The function of mass scholarly annotations is to point to the nightmare burden of the *realia* on the action. In the developed form of tragedy of fate there is no getting away from the stage-property. But alongside it there are dreams, ghostly-apparitions, the terrors of the end, and all of these are part of the stock-in-trade of its basic form, the *Trauerspiel*. All of these are more or less closely oriented around the theme of death, and in the baroque they are fully developed, being transcendental phenomena whose dimension is temporal, in contrast to the immanent, predominantly spatial phenomena of the world of things. Gryphius, in particular, set great store by everything associated with the world of spirits. The German language has him to thank for the marvelous translation of deus ex machina in the following sentence: "*Obs jemand seltsam vorkommen dörffte, dass wir nicht mit den alten einen gott aus dem gerüste, sondern einen geist aus dem grabe herfür bringen, der bedencke, was hin und weider von den gespesten geschrieben.*"[11] He either devoted, or intended to devote *De Spectris*, to his ideas on this subject; nothing is known for certain about this. Like ghostly apparitions, prophetic dreams are an almost obligatory ingredient of the drama, which occasionally begins by relating them as a kind of prologue. They generally foretell the end of a tyrant. It may have been the belief of the dramaturgists of the age that this was a way of introducing the Greek oracle into the German theater; here it is worth pointing out that these dreams belonged to the natural domain of fate and so could only be related to certain Greek oracles, most likely the telluric ones. On the other hand, the assumption that the significance of these dreams lay in the fact that "the spectator [would be] prompted to make a rational comparison between the action and its metaphorical anticipation,"[12] is a delusion of intellectualism. As can be deduced from dream visions and ghostly happenings, night plays a major role. From here it is but a step to the drama of fate, where the witching hour plays a dominant part. *Carolus Stuardus* by Gryphius, and *Agrippina* by Lohenstein begin at midnight; others do not only take place at night, as the unity of time frequently required, but, like *Leo Aremenius, Cardenio und Celinde,* and *Epicharis,* contain great scenes which derive their poetic quality from the night. There is a good reason for associating the dramatic action with night, especially midnight. It lies in the widespread notion that at this hour time stands still like the tongue of a scale. Now since fate, itself the true order of eternal recurrence, can only be described as temporal in an indirect, parasitical sense,[13] its manifestations seek out the temporal dimension. They stand in the narrow frame of midnight, an opening in the passage of time, in which the same ghostly image constantly reappears. One way of illuminating to its very depths the gulf which separates tragedy from *Trauerspiel* is to read in the strictest literal sense the excellent comment of the Abbé Bossu, author of a *Traité sur la poésie epique,* which is quoted by Jean Paul. It says that "no tragedy should be set at night-time." The midnight hour of the *Trauerspiel* stands in contrast to the daytime setting required by every tragic action. "Tis now the very witching time of night, / When churchyards yawn, and hell itself breathes out / Contagion to this world."[14] The spirit world is ahistorical. To it the *Trauerspiel* consigns its dead.

> *O wehe, ich sterbe, ia, ia, Verfluchter, ich sterbe, aber du hast die Rache von mir annoch zu befürchten: auch unter der Erden werd ich dein grimmiger Feindt und rachgieriger Wüttrich dess Messinischen Reichs verbleiben. Ich werde deined Thron erschittern, das Ehebeth, deine Liebe und Zufriedenheit beunruhigen und mit meinem Grimme dem König und dem Reich möglichsten Scharden zufügen.*[15]

It has been rightly said of the English *Trauerspiel* before Shakespeare that it has "no proper end, the stream continues on its course."[16] This is true of the

Trauerspiel in general; its conclusion does not mark the end of an epoch, as the death of the tragic hero so emphatically does in both a historical and an individual sense. This individual sense—what also has the historical meaning of the end of the myth—is explained in the words that tragic life is "the most exclusively immanent of all kinds of life. For this reason its limits always merge into death . . . For tragedy death—the ultimate limit—is an immanent reality, which is inextricably bound up with each of its occurrences."[17] Death, as the form of tragic life, is an individual destiny; in the *Trauerspiel* it frequently takes the form of a communal fate, as if summoning all the participants before the highest court. "*In dreien Tagen solln zu Recht sie stehen: / Sie sind geladen hin vor Gottes Throne; / Nun lasst sie denken, wie sie da bestehen.*"[18] Whereas the tragic hero, in his 'immortality', does not save his life, but only his name, in death the characters of the *Trauerspiel* lose only the name-bearing individuality, and not the vitality of their role. This survives undiminished in the spirit-world. "After a *Hamlet* it might occur to another dramatist to write a *Fortinbras*; no one can stop me from allowing all the characters to meet again in hell or in heaven, and settling their accounts anew."[19] The author of this remark has failed to perceive that this is determined by the law of the *Trauerspiel*, and not at all by the work referred to, let alone its subject-matter. In the face of such great *Trauerspiele* as *Hamlet*, which has constantly been the subject of renewed critical attention, the irrelevance of the absurd concept of tragedy which has been used to judge these works ought to have been clear long ago. For, with reference to the death of Hamlet, what is the point of attributing to Shakespeare a final "residue of naturalism and imitation of nature, which causes the tragic poet to forget that it is not his job to provide a physiological reason for death"? What is the point of arguing that in *Hamlet* death has absolutely no connection with the conflict? Hamlet, who is inwardly destroyed because he could find no other solution from the problem of existence than the negation of life, is killed by a poisoned rapier! That is, by a completely external accident: "Strictly speaking this naïve death-scene completely destroys the tragedy of the drama."[20] This is what is produced by a criticism which, in the arrogance of its philosophical knowledgeability, spares itself any profound study of the works of a genius. The death of Hamlet, which has no more in common with tragic death than the Prince himself has with Ajax, is in its drastic externality characteristic of the *Trauerspiel*; and for this reason alone it is worthy of its creator: Hamlet, as it is clear from his conversation with Osric, wants to breathe in the suffocating air of fate in one deep breath. He wants to die by some accident, and as the fateful stage-properties gather around him, as around their lord and master, the drama of fate flares up in the conclusion of this *Trauerspiel*, as something that is contained, but of course overcome, in it. Whereas tragedy ends with a decision—however uncertain this may be—there resides in the essence of the *Trauerspiel*, and especially in the death-scene, an appeal of the kind which martyrs utter. The language of the pre-Shakespearian *Trauerspiel* has been aptly described as a "bloody legal dialogue" [*blutiger Aktendialog*].²¹ The legal analogy may reasonably be taken further and, in the sense of the mediaeval literature of litigation, one may speak of the trial of the creature whose charge against death—or whoever else was indicted in it—was only partially dealt with and is adjourned at the end of the *Trauerspiel*. Its resumption is implicit in the *Trauerspiel*, and sometimes it actually emerges from its latent state. Through this, of course, is also something which only happens in the richer, Spanish variant. In *La vida es sueño* the repetition of the principal situation is placed right at the centre. Again and again the *Trauerspiele* of the seventeenth century treat the same subjects, and treat them in such a way as to permit, indeed necessitate, repetition. But the same old theoretical prejudices have meant that this has not been understood, and Lohenstein has been accused of "curious errors" about the nature of the tragic, "such as the error that the tragic effect of the action is intensified if the scope of this action is extended by the addition of similar occurrence. Instead of giving his action greater plasticity and bringing it to a head with new, important events, Lohenstein prefers to embellish its principal elements with arbitrary arabesques, as if a statue would be made more beautiful by the doubling of its most artistically sculpted limbs!"²² These dramas should not have had an odd number of acts, as was the case in imitation of the drama of the Greeks; an even number is much more appropriate to the repeatable actions which they describe. In *Leo Armenius*, at least, the action is complete by the end of the fourth act. With its emancipation from the three-act and five-act scheme, modern drama has secured the triumph of one of the tendencies of the baroque.²³

Ich finde nirgends Ruh
muss selber mit mir zancken
Ich sitz
ich lieg
ich steh
ist alles in Gedancken.
    —Andreas Tscherning: *Melancholey Redet selber*²⁴

The great German dramatists of the baroque were Lutherans. Whereas in the decades of the Counter-Reformation Catholicism had penetrated the secular life with all the power of its discipline, the relationship of Lutheranism to the everyday had always been antinomic. The rigorous morality of its teaching in respect of the civic conduct stood in sharp contrast to its renunciation of 'good works'. By denying the latter any special miraculous spiritual effect, making the soul dependent upon the grace through faith, and making the secular-political sphere a testing ground for a life which was only indirectly religious, being intended for the demonstration of civic virtues, it did, it is true, instill into the people a strict sense of obedience to duty, but in its great men it produced melancholy. Even in Luther himself, the last two decades of whose life are filled with an increasing heaviness of the soul, there are signs of a reaction against the assault on good works. 'Faith', of course, carried him through, but it did not prevent life from becoming stale. 'What is a man, / If his chief good and market of his time / Be but to sleep and feed? a beast, no more. / Sure, he that hath made us with such large discourse, / Looking before and after, gave us not / That capacity and god-like reason / To fust in us unused"[25]—these words of Hamlet contain both the philosophy of Wittenberg and a protest against it. In that excessive reaction which ultimately denied good works as such, and not just their meritorious and penitential character, there was an element of German paganism and the grim belief in the subjection of man to fate. Human actions were deprived of all value. Something new arose: an empty world. In Calvinism—for all of its gloominess—the impossibility of this was comprehended and in some measure corrected. The Lutheran faith viewed this concession with suspicion and opposed it. What was the point of human life if, as in Calvinism, not even faith had to be proved? If, on the other hand, faith was naked, absolute, effective, but on the other, there was no distinction between human ordinary people—'honesty in small things', 'upright living'—which developed at this time, forming a contrast to the *taedium vitae* of richer natures. For those who looked deeper saw the scene of their existence as a rubbish heap of partial, inauthentic actions. Life itself protested against this. It feels deeply that it is not there merely to be devalued by faith. It is overcome by deep horror at the idea that the whole of existence might proceed in such a way. The idea of death fills it with profound terror. Mourning is the state of the mind in which feeling revives the empty world in the form of a mask, and derives an enigmatic satisfaction in contemplating it. Every feeling is bound to an a priori object, and the representation of this object is its phenomenology. Accordingly, the theory of mourning, which emerged unmistakably as a pendant to the theory of tragedy, can only be developed in the description of that world which is revealed under the gaze of the melancholy man. For feelings, however vague they may seem when perceived by the self, respond like a motorial reaction to a concretely structured world. If the laws which govern the *Trauerspiel* are to be found, partly explicit, partly implicit, at the heart of mourning, the representation of these laws does not concern itself with the emotional condition of the poet or his public, but with a feeling which is released from any empirical subject and is ultimately bound to the fullness of an object. This is a motorial attitude which has its appointed place in the hierarchy of intentions and is only called a feeling because it does not occupy the highest place. It is determined by an astounding tenacity of intention, which, among the feelings is matched perhaps only by love—and not that playfully. For whereas in the realm of the emotions it is not unusual for the relation between an intention and its object to alternate between attraction and repulsion, mourning is capable of a special intensification, a progressive deepening of its intention. Pensiveness is characteristic above all of the mournful. On the road to the object—no: within the object itself—this intention progresses as slowly and solemnly as the processions of the rulers advance. The passionate interest in the pomp of the *Haupt- und Staatsaktionen*, in part an escape from the restrictions of pious domesticity, was also a response to the natural affinity of pensiveness for gravity. In the latter it recognizes its own rhythm. The relationship between mourning and ostentation, which is so brilliantly displayed in the language of the baroque, has one of its sources here; so too does the self-absorption, to which these constellations of the worldly chronicle seem but a game, which may, it is true, be worthy of attention for the meaning which can reliably be deciphered from it, but whose never-ending repetition secures the bleak rule of the melancholic distaste for life. Even from the heritage of the Renaissance did this age derive material which could only deepen the contemplative paralysis. It is only one step from stoic ἀπάθεια to mourning, but a step which only becomes possible in Christianity. Like all other antique qualities of the baroque, its stoicism too is pseudo-antique. The influence of rational pessimism is less important than the desolation with which the practice of stoicism confronts man. The deadening of the emotions, and the ebbing away of the waves of life which are the source of these emotions in the body, can increase the distance between self and the surrounding world to the point of alienation from the body. As soon as the symptom of depersonalization was seen as an intense degree of mournfulness, the concept of the pathological state, in which the most simple object appears to be a symbol of some enigmatic wisdom because it lacks any natural, creative relationship to us, we set in an incomparably productive context. It accords with this that in the proximity of Albrecht Dürer's figure, *Melancholia*, the utensils of active life are lying around unused on the floor, as objects of contemplation. This engraving anticipates the baroque in many respects. In it the knowledge of the introvert and the investigations of the scholar have merged as intimately as the men in the baroque. The Renaissance explores the universe; the baroque explores libraries. Its meditations are devoted to books. "*Kein grösserers Buch weiss die Welt als sich selbst; dessen fürnehmstes Theil aber ist der Mensch, welchem Gott anstatt eines schönen Titubildes sein unvergleichliches, Ebebenbild hat vorge- druckt, überdas ihn zu einem Auszuge, Kern und Edelgesteine der übringen Theile solches grossen Weltbuches gemacht.*"[26] The "Book of nature" and the "Book of the times" are objects of baroque meditation. In them it possesses something housed and roofed. But they also contain evidence of the social prejudice of the imperially crowned poet, who had long since fortified the dignity of Petrarch, and here looks down in superiority on the divertissements of his 'leisure hours'. Not least the book served as a permanent monument in a natural scene rich in emphasis that is placed on melancholy as the mood of the times, the publisher seeks to recommend the book as an *arcanum*, immune to the assaults of melan- choly.

> *In bedenckung dessen, das die Pyramides, Seulen und Büldnussen allerhand materien mit der zeit schadhafft oder durch gewalt zerbrochen werden oder wol gar verfallen ... das wol gantze Städt versuncken, untergangen und mit wasser bedeckt seien, da hergegen die Schrifften und Bücher dergleichen untergang befreyet, dann was jrgendt in einem Landt oder Ort ab und untergehet, das findet man in vielen andern und unzehlichen orten unschwer wider, also das, Menschlicher weiss davon zu reden, nichts Tauerhaffters und unsterblichers ist, als eben die Bücher.*[27]

It is a consequence of this same mixture of complacency and contemplativeness that "baroque nationalism" "never took a form of political action ... any more than baroque hostility to convention ever became concentrated into something similar to the revolutionary will of the *Sturm und Drang* or the romantic on- slaught on the philistinism of state and public life."[28] The vain activity of the intriguer was regarded as the undignified antithesis of passionate contempla- tion, to which alone was attributed the power to release those in high places from the satanic ensnarement of history, in which the baroque recognized only the political aspect. And yet: innovation also led only too easily in the abyss. This is illustrated by the theory of the melancholy disposition ...

... In the German *Trauerspiel* the characteristic attitude is that of the reaction of the Counter-Reformation, and so the determining factor in the creation of dramatic types is the mediaeval scholastic image of melancholy. But in its formal totality this drama diverges fundamentally from such a typology; its style and language are inconceivable without that audacious twist thanks to which the speculations of the Renaissance were able to recognize in the features of the sorrowful Contemplator[29] the reflection of a distant light, shining back from the depths of self-absorption. This age succeeded (at least once) in conjuring up the human figure who corresponded to this dichotomy between the neo-antique and the mediaeval light in which the baroque saw the melancholic. But Germany was not the country which was able to do this. The figure is Hamlet. The secret of his person is contained within the playful, but for that very reason firmly circumscribed, passage through all the stages in this complex of intentions, just as the secret of his fate is contained in an action which, according to this, his way of looking at things, is perfectly homogenous. For the *Trauerspiel* Hamlet alone is a spectator by the grace of God; but he cannot find satisfaction in what he sees enacted, only in his own fate. His life, the exemplary object of his mourning, points, before its extinction, to the Christian providence in whose bosom his mournful images are transformed into a blessed existence. Only in a princely life such as this is melancholy redeemed by being confronted with itself. The rest is silence. For everything that has not been lived sinks beyond recall in this space where the word of wisdom leads but a deceptive, ghostly existence. Only Shakespeare was capable of striking Christian sparks from the baroque rigidity of the melancholic, un-stoic as it is un-Christian, pseudo-antique as it is pseudo-pietistic. If the profound insight with which Rochus von Liliencron recognized the ascendancy of Saturn and marks of *acedia* in Hamlet[30] is not to be deprived of its finest object, then this drama will also be recognized as the unique spectacle in which these things are overcome in the spirit of Christianity. It is only in this prince that melancholy self-absorption attains to Christianity. The German *Trauerspiel* was never able to inspire itself to new life; it was never able to awaken within itself the clear light of self-awareness. It remained astonishingly obscure to itself, and was able to portray the melancholic only in the crude and washed-out colours of the mediaeval complexion-books. What then is the purpose of this excursus? The images and figures presented in German *Trauerspiel* are dedicated to Dürer's genius of winged melancholy. The intense life of its crude theater being in the presence of this genius.

7   "Othello," from *An Essay on the Tragic*

1

Shakespeare's literary model is an Italian novella, *The Moor of Venice*. The title refers to one of the antagonistic elements that determine the tragic events. Othello is a Moor and a Venetian. As a Venetian, he is allowed to have command of the fleet; as a Moor, he is not allowed to wed a Venetian. The city's inhabitants consider the warrior to be their equal, but the lover to be a black animal. In a turbulent counterpoint, the first act illustrates this division of Othello: In the nocturnal streets of Venice, two sides search for him. The father whose daughter he stole pursues him to deliver him over to the courts, while the doge looks for Othello to entrust him with the command of the fleet. It is particularly characteristic of *Othello* that the conflict is not fought out in the doge's palace, but only later within Othello himself. Corneille's heroes are also painfully aware that as lovers and warriors they cannot be one and the same person. Their tragic conflict—"the crossing of two necessities"—is, however, capricious in origin and external to them.[1] Admittedly, Corneille's heroes can neither follow their inclination and their duty simultaneously nor disregard one of them. But they are not attacked in their inner being: Neither as lover nor as warrior are they called into question. Othello, on the contrary, immediately succeeds in obtaining from the doge both the honorable appointment as fleet commander and the approval of his marriage. But in his heart, he takes away from this success his own self-doubt. Man often views himself through the eyes of another, and although Othello knows himself to be of royal lineage, in Cyprus, he will never be able to forget how he saw himself in the Venetian mirror. Although Desdemona gave Othello proof of her love, Othello's self-confidence is undermined by Desdemona's father's not only disapproving of this love, but also disbelieving it—and therefore actually accusing Othello of magic. Upon this ground of shaken belief in oneself, Iago brings jealousy into bloom.

2

Unlike the other passions, jealousy bears within itself the possibility of the tragic. Even before colliding with another power, the one seized by jealousy is branded a tragic hero. The essence of jealousy lies in the dialectic, which admittedly also allows it to turn into the comical. Jealousy is love that destroys by wanting to preserve. Othello's parting kiss is accompanied by the words: "O balmy breath, that dost almost persuade / Justice to break her sword. One more, one more! / Be thus when thou art dead, and I will kill thee / And love thee after."[2]

3

Othello is a victim of Iago's revenge. Iago is an ironist; his method is Socratic. Therefore, Iago's image of himself trickling poison into Othello's ear is not entirely accurate. Just as Socrates finds his students guilty of ignorance, Iago finds Othello guilty of jealousy. His plan is characterized by an ironic joy in finding and imparting opposites, in turning good into evil. "So will I turn her virtue into pitch; / And out of her own goodness make the net / That shall enmesh them all," Iago says of Desdemona, who, by helping the dismissed Cassio, supposedly betrays her adulterous love for him.[3] But the scene in which Iago induces the birth of Othello's jealousy (to use the Socratic metaphor) is probably the most perfect realization of the irony of action, which is far more rare than the irony of observation. Iago, a second Socrates, acts in "absolute negativity" in relation to Othello.[4] What Iago achieves, he always achieves through its opposite. His questions are answers, his answers questions; his "yes" conceals a "no," his "no" a "yes." Othello's disquiet is the work of Iago's attempts to quiet him; Othello's doubt is the effect of Iago's attempts to convince him. Iago names the destination to which he wants to lead Othello under the pretense of warning him against going there. Othello thus arrives there by his own doing; just as he also first mentioned Cassio's name. Iago's irony thereby heightens the tragic in Othello. Not only does Othello destroy by wanting to preserve, but he also destroys no longer as a victim of Iago, but as a victim of himself. The divine irony that stood opposite the tragic hero in antiquity is replaced in the Baroque by the irony of the villain.

4

"Give me the ocular proof," Othello exclaims as his jealousy takes possession of him.[5] This tormenting demand for proof belongs to the dialectic of doubt, which has its tragic side. The doubt about a wife's fidelity—born out of fear of her infidelity—seeks its proof not in fidelity, but in infidelity. Othello's doubts can be put to rest only by the evidence that proves him right, not by the evidence that proves him a liar. And this is his only wish. What Othello fears most is, then, precisely what he longs for the most. Iago knows that the least of evidence will be sufficient enough for the jealous one. What he offers Othello is the handkerchief that Othello once gave to Desdemona as a present and is now in Cassio's hands. Like the letter in Schiller's *Don Carlos*, the handkerchief takes on a pernicious power over Othello, a power that is tragic because he hands himself over to this power. The possibility of doubting the proof is foreign to Othello. This is the case not only because he yearns to quench the doubts that plague him like thirst, but also because he seeks refuge from the man he does not trust (for Iago can don any role) in the object he does trust (for he believes the handkerchief is capable of doing no harm). Precisely because the object cannot tell its own lies, it is difficult to see through its lies. For Othello, the fact that Desdemona gives away the handkerchief, which he then sees in Cassio's possession, counts as proof of his wife's infidelity. Yet Desdemona's giving of the handkerchief is her gesture of love for Othello, for she does so to soothe his headache. When Othello turns it down, Emilia takes it and gives it to Iago, who brings it into Cassio's room. The headache that Othello claims to suffer from is only the alias for his passion. The handkerchief thus becomes an emblem for an element in Desdemona's tragic fate. With the handkerchief she unknowingly sets ablaze what she sought to extinguish: Othello's jealousy.

5

Desdemona is accompanied to Cyprus by her father's curse: "Look to her, Moor, if thou hast eyes to see: / She has deceived her father, and may thee."[6] This argument has its place in Iago's plan. Because Othello is not naturally distrustful, Iago must make Othello believe that Desdemona could deceive him, and therefore reminds him of the deception to which he owes her love for him. Othello is now finally ready to disregard Desdemona's affirmations and to trust only the handkerchief. What had united Othello and Desdemona in front of all of Venice divides them in his soul. Their marriage falls apart on the very thing that had established it. What Desdemona did for Othello's sake now proves only that she is capable of doing it again, now in an act of unfaithfulness to Othello. The proof of her love turns into the proof of her infidelity. The ironist's dialectical method thereby transforms man into the opposite of himself. The loving wife appears as the adulteress; the lover becomes the murderer of the one he loves.

SECTION II

8   From *Economic and Philosophical*
              Manuscripts of 1844

"The Power of Money"

If man's feelings, passions, etc., are not merely anthropological phenomena in the (narrower) sense, but truly ontological affirmations of being (of nature), and if they are only really affirmed because their object exists for them as a sensual object, then it is clear that:

1. They have by no means merely one mode of affirmation, but rather that the distinct character of their existence, of their life, is constituted by the distinct mode of their affirmation. In what manner the object exists for them, is the characteristic mode of their gratification.

2. Wherever the sensuous affirmation is the direct annulment of the object in its independent form (as in eating, drinking, working up of the object, etc.), this is the affirmation of the object.

3. Insofar as man, and hence also his feeling, etc., is human, the affirmation of the object by another is likewise his own gratification.

4. Only through developed industry—i.e., through the medium of private property—does the ontological essence of human passion come into being, in its totality as well as in its humanity; the science of man is therefore itself a product of man's own practical activity.

5. The meaning of private property—apart from its estrangement—is the existence of essential objects for man, both as objects of enjoyment and as objects of activity.

By possessing the property of buying everything, by possessing the property of appropriating all objects, money is thus the object of eminent possession. The universality of its property is the omnipotence of its being. It is therefore regarded as omnipotent. . . . Money is the procurer between man's need and the object, between his life and his means of life. But that which mediates my life for me, also mediates the existence of other people for me. For me it is the other person.

> What, man! confound it, hands and feet
> And head and backside, all are yours!
> And what we take while life is sweet,
> Is that to be declared not ours?
>
> Six stallions, say, I can afford,
> Is not their strength my property?
> I tear along, a sporting lord,
> As if their legs belonged to me.
>> —Goethe: *Faust* (Mephistopheles)

Shakespeare in *Timon of Athens*:

> Gold? Yellow, glittering, precious gold?
> No, Gods, I am no idle votarist! . . .
> Thus much of this will make black white, foul fair,
> Wrong right, base noble, old young, coward valiant.
> . . . Why, this
> Will lug your priests and servants from your sides,
> Pluck stout men's pillows from below their heads:
> This yellow slave
> Will knit and break religions, bless the accursed;
>
> Make the hoar leprosy adored, place thieves
> And give them title, knee and approbation
> With senators on the bench: This is it
> That makes the wappen'd widow wed again;
>
> She, whom the spital-house and ulcerous sores
> Would cast the gorge at, this embalms and spices
> To the April day again. Come, damned earth,
> Thou common whore of mankind, that put'st odds
> Among the rout of nations.

And also later:

> O thou sweet king-killer, and dear divorce
> 'Twixt natural son and sire! thou bright defiler
> Of Hymen's purest bed! thou valiant Mars!
> Thou ever young, fresh, loved and delicate wooer,
>
> Whose blush doth thaw the consecrated snow
> That lies on Dian's lap! Thou visible God!

That solder'st close impossibilities,
And makest them kiss! That speak'st with every tongue,

To every purpose! O thou touch of hearts!
Think, thy slave man rebels, and by thy virtue
Set them into confounding odds, that beasts
May have the world in empire!

Shakespeare excellently depicts the real nature of money. To understand him,
let us begin, first of all, by expounding the passage from Goethe.

That which is for me through the medium of money—that for which I can
pay (i.e., which money can buy)—that am I myself, the possessor of the money.
The extent of the power of money is the extent of my power. Money's properties are my—the possessor's—properties and essential powers. Thus, what I
am and am capable of is by no means determined by my individuality. I am
ugly, but I can buy for myself the most beautiful of women. Therefore I am not
ugly, for the effect of ugliness—its deterrent power—is nullified by money. I,
according to my individual characteristics, am lame, but money furnishes me
with twenty-four feet. Therefore I am not lame. I am bad, dishonest, unscru-
pulous, stupid; but money is honoured, and hence its possessor. Money is the
supreme good, therefore its possessor is good.

Money, besides, saves me the trouble of being dishonest: I am therefore presumed honest. I am brainless, but money is the real brain of all things and how
then should its possessor be brainless? Besides, he can buy clever people for
himself, and is he who has a power over the clever not more clever than the
clever? Do not I, who thanks to money am capable of all that the human heart
longs for, possess all human capacities? Does not my money, therefore, transform all my incapacities into their contrary?

If money is the bond binding me to human life, binding society to me, con-
necting me with nature and man, is not money the bond of all bonds? Can it
not dissolve and bind all ties? Is it not, therefore, also the universal agent of separation? It is the coin that really separates as well as the real binding agent—the
. . . chemical power of society.

Shakespeare stresses especially two properties of money:

1. It is the visible divinity—the transformation of all human and natural
properties into their contraries, the universal confounding and distorting of
things: impossibilities are soldered together by it.

2. It is the common whore, the common procurer of people and nations.
The distorting and confounding of all human and natural qualities, the frater-

nisation of impossibilities—the divine power of money—lies in its character as men's estranged, alienating and self-disposing species-nature. Money is the alienated ability of mankind. That which I am unable to do as a man, and of which therefore all my individual essential powers are incapable, I am able to do by means of money. Money thus turns each of these powers into something which in itself it is not—turns it, that is, into its contrary. If I long for a particular dish or want to take the mail-coach because I am not strong enough to go by foot, money fetches me the dish and the mail-coach: that is, it converts my wishes from something in the realm of imagination, translates them from their meditated, imagined or desired existence into their sensuous, actual existence—from imagination to life, from imagined being into real being. In effecting this mediation, [money] is the truly creative power.

No doubt the demand also exists for him who has no money, but his demand is a mere thing of the imagination without effect or existence for me, for a third party, for the [others], and which therefore remains even for me unreal and objectless. The difference between effective demand based on money and ineffective demand based on my need, my passion, my wish, etc., is the difference between being and thinking, between the idea which merely exists within me and the idea which exists as a real object outside of me.

If I have no money for travel, I have no need—that is, no real and realisable need—to travel. If I have the vocation for study but no money for it, I have no vocation for study—that is, no effective, no true vocation. On the other hand, if I have really no vocation for study but have the will and the money for it, I have an effective vocation for it. Money as the external, universal medium and faculty (not springing from man as man or from human society as society) for turning an image into reality and reality into a mere image, transforms the real essential powers of man and nature into what are merely abstract notions and therefore imperfections and tormenting chimeras, just as it transforms real imperfections and chimeras—essential powers which are really impotent, which exist only in the imagination of the individual—into real essential powers and faculties. In the light of this characteristic alone, money is thus the general distorting of individualities which turns them into their opposite and confers contradictory attributes upon their attributes.

Money, then, appears as this distorting power both against the individual and against the bonds of society, etc., which claim to be entities in themselves. It transforms fidelity into infidelity, love into hate, hate into love, virtue into vice, vice into virtue, servant into master, master into servant, idiocy into intelligence, and intelligence into idiocy.

Since money, as the existing and active concept of value, confounds and confuses all things, it is the general confounding and confusing of all things—the world upside-down—the confounding and confusing of all natural and human qualities.

He who can buy bravery is brave, though he be a coward. As money is not exchanged for any one specific quality, for any one specific thing, or for any particular human essential power, but for the entire objective world of man and nature, from the standpoint of its possessor it therefore serves to exchange every quality for every other, even contradictory, quality and object: it is the fraternisation of impossibilities. It makes contradictions embrace.

Assume man to be man and his relationship to the world to be a human one: then you can exchange love only for love, trust for trust, etc. If you want to enjoy art, you must be an artistically cultivated person; if you want to exercise influence over other people, you must be a person with a stimulating and encouraging effect on other people. Every one of your relations to man and to nature must be a specific expression, corresponding to the object of your will, of your real individual life. If you love without evoking love in return—that is, if your loving as loving does not produce reciprocal love; if through a living expression of yourself as a loving person you do not make yourself a beloved one, then your love is impotent—a misfortune.

9   From *The Birth of Tragedy*

Dionysian man has similarities to Hamlet: both have had a real glimpse into the essence of things. They have understood, and it now disgusts them to act, for their action can change nothing in the eternal nature of things. They perceive as ridiculous or humiliating the fact that they are expected to set right a world which is out of joint. Knowledge kills action, for action requires a state of being in which we are covered with the veil of illusion—that is what Hamlet has to teach us, not that really venal wisdom about John-a-Dreams, who cannot move himself to act because of too much reflection, because of an excess of possibilities, so to speak. It is not a case of reflection. No!—the true knowledge, the glimpse into the cruel truth overcomes every driving motive to act, both in Hamlet as well as in the Dionysian man. Now no consolation has any effect any more. His longing goes out over a world, even beyond the gods themselves, toward death. Existence is denied, together with its blazing reflection in the gods or in an immortal afterlife. In the consciousness of once having glimpsed the truth, the man now sees everywhere only the horror or absurdity of being; now he understands the symbolism in the fate of Ophelia; now he recognizes the wisdom of the forest god Silenus. It disgusts him.

Here, when the will is in the highest danger, art approaches, as a saving, healing magician. Art alone can turn those thoughts of disgust at the horror or absurdity of existence into imaginary constructs which permit living to continue. These constructs are the Sublime as the artistic mastering of the horrible and the Comic as the artistic release from disgust at the absurd. The chorus of satyrs in the dithyramb is the saving fact of Greek art. Those emotional moods I have just described play themselves out by means of these Dionysian attendants . . .

. . . Dionysian art thus wishes to convince us of the eternal delight in existence: except that we are to seek this delight, not in appearances, but behind them; we are to recognize how everything which comes into being must be ready for painful destruction; we are forced to gaze directly into the terror of individual existence—and nonetheless are not to become paralyzed: a metaphysical consolation tears us momentarily out of the hustle and bustle of changing forms. For a short time we really are the primordial essence itself and feel its unbridled lust for and joy in existence; the struggle, the torment, the destruction of appearances now seem to us necessary, on account of the excess of innumerable forms of existence pressing and punching themselves into life and of the exuberant fecundity of the world will; we are transfixed by the raging barbs of this torment in the very moment when we become, as it were, one with the immeasurable primordial delight in existence and when, in Dionysian rapture, we sense the indestructible and eternal nature of this joy. In spite of fear and pity, we are fortunate vital beings, not as individuals, but as the one living being, with whose procreative joy we have been fused.

The story of how Greek tragedy arose tells us now with clear certainty how the Greeks' tragic work of art really was born out of the spirit of music. With this idea we think we have, for the first time, done justice to the original and astonishing meaning of the chorus. At the same time, however, we must concede that the significance of the tragic myth established previously was never conceptually and transparently clear to the Greek poets, to say nothing of the Greek philosophers. Their heroes speak to a certain extent more superficially than they act; the myth really does not find its adequate objectification in the spoken word.

The structure of the scenes and the vivid images reveal a deeper wisdom than the poet himself can grasp in words and ideas. We can make the same observation about Shakespeare, whose Hamlet, for example, in a similar sense speaks more superficially than he acts, so that we derive the doctrine of Hamlet we discussed earlier, not from the words, but from the deeper view and review of the totality of the work. With respect to Greek tragedy, which, of course, comes to us only as a drama of words, I have even suggested that the incongruity between myth and word can easily seduce us into considering it shallower and more empty of meaning than it is and thus also to assume a more superficial effect than it must have had according to the testimony of the ancients, for we easily forget that what the poet as a wordsmith could not achieve, the attainment of the highest intellectualization and idealization of myth, he could have achieved successfully at any moment as a creative musician!

10   "Shakespeare and Modern Drama"

Appearing before you as part of this lecture series, that sang and continues to sing the glory of our great poet, whose stage works are recalled with ecstasy, you may not find—nor do I—my assigned role the most appealing or sympathetic one. . . . For it is not Shakespeare's richness, but his boundaries, not his splendours, but his dangers that I wish to address. In fact, my topic is not Shakespeare himself but his influence. The potential of his influence and whether it is good or dangerous.

What does the question mean? What does it mean that that long departed and long gone age can and does influence contemporary art? Let me hasten to add that what I have in mind is neither imitation nor a facile transference of some superficial external features, but whether the essence of any art can be appropriated and developed. Whether the key principles that enable an artist to create his own world, arrange and exclude it from the external world, make it self-enclosed and different from any other created world, whether the key compositional principles—even if their essence is misunderstood—can be appropriated. I have in mind, for instance, the art of Velazquez[1] and Frans Hals[2] that contributed to the development of Impressionist painting, or the way the romantic and humouristic novel, in the late eighteenth century, discovered the decisive features of its style in Rabelais and Cervantes.

The question I wish to raise, rather than exhaust, is this. What are the essential features of Shakespeare's dramatic composition, and to what degree can they be utilized to create, if need be, a contemporary drama that would hold up a mirror to our life as he did in his own life? Such a modern drama would embody and immortalize our life just as Shakespeare's art embodies his own age.

History gives us the right to raise the question. From the very moment that Shakespeare emerged, so to speak, from the great crowd of his contemporaries, he wielded a dominant influence on the style of the great European drama. (Not to mention the quickly fading popular dramas!) That this is not something un-equivocally positive, that we face a real problem here, that Shakespeare's style has its inherent dangers is historically attested by the concealed or open opposi-tion which the greatest thinkers and finest artists, from Voltaire to Tolstoy[3] and Bernard Shaw[4], showed toward the dramatist. I am also thinking of Lessing's shocked discovery that he could not transplant into the praxis of *Sturm und Drang* what he professed and yet guarded against in Shakespeare's art.

There is also Goethe and Schiller's anti-Shakespearean cult of the Greek drama—though they didn't admit it, it is de facto—and Byron's open,[5] and Hebbel and Grillparzer's secret[6] opposition to Shakespeare. And just recently, the subtlest exponent of stylized modern art, Paul Ernst, severely criticized Shakespeare's compositions. I am also thinking that where Shakespeare had a total impact (*Sturm und Drang*, the French romantic drama and, in many respects, the German), the movements nonetheless remained sterile. Let's also remember that the great English poets who, as Swinburne put it, wrote for an imaginary Globe or Blackfriars theatre, never produced a lively great drama. That those who diligently searched for and grasped Shakespeare's central prob-lem have reached a dead end, just as—to mention the greatest example—did the unfortunate, profound and great artist, Otto Ludwig.[7]

That there is a problem is attested, if by nothing else, by the very question whether Shakespeare's style is really dramatic. We know that Goethe, mature and well versed in great theatrical praxis, had denied this.[8] Many theoretical writers claim that if we really analysed Shakespeare's drama in depth, and com-pared it with the Greek drama, Shakespeare would prove to be an epic writer. In my view, these polemics are unfair to Shakespeare, but their symptomatic importance is undeniable. If serious people and artists who take their art seri-ously can question the dramatic nature of Shakespeare's method of composi-tion, then it is legitimate to ask whether it is dramatic in the modern sense of the term. Our question therefore is whether the compositional essence of Shakespeare's dramas is the same as what we demand today from the drama. In short, can modern drama follow in the footsteps of Shakespeare?

How does Shakespeare motivate his characters? Our feeling is that the problem of motivation practically defines the whole problem of drama; that the essence of dramatic structure is the forceful joining of cause and effect. What is Shakespeare's feeling on this? First of all, the territory of motivation is much more confined for him than it is in modern drama. He can dispense with the causal explanation of the events, eternal to the drama and yet integral to it. He never bothers with the causal explanation of historical events. In all Shakespearean dramas, the historical events must be accepted as they are or, more properly, as Shakespeare adopted them from their sources. Think of the introductory part of *King Lear*, in which the chronicle of 'history'—fantastic, fairytale-like, unbelievable and inextricable—gives rise to a powerful and spellbinding tragedy. That is, of course, provided that we accept the 'history', forego its analysis, and neither demand nor derive the conclusions from it that would affect the dramatic character of Lear. Think also of the pre-dramatic events in *The Merchant of Venice* and *Cymbeline*. (I deliberately chose examples from Shakespeare's different periods.)

Everyone feels a dissonance here. And precisely because one feels it, and feels it with the same intensity in Shakespeare's late period, we attempt to achieve a balance and, subsequently, create a unity where there is no unity. There is no unity because the demand for it, as advanced by us—later we will explain why—was unknown to Shakespeare and his age. They say that Shakespeare's dramas are dramatic tales, and the tale tolerates inconsistency that the drama would not allow. I cannot discuss here whether this is true or not. Namely, to what extent Shakespeare's audience felt that his dramas were tales and to what extent the audience held, with the same conviction, that they were realistic like, for instance, the dramas of Ibsen. I consider the last proposal plausible. But the requirement of logical structure is, for drama, the requirement of form. The drama is not written to awaken the illusion of reality, for which the drama is inapplicable. Consequently, if we declare drama to be a dramatic tale, all we have really said is that the rigorous system of cause and effect joins various facts and people; that though the content of cause and effect changes, the content has no bearings on the cause and the effect.

Think of Grillparzer's mythological dramas,[9] of Kleist's *Kätchen von Heilbronn*, of Mihaly Vörösmarty's *Csongor és Tünde*, and [Gerhart Hauptmann's] *The Sunken Bell*. In all these works, the source materials and the tale grew from the same world and obey the same laws, the same human beings act in both, and just as nothing is forgotten, nothing overlooked. They reconstruct Cordelia's whole past in order to make her relationship with Lear necessary. Hebbel had utilized modern theories—like milieu and hereditary transmission—to infuse the actions of Goneril and Regan with relative rights and determinism.

Needless to say, all these attempts have proved futile because they offer arbitrary interpretations, and, as such, are deficient as real explanations. They are deficient because Shakespeare and his age—among his contemporaries, he formulated the motives best—felt no need for motives. We know of an older play [*The True Chronicle History of King Lear, and His Three Daughters, Gonorill, Ragan, and Cordella* (1605)] that inspired Shakespeare's *King Lear*. In the anonymous play there was an attempt, naïve and primitive, to provide motives for the actions of Lear, Goneril, Regan and Cordelia. Shakespeare discarded these motives. He also discarded Cinthio's novel [*Hecatommithi, Parte Prima, Deca Terza, Novella 7*], from which he borrowed the theme of *Othello*, the motives for Iago's intrigues. In Plutarch, he discarded the motives for Cassius' hatred of Caesar. We are dealing here with Shakespeare's intentions, rather than accidents. Specifically, what he kept from readymade sources, what he developed and what he discarded. We know that Othello, in the original novel, was not a noble hearted tragic hero. Shakespeare made him into that, and it is inconceivable, even if we presuppose a spontaneous, direct but still conscious artistic intention in *Othello*, that it was otherwise in cases where Shakespeare decided to omit certain things.

We also know that in developing the plot of *Othello*, Shakespeare minimizes the role of motive.[10] The most decisive facts and catastrophes are the result of accidents and misunderstandings, rather than the inevitable, logical sequence of events. Shakespeare needs great, pathetic situations that reveal man's whole soul. He is not concerned, just as his age was not concerned, how he arrived at these situations. Let me cite a few examples. Cassius' suicide is the result of accidents and misunderstandings, as is the relationship of Gloucester, Edgar and Edmund. And to cite the greatest example, the tragic end of *Romeo and Juliet* is based on a brutal accident. The tragedy of Othello and Desdemona—where accident has a deep psychological background—resembles an unpredictable game of cards, where the good outcome is just a hairsbreadth away.

How is this possible? Why is Shakespeare so unconcerned with the pragmatic interaction of things, and why is it so important for us? What is Shakespeare's creative objective, what objective decides that he selects some elements and omits others? What was his purpose in composing his tragedies? And what is the purpose of contemporary playwrights? Hebbel—who is as typical a representative of modern drama as Shakespeare was of his own age—reflecting on his own praxis, said that the ultimate goal is to "plug up every mouse and rat hole," to make the drama self-enclosed and subject to inexorable necessity. It is only from Shakespeare's own works that we can guess his goals, and therefore it is more difficult to formulate, or compress them into a single sentence.

Though fully aware that every formula, by leaving out many things, falsifies reality, I would sum things up as follows. Shakespeare's plays are based on individuals, on characters and on their interplay. The new drama is based on situations, or, more precisely, on men's relation to situations. To put it at its simplest, Shakespeare's conflicts are concrete, those of modern drama are abstract.

What does this mean? It means that Shakespeare's tragic vision pits one individual against another, or others who are just as real and who, as they are and what they are, can never and nowhere be duplicated. Othello's tragedy is that he is what he is, and Iago and Desdemona are what they are, and these characters have met. Their encounter is a fact, a reality, an event with a history, it is as it is, and beyond dispute. This is what is required for *Othello*, whose tragic essence is precisely that the three characters have come into contact. In a profound sense we can claim that every tragedy is based on accident—and precisely so from the Shakespearean standpoint.[11] The crossing of the paths of certain individuals can only be accidental, and Shakespeare's profound insight is that he sees life as a series of accidents. In the light of this, it is irrelevant and must remain so that accidents keep piling up (in the first part of *King Lear*), or strongly interact with the tragedy (at the end of *Romeo and Juliet*).

A negative definition can help us to clarify this. We have posed the question: what does Shakespeare's tragic vision contain? And now we ask, what is missing from it? The simple answer is: the abstract. What does this mean? It means that the tragic content of *Julius Caesar* is the strange character of four men, Caesar, Brutus, Cassius and Antonius, whose interaction spells tragedy for Brutus. It means that the play contains nothing of the abstract struggles from that age, a struggle between the declining Roman aristocratic republic and the new Caesarism. It means that in *Coriolanus* it is not the confrontation of aristocrats and plebeians,[12] but the baseness of Sicinius, Brutus and Aufidius, and Volumnia's great nobility that leads to Coriolanus' death. It means, that in the historical struggles portrayed in Shakespeare's dramas of English history, it is not English feudalism that collapses, because of the bloody internecine wars, whose outbreak and tenacity were symptomatic of that period of great disintegration. True, the characters display better animosities and enact bloody acts. But in the end, Henry VII marks not the triumph of the new over the old, but the success of the noble hero against the monumental villain [*Richard the Third*]. The abstraction was a potential presence in Shakespeare's English history plays. But Shakespeare left it out, deliberately abandoned it, or did not even notice it. He located the problems elsewhere and saw no problems here.[13]

Consider the opening scene of *Julius Caesar*, the roles of Flavius and Marullus were readymade for Shakespeare, and yet when the tribunes scold the people for fawning on Caesar, they talk only about the people's ingratitude to Pompey, and not about the struggle against tyranny. Moreover, the essence of Cassius' argument is to question why Caesar should rule, for he is no better than Brutus or Cassius. Brutus of course was a lover of freedom. It is noteworthy, that not even Brutus is as resolutely and theoretically opposed to the crowing of Caesar as he should have been, freedom and tyranny confront each other here. Brutus is guided and possessed by the fear that kingly power could change Caesar's character. But as Coleridge rightly pointed out, Brutus' fear is historically untenable. Consequently, Brutus' conviction is just as integral to his character (and not to the great historical situation) as is envy to Cassius' character.

The tragic turning point occurs when Brutus, out of noble minded short-sightedness spares Mark Antony's life and, in fact, allows him to deliver a funeral oration over Caesar's body. The fickle nature of the crowd here is not due to the historical situation (that is to say, abstract). Every crowd in Shakespeare acts this way. But while Antony takes this into account, Brutus does not. And herein lies the key to his tragedy. Recall the episodical treatment of the people's misery (the question of bread), and how much attention is given to the tribunes who, full of hatred, want to deprive Coriolanus of power and destroy him completely. In the same way, in *Antony and Cleopatra* the world's fate depends on—the episodical—Sextus Pompeius' character.

I deliberately choose such illustrations because these dramas, by their very substance, contain the great, historical, abstract necessity. All this could be read without any difficulties into these dramas, once the need and the demand had been made for the drama to express the abstract necessities that reign over life. That this has taken place, I believe hardly needs to be proved by many examples. In the early and mid-nineteenth century, the outstanding German aestheticians, under the pretext of studying Shakespeare, have persisted in their attempt to read into Shakespeare the conflicts of modern life. They tried to reconcile Shakespeare's approach to problems with actual problems.

The best known case—and the most interesting—is that of Hegel who, in his interpretation of *Macbeth*, traces the conflict to disputes between different systems of hereditary rights. According to Hegel, Macbeth, as the next eldest male relative of Duncan, is therefore strictly heir to the throne. Indeed, Macbeth suffered injustice when Duncan named his own son as his successor. Hegel in fact reproaches Shakespeare for altogether omitting this motive, this justification of Macbeth, and thus representing him as a criminal. In Hegel's view, Shakespeare's treatment of Macbeth was nothing but a genuflection to King James.[15] Hegel also criticizes Shakespeare for not letting Macbeth murder Duncan's sons too, but allowing them to escape, while none of the nobles gives them a thought either.

— That such a profound philosopher of art, such as Hegel, could so misunderstand what is perhaps one of Shakespeare's most wonderfully composed tragedies, demonstrates just how deeply modern drama has already influenced our perceptions. For all practical purposes, what Shakespeare really described is how Schiller, Grillparzer or Hebbel, or any of the modern playwrights—despite all their differences—would have handled the Macbeth theme if they came across it first in Holinshed's *Chronicles*. We can see what misunderstanding, bordering on the ridiculous, this can lead to when applied to Shakespeare, even on the part of a great thinker like Hegel.

Purely from an artistic standpoint, the essence of Shakespeare's composition is a powerful sequence of great scenes that depict and portray the tragic feelings of tragic figures. The fundamental elements that connect these scenes reside in the individual, in his character; in the atmosphere which surrounds the individual, his adversaries, and in his interactions with them, rather than in the possibility or necessity of the atmosphere itself. Hebbel saw this clearly and summed it up by saying that, for Shakespeare, the dialectics of drama resides in the character, while for the new drama it resides in the idea, in the abstract.

What holds together every Shakespearean tragic play is that, for instance, the Othello-Iago-Desdemona relationship must lead to tragedy. Tragedy is a necessity, but how it takes place is not a necessity. This question—not being raised as an abstract problem—was a mute question for Shakespeare. He was only interested in how the tragic feelings, based on the relationship of Othello, Iago and Desdemona, manifest themselves. This is the reason why he concentrated on scenes that impart immediacy and force to tragic feelings. It would be unfair to make any other demands on Shakespeare's scenes, expecting them to yield what was not intended in the first place; thus the success or failure of what was not intended cannot be in question.

In Shakespeare's dramas individuals dominate the events. The role of events and circumstances is to provide the individuals with an opportunity to express his spiritual feelings, and give these feelings a beautiful colorful background. Events and circumstances have no life of their own. Abstracted from the life of the individual, in whose life they play a role, events and circumstances are non-existence. (Here let me just add in parenthesis that the great theme that dominates modern drama, variations of which are evident in every great modern writer, is none other than the conflicts and collisions produced by the circumstances, by the separate existence of the external world. So much so, that it would hardly be an exaggeration to say that these conflicts are the central and dominant theme of modern drama.)

Let me remind you of the war in Cyprus in *Othello*, of the Fortinbras episode in *Hamlet* [5.2]; consider that no single circumstance prevents Macbeth's ascension to the throne, and everything is against him when he is doomed. Goethe once remarked that nobody ever designed men's material costumes the same way as did Shakespeare, and perhaps this is more apt than even Goethe thought. For in Shakespeare everything turns into a material costume: place, time, circumstance, action, everything, even spiritual characteristics, which sheds no light on his characters' souls, though large and rich, and the real scene of tragic events.

Apart from some central figures, everyone else merely serves as a background. Characters attain significance in relation to the central figure. This is why it is so futile to analyze in great depth, or by themselves, for instance such characters as, Claudius or Polonius. These figures, as [Walter] Raleigh[16] has observed, Shakespeare saw through the eyes of Hamlet, they are no more and no less than what Hamlet sees and needs in them to realize the tragedy of his soul, that gives off light in contact with others. But these figures, unlike those of the modern drama, have no separate life of their own. Shakespeare therefore can treat them with absolute arbitrariness. This is how Antigonus disappears in the middle of *The Winter's Tale*, no longer being needed in the drama of principal characters; and this is how Clotten is got rid of in *Cymbeline* [4.2].

But to offer more substantial illustrations, this is how Lepidus and Sextus Pompeius disappear in *Antony and Cleopatra* when Antony and Octavius Caesar fight to decide who will rule the empire. And after the great storm scene, there is no place for the fool next to Lear, and he disappears—taking leave of the world in a barely audible sentence—never to be heard of again. Perhaps *The Merchant of Venice* is Shakespeare's only drama in which one character, none other than Shylock, actually outgrows the framework, attains a self-contained life, a life that is independent of the dramatic process. However—as confirmed by conflicting interpretations—Shylock explodes the play, splits it into two plays, and in fact, as far as we are concerned, in essence kills the other play, the genuine one, the Antonio-Bassanio-Portia circular-drama.

In fact, this problem raises the question of the significance of background. In Shakespeare, a few principal characters dominate the whole play, and nothing else can equal or even approach their importance. However, these other things—and I cannot analyze the reasons for it here—have attained quite different meanings since Shakespeare's time. For no matter how useful Shakespeare's creative method is, from a purely artistic perspective, it would be useless if one were to emphasize other than the principal characters. One example from the fine arts, perhaps, can shed light on this. It is hardly accidental that modern painters whose style is the most consistent display the strongest feeling for Giotto's so-called primitivism, and its indescribable and inestimable advantage for his art. That, for instance—this is merely an example—he borrowed from nature and architecture exactly what he needed, when he needed it, to compose the background for his human figures, irrespective of their self-centered life and its visual expression. Virtually everything that is external to the soul of Shakespeare's principal characters recalls the nature that surrounds Giotto's figures.[17] But as soon as the intrinsic value of nature is recognized—in Venice it started with Bellini and Giorgione—new designs had to be found to accommodate the new perception of nature in great compositions and today—in the wake of Impressionism—once more there is a search for new designs. This is also the situation of new drama in relation to Shakespeare.

Strangely enough, the superficial seems to express the profoundest things the most vividly. When Goethe criticized Shakespeare's drama, perhaps he objected to its colorfulness or, most likely, he had in mind the difficulty of adapting it for the modern stage. For Goethe, Shakespeare's complex actions, based on many short scenes, prove difficult if not impossible, for the modern stage, without sacrificing their most beautiful and appealing features. Undeniably, if the performance of Shakespeare's plays cannot satisfy us completely, this is all the more true in other aspects. The reasons for this, in my view, lie deeper than the theater's technical ability to overcome the problem of many scenes.

I would summarize this—in a somewhat paradoxical form—by saying that every literary work, especially drama, is the result of the mixture of concrete and abstract elements, and that neither the one nor the other can ever dominate the whole. Thus, in the case of Shakespeare, as we saw, the conflict is concrete, and therefore, the place where the conflict takes place can be abstract. In modern drama, the conflict is abstract, and this conflict needs a concrete place and time in which to express itself.

What do I mean when I assert that the locale and time of Shakespeare's dramas are abstract? Among other things, I mean that they resemble the background in, for instance, the *Mona Lisa*, as distinct from the background in a Manet landscape, or a figure in Pieter de Hooch's interiors.[18] I mean that place and time in Shakespeare have no substance, only pictorial quality, and this picturesqueness is the visual, symbolic projection of the momentary feelings and moods of the characters who dwell in it. From this perspective—apart from the accidental nature of historical circumstances—Shakespeare's frequent changes of scene attain a great and deep meaning. Specifically, the background accompanies his characters everywhere and everything external merely serves as a background. But at the same time, this background best symbolizes what takes place in the character internally.

Think of the court of Macbeth's castle, in Inverness, on the morning after the murder; think of the *churchyard* scene in *Hamlet*; think of the great storm scenes in *King Lear*. You soon realize that these scenes exert less influence on what is taking place internally, than does the atmosphere of modern drama. And you also become aware that no sooner do Shakespeare's characters change their mood, than the background also changes. The characters, however, receive nothing from their surroundings, and in fact, it only exists inside them. But precisely for this reason, location forms such an integral part of character, it assumes the form of an irretrievable moment, that more profound, sublime emotion demands a neutral setting. Once the great feeling becomes manifest, the neutral setting becomes its timeless symbol, and nothing else. So it is inconceivable that Shakespeare could have limited his dramas to one act. And it would have a dissonant effect if we tried to reduce the multiplicity of his symbols to a single one, or if we tried to transpose his symbolic backgrounds into something modern.

My limited time prevents me from discussing this issue in greater depth. Nor have I accomplished what I should have, namely, to examine and compare those two great trees, Shakespearean drama and modern drama, describe their features, the circumstances that produced them, and what facilitated and what endangered them. The best I could do is to provide a cross-section of the two tree trunks and, by comparing them, outline their different natures and tendencies. I could only draw the respective boundaries of Shakespearean and modern drama, without addressing the question of why those boundaries exist, and how they manifest themselves.

Of course, I made some critical points about Shakespeare's boundaries—as defined by his age—boundaries that grew from his own limitations rather than from his specific and unsurpassed beauties. It should be obvious that our perception of Shakespeare's boundaries is informed by the same profound and sympathetic admiration as are his dithyrambic praises. In fact, our love of Shakespeare may well be a truer love, because it wants to know what Shakespeare was really like, what he considered important and what less important. This love of ours instructed us to approach Shakespeare's dramas from the perspective of his own demands, to see its perfect solutions, without trying to read into them things he could not even think of, things without which, outside the context of his intentions, even his best composition would appear fragmentary.

11   "The Source of the Tragic,"
from *Hamlet or Hecuba*

What is the source of the tragic? What is the source of tragic action which gives life to tragedy? Once we recognize in the guilt of the queen and the figure of the avenger[1] two historical intrusions into the drama [of *Hamlet*], we confront the last and most difficult question: Should historical considerations be included in the discussion of a work of art?

The generality of this question is somewhat disconcerting. The first difficulty is purely technical. Owing to an extreme division of labor, academic fields and disciplines have become overly specialized. Literary historians work with different materials and from different approaches than political historians. Shakespeare and his *Hamlet* belong to the realm of literary historians, whereas Mary Stuart and James I are the responsibility of political historians. Consequently, Hamlet and James encounter each other only with great difficulty. The rift is too deep. Literary historians consider the source of a drama to be a literary source, either a precursor or a book which Shakespeare used: for *Julius Caesar,* Plutarch; or for *Hamlet* the Nordic saga of *Saxo Grammaticus* in its 16th century literary adaptations.

Another difficulty stems from the prevailing German philosophy of art and aesthetics. Its relation to the problem of the division of labor need not concern us here. Nevertheless, philosophers of art and teachers of aesthetics tend to understand the world of art as an autonomous creation unrelated to historical or sociological reality—something to be understood only in its own terms. To relate a great work of art to the actual politics of the time in which it was created would presumably obscure its purely aesthetic beauty and debase the intrinsic worth of artistic form. The source of the tragic then lies in the free and sovereign creative power of the writer.

Here we find sharp distinctions and fundamental divisions, boundaries and barriers of opposing approaches; complete value systems, which recognize only their own passports and certifications, validate only their own visas, allowing others neither entrance nor passage. We will attempt in our discussion of Shakespeare's *Hamlet* to avoid this dangerous fragmentation, to find a better approach. In so doing, we must bear in mind that these difficulties are exacerbated by the preconceptions of the German cultural tradition.

The Creative Freedom of the Writer

In Germany we have become accustomed to look upon the writer as a genius who can create from whatever sources he chooses. In view of Shakespeare's presumed arbitrariness, the cult of genius which arose during the German *Sturm und Drang* of the 18th century has become a *credo* of the German philosophy of art. The creative freedom of the writer becomes thereby a defense of artistic freedom in the general and a stronghold of subjectivity. If his genius so compels him, why should an artist not be able to utilize artistically whatever he wishes and in whatever manner he wishes, be it personal experience or the experiences of others, books or newspaper articles? He enters into and transports the stuff of life into the totally other realm of the beautiful, where historical and sociological questions become tactless and tasteless. The old poetics spoke of 'poetic license', which in German becomes an expression of the sovereignty of genius.

It is also significant that German aesthetic concepts are generally determined more by poetry than by drama. When discussing literature, we tend to think of a lyric poem more readily than a drama. The relation of lyric poem to literary experience is something much different than the relation of tragedy to its mythical or historical sources. In this sense, the lyric poem has no source; it is occasioned by a subjective experience. One of our greatest and most form-conscious writers, Stefan George says: Experience undergoes such a transformation through art that it becomes meaningless for the artist himself, even as knowledge of this experience is for others more confusing than redeeming. That may be true for a lyric poem and may refute the pedants who wish to garnish Goethe's love poems with his romantic experiences. But the freedom to create, which provides the lyric poet with such free play with respect to reality, cannot be conferred upon other types and forms of literary creation. The subjectivity of the lyric poet corresponds to a different type of creative freedom than that of the objectivity of the epic writer and the dramatist.

In Germany we have an image of the dramatist which, understandably, is drawn from the model of our great dramatic writers. Lessing, Goethe, Schiller,

Grillparzer and Hebbel all wrote their dramas as books for publication. They sat at their writing tables or stood at their lecterns as 'domestic workers' and delivered polished manuscripts to a publisher for an honorarium. The term 'domestic worker' (*Heimarbeiter*) is not used here disparagingly; it is merely the proper designation for a sociological fact that is important for our problem and indispensible for our discussion, because Shakespeare's plays originated in a completely different manner. He wrote them not for posterity but for his concrete and immediate London public. Strictly speaking, one could say he did not write but rather composed them for a very specific audience. Not one of Shakespeare's plays anticipated spectators who had read it beforehand and recognized it in a published book.

All the above-mentioned German conceptions of art and the work of art, of the drama and the dramatist, prevent an unbiased view of Shakespeare and his work. Let us leave aside the debate about Shakespeare the person. One thing is certain: he was no 'domestic worker' in the literary production of book-dramas. His plays originated in direct contact with the London court, the London public, and the London actors. An intentional or unintentional referencing of contemporary events and persons arose quite naturally, whether as mere allusion or true reflection. In times of political tension and agitation it was unavoidable. We recognize this in our own situation and need only remind ourselves of a formula that has become quite common in the last few years: *All characters and events in this production are fictitious and any resemblance to real persons and events is purely coincidental.* I certainly do not mean to equate the author of *Hamlet* with contemporary producers of films and period plays. But the analogy of references to current events is revealing, and Shakespeare would certainly have not been averse to prefacing his dramas with such as statement.

All this not only contributes to our understanding of the psychology and sociology of the playwright, but also to the concept of drama and our question concerning the source of tragic action. It is here that the limits of the invention of the writer become clear. An author of plays to be immediately performed before a similar audience not only stands in a psychological and sociological relation to this audience but also within a common public sphere. The established audience establishes through its concrete presence a public sphere which encompasses and incorporates the author, the director, the actors, and the audience itself. If the audience does not understand the action of a play, it simply does not remain engaged and the public sphere disintegrates or ends in theatrical scandal.

Such a public sphere places a strict limit on the creative freedom of the playwright. Observance of this limit is guaranteed by the fact that the audience will not follow the events of the stage; deviating too much from the audience's knowledge and expectations makes the process incomprehensible or meaningless. The knowledge of the audience is an essential factor of theater. Even the dreams the dramatist weaves into his play must be those that could be dreamed by the spectators, with all the complications and vagaries of recent events. The creative freedom of the lyric writer as well as the epic writer and the novelist is unique. But the subjectivity and inspired fabrication of the dramatist is severely restricted both by the presence of the spectators and by the public sphere established by this presence.[2]

One should not be fooled by the seemingly limitless freedom Shakespeare exercised with respect to his literary sources. He certainly took great liberties. One might even characterize him as "essentially antihistorical."[3] Yet his arbitrary utilization of literary sources is only the other side of a much firmer tie to this concrete London audience and its knowledge of past history. In historical dramas, which presuppose a knowledge of the past, the knowledge of the audience is incorporated differently than in dramas tied to current events. The historical drama identifies persons and events with familiar names and calls up certain conceptions and expectations relevant to the author's purpose. One of Jean Paul's expressions is applicable to this type of the spectator's knowledge: "When called upon by writers, a familiar historical character—for example, Socrates or Caesar—enters like a prince and presupposes his cognito. A name is here a collection of situations." The effect is different, but no less forceful, when a person from contemporary history appears under a different name but is nonetheless immediately recognizable to the spectators. In this case, the transparent incognito heightens the tension and the participation of the knowing spectators. This is true for the character of Hamlet-James I. However, the knowledge of the spectators is not the only essential factor in the theater; it is not only the audience which pays attention to the observance of the rules of the game.

Play and Tragedy

The theater itself is essential play (*Spiel*). The play is not only played out on stage; it is play in and of itself. Shakespeare's plays, in particular, are true plays: comic plays (*Lustspiel*) or tragic plays (*Trauerspiel*). The play has its own sphere and creates a space for itself within which a certain freedom of literary materials as well as original situations reigns. Thus it creates its own field of play in both space and time. This makes possible the fiction of a completely self-contained, internally self-sufficient process. Thus Shakespeare's plays can be performed as pure play, without reference to any historical, philosophical or allegorical interpretations or other extraneous consideration. This is true also for *Hamlet,* wherein most of the action and most of the scenes are pure play.[4]

I do not expect anyone to think of James I when Hamlet is on stage. I would also not take the measure of Shakespeare's Hamlet with the historical James I or the reverse. It would be absurd, after viewing a well-played performance of *Hamlet,* to be distracted by the historical reminiscences. Nevertheless, we must distinguish between *Trauerspiel* and tragedy. Unfortunately, we Germans have become accustomed to translate the word 'tragedy' into *Trauerspiel,* thus eliminating the distinction. Shakespeare's dramas, which end with the death of the hero, are called 'tragedies'; even *Hamlet* is called a 'tragical history' or a 'tragedy'. It is still necessary to distinguish and divorce *Trauerspiel* and tragedy, so as not to lose sight of the specific quality of the tragic, so that the seriousness of a genuine tragedy is not lost.

There is today an extensive philosophy and even theology of play. However, there has long been a genuine piety which understands itself and its earthly existence as a game of God, as in the evangelical hymn: "In Him all things find their purpose and aim; Even what man achieves is God's great game." With reference to the Cabbalists, Luther spoke of the game that God plays with the leviathan for several hours a day. A Lutheran theologian even took Shakespeare's drama for a "Wittenbergian play" and made Hamlet into one of "God's players."[5] Both Catholic and Protestant theologians quote Luther's translation of a Solomonic passage from the Proverbs: "When he appointed the foundations of the earth, I was by him, as one brought up with him, and was daily his delight, rejoicing always before him, rejoicing the habitable part of his earth."[6]

In German the word 'play' has numerous aspects and contrasting applications. Anyone who strokes a violin, blows a flute or beats a drum following notes on a score calls it 'playing'. Whoever throws or hits a ball according to the rules of a game is also 'playing'. Little children and lively cats play with a special intensity, delighting in the fact that they do *not* play according to rules but in perfect freedom. From the complete control of an omnipotent and omniscient God to the activity of irrational beings, all possible and contradictory rules are thus circumscribed by the concept of 'play'. Even so, in play lies the fundamental negation of the serious situation, the state of emergency.[7] The tragic ends where play begins, even when this play is melancholic—a melancholic play for melancholic spectators, a deeply moving *Trauerspiel*. It is absolutely impossible to overlook, with regard to Shakespearean *Trauerspiel*, that the tragic is by definition not 'playable'; on the other hand, even in the so-called tragedies there comes to light in Shakespeare a character of play.

The Play Within the Play: Hamlet or Hecuba

All the world's a stage, or so it had become in the already intensely baroque atmosphere around 1600—a *Theatrum Mundi, Theatrum Naturae, Theatrum Europeum, Theatrum Belli, Theatrum Fori*. Men of action in this epoch saw themselves on a rostrum before spectators, understood themselves and their activities in terms of the theatricality of their roles. Such a stage existed in other times, but in the baroque epoch it was especially intense and widespread. Action in the public sphere was action on a stage and thus role-playing: "No life evidences more play and theater than that which elects the life of the court."[8] James I also admonished his son to remember always that as a king he would be on stage and all eyes would be upon him.

In Shakespeare's Elizabethan England the baroque theatrification of life was still unfounded and elementary—not yet incorporated into the strict framework of the sovereign state and its establishment of the public peace, security and order, as was the theater of Corneille and Racine in the France of Louis XIV. In comparison with this classical theater, Shakespeare's play in its comic as well as melancholic aspects was coarse and elementary, barbaric and not yet 'political' in the sense of the state at that time. As rudimentary theater it was all the more intensely integral to its current reality, a part of the present in a society which largely perceived its own action as theater—a theater which did not for this reason oppose the situation of the play to the concrete contemporary situation. Society, too, was seated on the rostrum. The play on stage could appear without artificiality as theater within a theater, as living play within the immediate play of real life. The play on stage could magnify itself as play without abstracting itself from the present reality. Even a double magnification became possible: the play within the play, which found astonishing realization in Act 3 of *Hamlet*. Here one can speak even of a triple magnification because the preceding pantomime, the "dumb show," once again mirrors the core of the action.

This play within a play is something other than a look behind the scenes. Above all it must not be confused with the actor's play, which originated in the 19th century in the wake of social revolution. In the actor's play the scenery is torn down, the mask is removed on stage, and the actor presents himself in his naked humanity or as a member of an oppressed class. In the 19th century the elder Dumas made the famous Shakespearean actor, Edmund Kean, into the hero of the play; in our own century, Jean-Paul Sartre has done something similar without adding anything essentially new. In both cases, a false public sphere is revealed on the rostrum, i.e., in the public sphere of its own theater. Masks and scenery are thrown out; to be sure, only in the theater and only as theater. The spectators receive information about an individual psychological or social problem. The play turns into a discussion or propaganda. Modifying one of Karl Marx's angry outbursts, one can say here: the emancipation of the actor is achieved in such a way that he becomes the hero and the hero becomes the actor.

In Shakespeare's *Hamlet* the play within a play in Act 3 is no look behind the scenes. One might consider Hamlet's meeting with the actors in Act II as such—the conversation with them, their declamations, and the advice Hamlet gives them could be the prelude to a genuine actor's play. But together these two acts are in fact the opposite. They don't serve an actor's play but rather the pure play within the play. The actor who declaims the death of Priam weeps for Hecuba. Hamlet does not weep for Hecuba. He is astonished that there are people who, in the performance of their duties, weep over something which does not concern them and has no impact on their actual existence or situation. From this realization he is strongly admonished to concentrate on his own situation and compelled to take action to fulfill his vow of vengeance.[9]

It is inconceivable that Shakespeare has nothing more in mind than to make his Hamlet into a Hecuba, that we are meant to weep for Hamlet as the actor wept for the Trojan queen. We would weep for Hamlet as for Hecuba if we wished to divorce the reality of our present existence from the play on stage. Our tears would then become the tears of actors. We would no longer have any purpose or cause because we would have sacrificed both to the aesthetic enjoyment of the play. That would be bad, for it would prove that the gods in the theater are different from those in the forum and the pulpit.

The play within the play in Act 3 of *Hamlet* is not only no look *behind* the scenes, it is the real play repeated *before* the curtains. This presupposes a realistic core of the most intense timeliness and significance. Otherwise the doubling would simply make the play more playful. More unlikely and more artificial—more untrue as a play, until finally it would become a "parody of itself." Only a strong core of reality could stand up to the double exposure of the stage upon stage. It is possible to have a play within a play, but not a tragedy within a tragedy. The play within a play in Act 3 of *Hamlet* is thus a phenomenal test of the hypothesis that a core of historical actuality and historical presence—the murder of the father and the marriage of the mother to the murderer—has the power to intensify the play as play without destroying the sense of the tragic.

What is significant about this fascinating play is that it does not exhaust itself without a trace. It contains other components than those of the play and, in this sense, is imperfect. There is no closed unity of time, no place and action, no internal process sufficient unto itself. It has two major openings through which historical time breaks into the time of the play, and this unpredictable current of ever-new possibilities of interpretation, of ever-new yet ultimately unsolvable puzzles flows into the otherwise very genuine play. Both intrusions—the tabu which surrounds the guilt of the queen, and the distortion of the avenger which leads to the Hamletization of the hero—are shadows, two dark areas. They are in no sense mere historical and political implications, neither simple allusions nor true reflections, but rather two given circumstances received in and respected by the play and around which the play timidly maneuvers. They disturb the unintentional character of pure play and, in this respect, are a *minus*. Nevertheless, they made it possible for the figure of Hamlet to become a true myth. In this respect they are a *plus*, because they succeeded in elevating *Trauerspiel* to tragedy.

Tragedy and Invention

In relation to every other form, including *Trauerspiel*, genuine tragedy has a special and extraordinary quality, a kind of surplus value that no play, however perfect, can attain because a play, unless it misunderstands itself, does not even want to attain it. This surplus value lies in the objective reality of tragic action itself, in the enigmatic involvement and entanglement of indisputably real events. This is the basis of the seriousness of tragic action which, being impossible to fictionalize or relativize, is also impossible to play. All participants are conscious of the ineluctable reality which no human mind has conceived—a reality externally given, imposed and unavoidable. This reality is the mute rock upon which the play founders and the form of genuine tragedy rises to the surface.

This is the final and insurmountable limit of literary invention. A writer can and should invent a great deal. He cannot invent the realistic core of tragic action. We can weep for Hecuba. One can weep for many things. Many things are sad and melancholy. But tragedy originates only from a given circumstance which exists for all concerned—an incontrovertible reality for the author, the actors and the audience. An invented fate is no fate at all. The most inspired creation is useless here. The core of tragic action, the source of genuine tragedy, is something so irrevocable that no mortal can invent it, no genius can compose it. On the contrary: the more original the invention, the more rigorously conceived the construction, the more perfectly the play works, the more certain the destruction of the tragic. In tragedy the common public sphere (which in every performance encompasses the author, the actors and the audience) is not based on the accepted rules of language and play but on a shared historical reality.

In spite of Nietzsche's famous formulation in *The Birth of Tragedy*, the source of tragic action cannot be music. In another and equally famous formulation, Wilamowitz-Muellendorff defines Attic tragedy in terms of myth or heroic legend.[10] He insists that he was quite aware that in his definition of tragedy he introduced the thought that tragedy is born from myth. So, myth is the source of tragedy. Unfortunately, he is not consistent. In the course of his discussion, myth becomes the "stuff" of tragedy in general and ultimately even the premise of a "story" (as one would say today) from which the writer "creates." That is again nothing more than a literary source. Nevertheless, the definition remains correct because it perceives myth as a form of heroic legend which is not a literary source of the writer but a vital understanding shared by the writer and his public—a part of reality to which all participants are bound by their historical existence. Attic tragedy is thus no simple play, because an element of reality flows into the performance from the spectators' actual knowledge of the myth. Tragic figures like Orestes, Oedipus and Hercules are not imaginary but real forms of a living myth introduced into the tragedy from an external present.

It is a different matter for Schiller's historical drama, where the question is whether or not the cultivated knowledge of history which can be presumed of the audience establishes a common public sphere. The answer to this question determines whether history becomes a source of tragic action or only the literary source for *Trauerspiel*; it has not risen to the level of myth. We know that he thought much about this question and developed his own philosophy of play. Art is for him a realm of autonomous representation. Only in play does one become human, does one transcend self-alienation and find true dignity. In such a philosophy, play must overcome seriousness. Life is serious, art is merry: yes, but the serious reality of the man of action is then ultimately only "miserable reality" and seriousness is always on the verge of becoming the law of the jungle. The autonomous and higher realm of art plays itself out against both seriousness and life. In 19th century Germany the spectators of classical Schiller drama saw world history as a world theater and enjoyed this play as self-edification in the sense of Schiller: "when you have seen the great play of the world, you will return much richer into yourself."

In Shakespeare's time the play was not yet a realm of human innocence, not yet divorced from its present reality. Sixteenth century England was far removed from the comfortable and cultivated enjoyment of 19th century Germany. The play still belonged to life itself—to a life certainly full of spirit and grace, but one not yet 'politicized'. It was a life at first stage of an elemental leap from the land to the sea, the transition from a terrestrial to a maritime existence. To the elite belonged such seafarers and adventurers as the Earl of Essex and Walter Raleigh. The play was still barbaric and elemental; it shunned neither morbidity nor buffoonery. Shakespeare, like Schiller, utilized and incorporated historical and literary sources. But even in his historical dramas he had a different relation to history.

We have already referred to Shakespeare's seemingly anti-historical arbitrariness. In his dramas based on English history, history is for him not even a literary source but simply a mouthpiece. His plays are always unencumbered theater—burdened neither with philosophical nor aesthetic problems. As much as the avenger is problematized in *Hamlet*, this drama of revenge does not attempt a deproblematization through play; neither a humanization through art, nor a birth of humanity in the play. The author of this consistent drama feared neither allusions nor reflections, but he allowed genuine historical intrusions. In the figure of Hamlet he came up against a concrete tabu and a historically concrete figure he respected as such. The son of the king and the murder of the father are, for Shakespeare and his public, present and inescapable realities from which one shrinks out of timidity, out of moral and political considerations, out of a sense of tact and natural respect. This accounts for the two historical intrusions into the otherwise closed circle of the play—the two doors through which the tragic element of an actual event enters into the world of the play and transforms the *Trauerspiel* into a tragedy, historical reality into myth.

The core of historical reality is not invented, cannot be invented, and must be respected as given. It enters into the tragedy in two ways, thus there are two sources of tragic action: one is the myth of classical tragedy, which mediates the tragic action; the other, as in *Hamlet*, is the given historical reality which encompasses the playwright, the actors and the audience. Whereas the tragedies of classical antiquity have the myth before them and create from it the tragic action, in the case of *Hamlet* we encounter the rare (but typically modern) case of a playwright who establishes myth from a reality he directly confronts. But neither in antiquity nor in modern times could the playwright invent the tragic action. Tragic action and invention are irreconcilable and mutually exclusive.[12]

Shakespeare's incomparable greatness lies in the fact that, moved by reserve and consideration, led by tact and respect, he was capable of extracting from his contemporary political situation the form capable of being raised to the level of myth. His success in conceiving the core of a tragedy and achieving the myth was the reward for that reserve and respect which honored the tabu and transformed the figure of an avenger into a Hamlet. Thus was the myth of Hamlet born. A *Trauerspiel* rose to tragedy and could thus convey to future ages and generations the living reality of a mythical figure.

12   "Othello and the Stake of the Other,"
from *Disowning Knowledge*

To study the imagination of the body's fate under skepticism, I ask how it is that we are to understand, at the height of *The Winter's Tale*, Hermione's reappearance as a statue. Specifically I ask how it is that we are to understand Leontes' acceptance of the "magic" that returns her to flesh and blood, and hence to him. This is a most specific form of resurrection. Accepting it means accepting the idea that she had been turned to stone; that that was the right fate for her disappearance from life. So I am asking for the source of Leontes' conviction in the rightness of that fate. Giving the question that form, the form of my answer is now predictable: For her to return to him is for him to recognize her; and for him to recognize her is for him to recognize his relation to her; in particular to realize what his denial of her has done to her, hence to him. So Leontes recognizes the fate of stone to be the fate of his particular skepticism. One can see this as the projection of his own sense of numbness, of living death. But then why was this *his* fate? It is a most specific form of remorse or of (self-)punishment.

Its environment is a tale of harrowing jealously, and a consequent accusation of adultery, an accusation known by every outsider, everyone but the accuser, to be insanely false. Hence Leontes is inevitably paired with *Othello*. I call attention to two further ways in which *The Winter's Tale* is a commentary upon *Othello*, and therefore contrariwise. First, both plays involve a harrowing of the power of knowing the existence of another (as chaste, intact, as what the knower knows his other to be). Leontes refuses to believe a true oracle, Othello insists upon believing a false one. Second, in both plays the consequence of man's refusal of knowledge of his other is an imagination of stone. It is not merely an appetite for beauty that produces Othello's most famous image of his victim, as a piece of cold and carved marble ("whiter skin of hers than snow, / And smooth, as monumental alabaster" [5.2.4–5]). Where does his image come from?

To introduce what I have to say about Othello, I want to give a final source for thinking about tragedy as a kind of epistemological problem, or as the outcome of the problem of knowledge—of the dominance of modern political thought by it. When I said toward the end of the introduction of this book, recalling how the beginning of a line of thought began from one, that "the pivot of Othello's interpretation of skepticism is Othello's placing of a finite woman in the place of God," was recalling a claim of mine to have given a certain derivation for the problem of the other. But I was also echoing one formulation Descartes gives his motive in wanting to secure God beyond doubt, viz., to know beyond doubt that he is alone in the world (*Third Meditation*). Now I ask, in passing but explicitly, why it is Descartes does not try to defeat that possibility of isolation in what would seem (to whom?) the most direct and surest way, by locating the existence of one other *finite* being.

He says simply that he can easily imagine that ideas "which represent men similar to myself" could be "formed by the combination of my other ideas, of myself, of corporeal objects, and of God, even though outside of me there were no other men in the world." He is setting up, of course, a powerful move toward God. And we can gather from this, something that seems borne out in the sequel of his *Meditations*, that the problem of others (other finite beings) is not discovered or derived by Descartes to be a special problem of knowledge; this is surely one reason it would not have been discovered to be such in subsequent epistemology. But the more one meditated upon the unique place Descartes makes for his relation to his own body, the less clear and distinct it is that he has available to himself the formulation of the idea of another body as having a unique relation to its mind in the special quasi-substantial way that he asserts is not like the way a ship is related to its pilot. But without such an idea, what is the content of the idea of "men similar to myself"? I do not conceive of Descartes' appealing to the route of analogy here, since he must be far surer that other human bodies go with minds than any sureness he can extract by inferring from another body's behavior alone. After all, the body has essentially nothing to do with the soul! I might express his difficulty as follows. His sense of himself as composed of his contrary natures (of what he means by mind and body, the one characterized in opposition to the other, each essentially what the other is not) is the idea of double nature, symbolized centrally in the culture we share with him (but perhaps now only in literature) as the figure of Christ. So the thing in incarnation, the mysterious meeting of heaven and earth, occurs in Descartes' thought not alone in the inspirer of Christianity but in each individual human being. From here you may conclude that the human problem in recognizing other human beings is the problem of recognizing another to be Christ for oneself. (What is the significance of the charge that Descartes proves the existence at best of a philosopher's God?)

In the light of this passing of the question of the other, a change is noticeable in the coda Descartes supplies his arguments at the end of this *Third Meditation*:

> The whole force of the argument I have here used to prove the existence of God consists in the fact that I recognize that it would not be possible for my nature to be what it is, possessing the idea of a God, unless God really exists—the same God, I say, the idea of whom I possess, the God who possesses all these high perfections . . . [who] cannot be a deceiver.

The main point of summary is that I could not produce the idea I have of God, for it can come from nothing less than God himself. But a new note of necessity is also struck, that without the presence of this idea in himself, and (hence) the presence of the fact of which it is the imprint, my own nature would necessarily not be what it is. (Nietzsche's idea of the death of God can be understood to begin by saying roughly or generally as much: the idea of God is part of (the idea of) human nature. If that idea dies, the idea of human nature equally dies.) So not only the fact, as it were, of my existence, but the integrity of it, depends upon this idea. And so these meditations are about the finding of self-knowledge after all; of the knowledge of a human self by a human self. That the integrity of my (human, finite) existence may depend on the fact and on the idea of another being's existence, and on the possibility of *proving* that existence, an existence conceived from my very dependence and incompleteness, hence conceived as perfection, and conceived as producing me "in some sense, in [its] own image"—these are thoughts that take me to a study of *Othello*. Briefly, to begin with, we have the logic, the emotion, and the sense of skepticism epitomized. The logic: "My life upon her faith" (1.3.294) and "when I love thee not / chaos is come again" (3.3.91–92) set up the stake necessary to best cases; the sense I expressed by the imaginary major premise "If I know anything, I know this." One standing issue about the theme of *Othello*'s plot is that the progress from the completeness of Othello's love to the perfection of his doubt is too precipitous for the fictional time of the play. Such precipitousness is just the rhythm of skepticism; all that is necessary is the stake. The emotion: Here I mean not Othello's emotion toward Desdemona: call it jealousy; but

the structure of his emotion as he is hauled back and forth across the keel of
his love. Othello's enactment, or sufferance, of the torture is the most extraordinary representation known to me of the "astonishment" in skeptical doubt.
In Descartes' *First Meditation*: "I realize so clearly that there are no conclusive
indications by which waking life can be distinguished from sleep that I am
quite astonished, my bewilderment is such that it is almost able to convince me
that I am sleeping." (It does not follow that one is *convinced* that one is awake.)
When Othello loses consciousness ("Is't possible?—Confess? Handkerchief?—
O devil!" [4.1.42–43]), it is not from conviction in a piece of knowledge but in
an effort to stave the knowledge off. The scene: Here I have in mind the per-
vasive air of the language and the action of this play as one in which Othello's
mind continuously outstrips reality, dissolves it in the trance or dream or in the
beauty or ugliness or his incantatory imagination; in which he visualizes possibilities that reason, unaided, cannot rule out. Why is he beyond aid? Why are
the ear and the eye in him disjoined? We know that by the time he formulates
his condition this way:

> By the world,
> I think my wife be honest, and think she is not,
> I think that thou are just, and think thou are not;
> I'll have some proof (3.3.389–92)

he is lost. Two dozen lines earlier he had demanded of Iago "the ocular proof,"
a demand that was no purer a threat than it was a demand, as if he does indeed
wish for this outcome, as if he has a use for Iago's suspicions, hence a use for
Iago that reciprocates Iago's use of him. Nothing I claim about the play here
will depend on an understanding of the relation between Iago and Othello, so
I simply assert what is suggested by what I have just said, that such a question
as "Why does Othello believe Iago?" is badly formed. It is not conceivable that
Othello believes Iago and *not* Desdemona. Iago, we might say, offers Othello
an opportunity to believe something, something to oppose to something else
he knows. What does he know? Why does it require opposition?—What do we
know?

We have known (say, since G. Wilson Knight's "The *Othello* Music") that
Othello's language, call it his imagination, is at once his, and the play's, glory,
and his shame, the source of his power and of his impotence; or we should
have known (since Bradley's *Shakespearean Tragedy*) that Othello is the most
romantic of Shakespeare's heroes, which may be a way of summarizing the

same facts. And we ought to attend to the perception that Othello is the most Christian of the tragic heroes (expressed in Norman Rabkin's *Shakespeare and the Common Understanding*). Nor is there any longer any argument against our knowledge that Othello is black; and there can be no argument with the fact that he has just married, nor with the description, compared with the cases of Shakespeare's other tragedies, that this one is not political but domestic.

We know more specifically, I take it, that Othello's blackness means something. But what specifically does it mean? Mean, I mean, to him—for otherwise it is not Othello's color that we are interested in but some other generalized blackness, meaning perhaps "sooty" or "filthy," as elsewhere in the play. The difference may show in the way one takes Desdemona's early statement: "I saw Othello's visage in his mind" (1.3.252). I think it is commonly felt that she means she overlooked his blackness in favor of his inner brilliance; and perhaps further felt that this is a piece of deception, at least of herself. But what the line more naturally says is that she saw his visage as he sees it and she understands his blackness as he understands it as expression (or in his word, his manifestation) of his mind which is not overlooking it. Then how does he understand it?

As the color of a romantic hero. For he, as he was and is, manifested by his parts, his title, and his "perfect soul" (1.2.31), is the hero of the tales of romance he tells, some ones of which he wooed and won Desdemona with, others of which he will die upon. It is accordingly the color of one of enchanted powers and of magical protection, but above all it is the color of one of purity, of a perfect soul. Desdemona, in entering his life, hence in entering his story of his life, enters as a fit companion for such a hero; his perfection is now open toward hers. His absolute stake in his purity, and its confirmation in hers, is shown in what he feels he has lost in losing Desdemona's confirmation:

> my name, that was as fresh
> As Dian's visage, is now begrim'd, and black
> As mine own face. (3.3.392–94)

Diana's is a name for the visage Desdemona saw to be in Othello's mind. He loses its application to his own name, his charmed self, when he no longer sees his visage in Desdemona's mind but in Iago's, say in the world's capacity for rumor. To say he loses Desdemona's power to confirm his image of himself is to say that he loses his old power of imagination. And this is to say that he loses his grasp of his own nature; he no longer has the same voice in his history. So then the question becomes: How has he come to displace Desdemona's imagination by Iago's? However terrible the exchange, it must be less terrible than some other. Then we need to ask not so much how Iago gained his power as how Desdemona lost hers.

We know—do we not?—that Desdemona has lost her virginity, the protection of Diana by the time she appears to us. And surely Othello knows this! But this change in her condition, well a big enough fact to hatch millennia of plots, is not what Othello accuses her of. (Though would that accusation have been much more unfair than the unfaithfulness he does accuse her of?) I emphasize that I am assuming in Othello's mind the theme and condition of virginity to carry their full weight within a romantic universe. Here is some recent Northrop Frye on the subject:

> Deep within the stock convention of virgin-baiting is a version of human integrity imprisoned in a world it is in but not of, often forced by weakness into all kinds of ruses and stratagems, yet always managing to avoid the one fate which really is worse than death, the annihilation of one's identity. . . . What is symbolized as a virgin is actually a human conviction however expressed, that there is something at the core of one's infinitely fragile being which is not only immortal but has discovered the secret of invulnerability that eludes the tragic hero.[1]

Now let us consolidate what we know on this sketch so far. We have to think in this play not merely about marriage but about the marriage of a romantic hero and of a Christian man; one whose imagination has to incorporate the idea of two becoming one in marriage and the idea that it is better to marry than to burn. It is a play, though it is thought of as domestic, in which not a marriage but an idea of marriage, or let us say an imagination of marriage is worked out. "Why did I marry?" is the first question Othello asks himself to express his first raid of suspicion (3.3.246). The question has never been far from his mind. Iago's first question to him is "Are you fast married?" and Othello's first set speech ends with something less than an answer: "But that I love the gentle Desdemona, / I would not my unhoused free condition / Put into circumscription and confine / For the sea's worth." Love is at most a necessary not sufficient condition for marrying. And for some minds, a certain idea of love may compromise as much as validate the idea of marriage. It may be better, but it is not perfect to marry, as St. Paul implies.

We have further, to think in this play not merely generally of marriage, but specifically of the wedding night. It is with this that the play opens. The central of the facts we know is that the whole beginning scene takes place while Othello and Desdemona are in their bridal bed. The simultaneity is marked: "Even now, now, very now, an old black ram / Is tupping your white ewe" (1.1.88–89). And the scene is one of treachery, alarms, of shouts, of armed men running through a sleeping city. The conjunction of the bridal chamber with the scene of emergency is again insisted on by Othello's reappearance from his bedroom to stop a brawl with his single presence; a reappearance repeated the first night in Cyprus. As though an appearance from his place of sex and dreams is what gives him the power to stop an armed fight with a word and a gesture.—Or is this more than we know? Perhaps the conjunction is to imply that their "hour of love" (1.3.298–99), or their two hours, have each been interrupted. There is reason to believe that the marriage has not been consummated, anyway reason to believe that Othello does not know whether it has. What is Iago's "Are you fast married?" asking? Whether a public, legal ceremony has taken place or whether a private act; or whether the public and the private have ratified one another? Othello answers by speaking of his nobility and his love. But apart from anything else this seems to assume that Iago's "you" was singular, not plural. And what does Othello mean in Cyprus by these apparently public words?

> come, my dear love,
> The purchase made, the fruits are to ensue
> The profit's yet to come 'twixt me and you (2.3.8–10)

What is the purchase and what the fruits or profit? Othello has just had claimed a general celebration at once of the perdition of the Turkish fleet and of his nuptials (2.2). If the fruits and profit are the resumption of their privacy then the purchase was the successful discharge of his public office and his entry into Cyprus. But this success was not his doing; it was provided by a tempest. Is the purchase their "public" marriage? Then the fruits and profit are their conjugal love. Then he saying that this is yet to come. It seems to me possible that the purchase, or price, was her virginity and the fruits or profit their pleasure. There could hardly be greater emphasis on their having had just one shortened night together, isolated from this second night by a tempest (always in these matters symbolic, perhaps here of a memory, perhaps of an anticipation). Or is it, quite simply, that this is something she wishes to *say* publicly, whatever the truth between them? (How we imagine Desdemona's reaction to this would then become all-important.)

I do not think that we must, nor that we can, choose among these possibilities in Othello's mind. On the contrary, I think Othello cannot choose among them. My guiding hypothesis about the structure of the play is that the thing denied our *sight* throughout the opening scene—the thing, the scene, that Iago takes Othello back to again and again, retouching it for Othello's enchafed imagination—is what we are shown in the final scene, the scene of murder. This becomes our ocular proof of Othello's understanding of his two nights of married love. (It has been felt from Thomas Rymer to G. B. Shaw that the play obeys the rhythm of farce, not of tragedy. One might say that in the beginning with the sexual scene denied our sight, this play opens exactly as a normal comedy closes, as if turning comedy inside out. I shall follow out this hypothesis here only to the extent of commenting on the final scene.

However one seeks to interpret the meaning of the great entering speech of the scene ("It is the cause, it is the cause, my soul. ... Put out the light, put out the light") I cannot take its mysteries, its privacies, magniloquence, as separate from some massive denial to which these must be in service. Othello must mean that he is acting impersonally, but the words are those of a man in a trance, in a dream state, fighting not to awaken; willing for anything but light. By "denial" I do not initially mean something requiring psychoanalytical, or any other theory. I mean merely to ask that we not, conventionally but insufferably, assume that we know this woman better than this man knows her—making Othello some kind of erotic, gorgeous, superstitious lunkhead; which is about what Iago thinks. However much Othello deserves each of these titles, however far he believes Iago's tidings, he cannot just believe them; somewhere he also *knows* them to be false. This is registered in the rapidity with which he is brought to the truth, with no further real evidence, with only a counterstory (about the handkerchief) that bursts over him, or from him, as the truth. Shall we say he recognizes the truth too late? The fact is, he recognizes it when he is ready to, as one alone can; in this case, when its burden is dead. I am not claiming that he is trying not to believe Iago, or wants not to believe what Iago has told him. (This might describe someone who, say, had a good opinion of Desdemona, not someone whose life is staked upon hers.) I am claiming that we must understand Othello, on the contrary, to want to believe Iago, to be trying, against his knowledge, to believe him. Othello's eager insistence on Iago's honesty, his eager slacking of his thirst for knowledge with that poison, is not a sign of his stupidity in the presence of poison but of his devouring need of it. I do not quite say that he could not have accepted slander about Desdemona so quickly, to the quick, unless he already believed it; but rather that it is a thing he would rather believe than something yet more terrible to his mind; that the

idea of Desdemona as an adulterous whore is more convenient to him than the
idea of her as chaste. But what could be more terrible than Desdemona's faith-
lessness? Evidently her faithfulness. But how?

Note that in taking Othello's entering speech as part of a ritual of denial,
in the context of taking the murder scene as a whole to be a dream enactment
of the invisible opening of the play, we have an answer implied to our original
question about this play, considering Othello's turning of Desdemona to stone.
His image denies that he scarred her and shed her blood. It is a denial at once
that he has taken her virginity and that she has died of him. (But it is at the
same time evidence that in suffering a replacement of the problem of God with
the problem of the other this man has turned both objects into stone, so that
we might at this moment understand his self-interpretation to be that of an
idolater, hence religiously as well as socially to be cast out.) The whole scene
of murder is built on the concept of sexual intercourse or orgasm as a dying.
There is a dangerously explicit quibble to this effect in the exchange

> OTH. Thou art on thy death bed
> DES. Ay, but not yet to die. (5.2.51–52)

The possible quibble only heightens the already heartbreaking poignance of
the wish to die in her marriage bed after a long life. Though Desdemona no
more understands Othello's accusation of her than, in his darkness to himself,
he does, she obediently shares the sense that this is their final night and that it
is to be some dream-like recapitulation of their former two nights. This shows
in her premonitions of death (the willow song, and the request that one of
the wedding sheets be her shroud) and in her mysterious request to Emilia,
"tonight / Lay on my bed our wedding sheets" (4.2.106–7), as if knowing, and
faithful to, Othello's private dream of her, her self preparing the scene of her
death as Othello, utilizing Iago's stage directions, imagines it must happen
("Do it not with poison, strangle her in her bed, even the bed she hath contaminated." "Good, good, the justice of it pleases, very good" [4.1.203–5]); as
if knowing that only with these sheets on their bed can his dream of her be
contested. The dream is of contamination. The fact the dream works upon is
the act of deflowering. Othello is reasonably literal about this, as reasonable as
a man in a trance can be:

> When I have pluck'd the rose,
> I cannot give it vital growth again,
> It must needs wither; I'll smell it on the tree,

A balmy breath, that doth almost persuade
Justice herself to break her sword; once more;
Be thus, when thou art dead, and I will kill thee,
And love thee after. (5.2.13–19)

(Necrophilia is an apt fate for a mind whose reason is suffocating in its sumptuous capacity for figuration, and which takes the dying into love literally to entail killing. "The death's unnatural that kills for loving" [5.2.41]; or that turns its object to live stone. It is apt as well that Desdemona senses death, or the figure of death, as the impending cause of death. And at the very end, facing himself, he will not recover from this. "I kissed thee ere I killed thee." And after too. And not just now when you died from me, but on our previous nights as well.)

The exhibition of wedding sheets in this romantic, superstitious, conventional environment can only refer to the practice of providing purity by staining—I mention in passing that this provides a satisfactory weight for the importance Othello attaches to his charmed (or farcical) handkerchief, the fact that it is spotted, spotted with strawberries. √

Well, were the sheets stained or not? Was she a virgin or not? The answers seem as ambiguous as to our earlier question whether they are fast married. Is this final? Fatal reenactment of their wedding night a clear denial of what really happened, so that we can just read off, by negation, what really happened? Or is it a straight reenactment without negation, and the flower was still on the tree, as far as he knew? In that case, who was reluctant to see it plucked, he or she? On such issues, farce and tragedy are separate by the thickness of a membrane. *cute*

We of course have no answer to such questions. But what matters is that Othello has no answers, or rather he can give none. For any answers to the questions, granted that I am right in taking the questions to be his, is intolerable. The torture of logic in his mind we might represent as follows: Either I shed her blood and scarred her or I did not. If I did not then she was not a virgin and this is a stain upon me. If I did then she is no longer a virgin and this is a stain upon me. Either way I am contaminated. (I do not say that the sides of this dilemma are of equal significance for Othello.)

But this much logic anyone but a lunkhead might have mastered apart from actually getting married. (He himself may say as much when he asks himself, too late, why he married.) Then what quickens this logic for him? Call whatever it is Iago. What is Iago? He is everything, we know, Othello is not. Critical and witty, for example, where Othello is commanding and eloquent; retentive where the other is lavish; concealed where the other is open; cynical where the other is romantic; conventional where the other is original; imagines flesh where the other imagines spirit; the imaginer and manager of the human guise; the bottom end of the world. And so on. A Christian has to call him devil. The single fact between Othello and Iago I focus on here is that Othello fails twice at the end to kill Iago knowing that he cannot kill him. This all but all-powerful chieftain is stopped at this nobody. It is the point of his impotence, and the meaning of it. Iago is everything Othello must deny and which, denied, is not killed but works on, like poison, like Furies.

In speaking of the point and meaning of Othello's impotence I do not think of Othello as having been in any everyday sense impotent with Desdemona. I think of him, rather, as having been surprised by her, at what he has elicited from her; at, so to speak, a success rather than a failure. It is the dimension of her that shows itself in that difficult and dirty banter between her and Iago as they await Othello on Cyprus. Rather than imagine himself to have elicited that, or solicited it, Othello would imagine it elicited by anyone and everyone else—Surprised, let me say, to find that she is flesh and blood. It was the one thing that he could not imagine for himself. For if she is flesh and blood, since they are one, so is he. But then although his potency of imagination can command the imagination of this child who is everything he is not, so that she sees his visage in his mind, she also sees that he is not identical with his mind, he is more than his imagination, black with desire, which she desires. Iago knows it, and Othello cannot bear what Iago knows, so he cannot outface the way in which he knows it, or knows anything. He cannot forgive Desdemona for existing, for being separate from him, outside, beyond command, commanding, her captain's captain.

It is an unstable frame of mind that compounds figurative with literal dying in love; and Othello unstably projects upon her, as he blames her:

O'perjured woman, thou dost stone thy heart
And makest me call what I intend to do
A murder, which I thought a sacrifice (5.2.64–66)

As he is the one who gives out lies about her, so he is the one who will give her a stone heart for her stone body, as if in words of stone which confound the figurative and literal there is the confounding of the incantations of poetry and of magic. He makes of her the thing he feels ("My heart is turned to stone" [4.1.178]), but covers the ugliness of his thought with the beauty of his imagery—a debasement of himself and of his art of words. But what produces the idea of sacrifice? How did he manage the thought of her death as a sacrifice? To what was he to sacrifice her? To his image of himself and of her, to keep his image intact, uncontaminated; as if *this* were his protection from slander's image of him, safe from a conventional view of his blackness. So he becomes conventional, sacrificing love to convention. But this was unstable: it could not be said. Yet better thought than the truth, which was that the central sacrifice of romance has been made by them: Her virginity, her intactness, her perfection had been gladly forgone by her for him, for the sake of their union, for the seeming of it. It is the sacrifice he could not accept, for then he was not himself perfect. It must be displaced. The scar is the mark of finitude, or separateness; it must be born whatever one's anatomical condition, or color. It is the sin or the sign of refusing imperfection that produces, or justifies, the visions and torments of devils that inhabit the region of this play.

If such a man as Othello is rendered impotent and murderous by aroused, or by having aroused, female sexuality—or let us say, if the man is horrified by human sexuality, in himself and in others—then no human being is free of this possibility. What I have wished to bring out is the nature of this possibility, or the possibility of this nature, the way human sexuality is the field in which the fantasy of finitude, of its acceptance and its repetitious overcoming is worked out; the way human separateness is turned equally toward splendor and toward horror. Mixing beauty and ugliness; turn toward before and after; toward flesh and blood.

—But Othello certainly knows that Desdemona exists! So what has his more or less interesting condition to do with skepticism?—

In what spirit do you ask that question? I too am raising it. I wish to keep suspicion cast on what it is we take to express skepticism, and here especially by casting suspicion on whether we know what it means to know that another exists; is flesh and blood; is separate from him; other. This is precisely the possibility that tortures him. The content of his torture *is* the premonition of the existence of another, hence of his own, his own as dependant, as partial. According to me further, his professions of skepticism over her faithfulness are a cover story for a deeper conviction; a terrible doubt covering a yet more terrible certainty, an unstable certainty. But this then is what I have throughout kept arriving at as the cause of skepticism—the attempt to convert the human condition, the condition of humanity, into an intellectual difficulty, a riddle. (To interpret "a metaphysical finitude as an intellectual lack.")[2]

Tragedy is the place we are not allowed to escape the consequences, or price, of this cover: that the failure to acknowledge a best case of the other is a denial of the other, presaging the death of the other, saved by stoning, or by hanging; and the death of our capacity to acknowledge as much, the turning of our hearts to stone, or their bursting. The necessary reflexiveness of spiritual torture.—But at any rate Othello is hardly in doubt that he can ever know whether Desdemona is, for example, in pain "perhaps suffering heartache" and for that reason in doubt that she exists; so again his problem cannot match the skeptical one.—But I ask again: Do we know what it is to be in such a doubt? And know this better than we know how to think of Othello's doubt? Moreover, is it even clear what it would mean to say that Othello does not doubt matters of Desdemona's consciousness such as that she has, or may have, some easily describable pain? If what he imagines is that she is stoned, then *can* he imagine that he is pain? ("Could one imagine a stone's having consciousness? And if anyone can do so—why should that not merely prove that such image-mongery is of no interest to us?" [*Investigations*, §390].)

Is the cover of skepticism—the conversion of metaphysical finitude into intellectual lack—a denial of the human or any expression of it? For of course there are those for whom the denial of the human *is* the human.[3] Call this the Christian view. It would be why Nietzsche undertook to identify the task of overcoming the human with the task of overcoming the denial of the human; which implies overcoming the human not through mortification but through joy, say ecstasy. If the former can be thought of as the denial of the body then the latter may be thought of as the affirmation of the body. Then those who are pushed, in attempting to counter a dualistic view of mind and body, to assert the identity of body and mind, are again skipping or converting the problem. For suppose my identity with my body is something that exists' only in my affirmation of my body. (As friendship may exist only in loyalty to it.) Then the question is: What would the body *become* under affirmation? What would become of *me*? Perhaps I would know myself as, take myself for, a kind of machine; perhaps as a universe.

I conclude with two thoughts, or perspectives, from which to survey one's space of conviction in the reading that I have started of Othello, and from which perhaps to guide it further.

First, what you might call a philosophy or the moral of the play seems all but contained in the essay Montaigne entitles "On Some Verses of Virgil," in such a remark as: "What a monstrous animal to be a horror of himself, to be burdened by his pleasures, to regard himself as a misfortune!" The essay concerns the compatibility of sex with marriage, of sex with age; it remarks upon, and upon the relations among, jealousy, chastity, imagination, doubts about virginity, upon the strength of language and the honesty of language; and includes mention of a Turk and of certain instances of necrophilia. One just about runs through the topics of *Othello* if to this essay one adds Montaigne's early essay "Of the Power of Imagination," which contains a Moor and speaks of a king of Egypt who, finding himself impotent with his bride, threatened to kill her, thinking it was some sort of sorcery. The moral would be what might have been contained in Othello's "one that lov'd not wisely, but too well," that all these topics should be food for thought and moderation, not for torture and murder; as fit for rue and laughter as for pity and terror; that they are not tragic unless one makes them so, takes them so; that we are tragic in what we take to be tragic; that one must take one's imperfections with a "gay and sociable wisdom" (in "Of Experience," Montaigne's final essay), not with a somber and isolating eloquence. It is advice to accept one's humanity, and one can almost see Iago as the slanderer of human nature (this would be his diabolism) braced with Othello as the enactor of the slander—the one thinking to escape human nature from below, the other from above. But to whom is the advice usable? And how do we understand how it cannot be taken by those in directest need of it? The urging of moderation is valuable only to the extent that it results from the knowledge of the human possibilities beyond its urging. Is Montaigne's attitude fully earned, itself without a tint of the wish for exemption from the human? Or is it Shakespeare's topic of the sheets and the handkerchief understandable as a rebuke to Montaigne, for refusing a further nook of honesty? A bizarre question, I suppose; but meant only to indicate how one might, and why one should, test whether my emphasis on the stain is necessary to give sufficient weight to one's experience of the horror and the darkness of these words and actions, or whether it is imposed.

My second concluding thought is more purely speculative, and arises in response to my having spoken just now of "the refusal of imperfection" as producing "the visions and torments of devils that inhabit the region of this play." I do not wish to dispute the evidence marshaled by Bernard Spivack in his *Shakespeare and the Allegory of Evil* showing Iago to be a descendant of the late morality figure of the Vice. I mean rather to explain the further appearance of that figure in this particular play, and, I guess, to suggest its humanizing, or human splitting off (the kind of interpretation Spivack's book seems to deplore). It is against the tradition of the morality play that I now go on to call attention—I cannot think I am the first to say it out loud—to the hell and the demon staring out of the names in Othello and Desdemona. I mention this curiosity to prepare something meant as a nearly pure conjecture, wishing others to prove it one way or another, namely that underlying and shaping the events of this play are certain events of witch trials. Phrases such as "the ocular proof" and "cords, or knives / Poison, or fire, or suffocating streams" (3.3.394–95) seem to me to call for location in a setting of judicial torture. And I confess to finding myself thinking of Desdemona's haunting characterization of a certain conception of her as "a moth of peace" when I read, from an 1834 study called *Folklore of the NE of Scotland*, "In some parts of Scotland moths are called 'witches'" (quoted in Kittredge, *Witchcraft in Old and New England*). But what prompts my thought primarily is the crazed logic Othello's rage for proof and for "satisfaction" seems to require (like testing for a woman's witchcraft by seeing whether she will drown, declaring that if she does she was innocent but if she does not she is to be put to death for a witch): What happened on our wedding night is that I killed her; but she is not dead; therefore she is not human; therefore she must die. ("Yet she must die, else she'll betray more men" [5.2.6].) He claims not to be acting personally, but by authority; here he has delivered a sentence. I recall that the biblical justification for the trial of witches was familiarly from the punishments in Exodus: "Thou shalt not suffer a witch to live." Othello seems to be babbling the crazed logic as he falls into his explicit faint or trance: "First, to be hanged, and then to confess; I tremble at it" (4.1.38–39), not knowing whether he is torturer or victim.

I introduced the idea of the trial for witchcraft as a conjecture, meaning immediately that it is not meant as a hypothesis: I do not *require* it for any interpretative alignment of my senses with the world of this play. It is enough, without supposing Shakespeare to have used literal subtexts of this sort, that the play opens with a public accusation of witchcraft, and an abbreviated trail, and is then succeeded with punctuating thoughts of hell and by fatal scenes of psychological torture, and concludes with death as the proof of mortality, i.e., of innocence (cf. "If that thou be'st a devil, I cannot kill thee" [5.2.283]). Enough, I mean, to stir the same depths of superstition—of a horror that proposes our lack of certain access to other minds—that under prompting institutions caused trial for witchcraft. *Othello* is at once, as we would expect of what we call Shakespeare's humanity, an examination of the madness and bewitchment of inquisitors, as well as of the tortures of love; as those tortures of which both victims and torturer are victims.

So they are there, on their bridal and death sheets. A statue, a stone, is something whose existence is fundamentally open to the ocular proof. A human being is not. The two bodies lying together form an emblem of this fact, the truth of skepticism. What this man lacked was not certainty. He knew everything, but he could not yield to what he knew, be commanded by it. He found out too much for his mind, not too little. Their differences from one another—the one everything the other is not—form an emblem of human separation, which can be accepted, and granted, or not. Like the separation from God; everything we are not.

So we are here, knowing they are "gone to burning hell," she with a lie on her lips, protecting him, he with her blood on him. Perhaps Blake has what he calls songs to win them back with, to make room for hell in a juster city. But can philosophy accept them back at the hands of poetry? Certainly not so long as philosophy continues, as it has from the first, to demand the banishment of poetry from its public. Perhaps if it could itself become literature. But can philosophy become literature and still know itself?

13   "Aphorism, Countertime"

1. Aphorism is the name.

2. As its name indicates, aphorism separates, it marks dissociation (*apo*), it terminates, delimits, arrests (*horizo*). It brings to an end by separating, it separates in order to end—and to define [*finir—et définer*].

3. An aphorism is a name but every name can take on the figure of aphorism.

4. An aphorism is exposure to contretemps.[1] It exposes discourse—hands it over to contretemps. Literally—because it is abandoning a word [*une parole*] to its letter.

(Already this could be read as a series of aphorisms, the alea of an initial anachrony. In the beginning there was contretemps. In the beginning there is speed. Word and deed are *overtaken*. Aphorism outstrips.)

5. To abandon speech [*la parole*], to entrust the secret to letters—this is the stratagem of the third party, the mediator, the Friar, the matchmaker who, without any other desire but the desire of others, organizes the contretemps. He counts on the letters without taking account of them.

> In the meantime, against thou shalt awake,
> Shall Romeo by my letters know our drift,
> And hither shall he come. (4.1.113–15)[2]

6. Despite appearances, an aphorism never arrives by itself, it doesn't come all alone. It is part of a serial logic. As in Shakespeare's play, in the trompe-l'oeil depth of its paradigms, all the *Romeo and Juliet*s that came before it, there will be several series of aphorisms here.

7. Romeo and Juliet, the heroes of contretemps in our mythology, the positive heroes. They missed each other, how they missed each other! Did they miss each other? But they also survived, *both of them*, survived *one another*, in their

name, through a studied effect of contretemps: an unfortunate crossing, by chance, of temporal and aphoristic series.[3]

8. Aphoristically, one must say that Romeo and Juliet will have lived, and lived on, through aphorism. *Romeo and Juliet* owes everything to aphorism. Aphorism can, of course, turn out to be a device of rhetoric, a sly calculation aiming at the greatest authority, an economy or strategy of mastery which knows very well how to potentialize meaning ("See how I formalize, in so few words I always say more than would appear"). But before letting itself be manipulated in this way, aphorism hands us over, defenseless, to the very experience of contretemps. Before every calculation but also across it, beyond the calculable itself.

9. The aphorism or discourse of disassociation: each sentence, each paragraph dedicates itself to separation, it shuts itself up, whether one likes it or not, in the solitude of its proper duration. Its encounter and its contact with the other are always given over to chance, to whatever may befall, good or ill. Nothing is absolutely assured, neither the linking nor the order. One aphorism in the series can come before or after the other, before *and* after the other, each can survive the other—and in the other series. Romeo and Juliet *are* aphorisms, in the first place in their name, which they are not (Juliet: "'Tis but thy name that is my enemy" ... Romeo: "My name, dear saint, is hateful to myself, / Because it is an enemy to thee. / Had I it written, I would tear the word" [2.2.38, 55–57]), for there is no aphorism without language, without nomination, without appellation, without a letter, even to be torn up.

10. Each aphorism, like Romeo and Juliet, each aphoristic series has its particular duration. Its temporal logic prevents it from sharing all its time with another place of discourse, with another discourse, with the discourse of the other. Impossible synchronization. I am speaking here of the discourse of time, of its marks, of its dates, of the course of time and of the essential digression which dislocates the time or desires and carries the step of those who love one another off course. But that is not sufficient enough to characterize our aphorism, it is not sufficient that there be language or mark, nor that there be dissociation, dislocation, anachrony, in order for aphorism to take place. It still must have a determined form, a certain mode. Which? The bad aphorism, the *bad* of aphorism is sententious, but every aphorism cuts and delimits by virtue of it sententious character[4]: it says the truth in the form of the last judgment, and this truth carries [*porte*] death.[5] The death sentence [*l'arrêt de mort*], for

Romeo and Juliet, is a contretemps which condemns them to death, both of them, but also a contretemps which arrests death, suspends its coming, secures for both of them the delay necessary in order to witness and survive the other's death.

11. Aphorism: that which hands over every rendezvous to chance. But desire does not let itself open to aphorism by chance. There is no time for desire without aphorism. Desire has no place without aphorism. What Romeo and Juliet experience in the exemplary anachrony, the essential impossibility of any absolute synchronization. But *at the same time* they live, as we do, this disorder of series. Disjunction, dislocation, separation of places, deployment or spacing of a story because of aphorism—would there be any theater without that? The survival of theatrical work implies that, theatrically, it is saying something about theater itself, about its essential possibility. And that it does so, theatrically, then, through the play of uniqueness and repetition, by giving rise every time to the chance of an absolutely singular event as it does to the untranslatable idiom of a proper name, to its fatality (the "enemy" that "I hate"), to the fatality of a date and of a rendezvous. Dates, timetables, property registers, place-names, all the codes that we cast like nets over time and space—in order to reduce or master differences, to arrest them, determine them—these are also contretemps-traps. Intended to avoid contretemps, to be in harmony with our rhythms by bending them to objective measurement, they produce misunderstanding, they accumulate the opportunities for false steps or wrong moves, revealing and simultaneously increasing this anachrony of desires: *in the same time*. What is this time? There is no place for a question in aphorism.

12. Romeo and Juliet, the conjunction of two desires which are aphoristic but held together, maintained in the dislocated now of a love or a promise. A promise in their name, but across and beyond their given name, the promise of *another name*, its request rather: "O be some other name" (2.2.42). The *and* of this conjunction, the theater of this "and," has often been presented, represented as the scene of a fortuitous contretemps, of aleatory anachrony: the failed rendezvous, the unfortunate accident, the letter which does not arrive at destination, the time of the detour prolonged for a *purloined letter*,[6] the remedy which transforms itself into poison when the stratagem of a third party, a brother, Friar Laurence, proposes simultaneously the remedy and the letter ("And if thou dar'st, I'll give thee remedy. . . . In the meantime, against thou shalt awake, / Shall Romeo by my letters know our drift, / And hither shall he come" [4.1.76, 113–15]). This representation is not false. But if this drama

has thus been imprinted, superimprinted on the memory of Europe, text upon text, this is because the anachronous accident came to illustrate an essential possibility. It confounds a philosophical logic which would like accidents to remain what they are, accidental. This logic, at the same time, throws out into the unthinkable an anachrony of structure, the absolute interruption of history as deployment of *a* temporality, of a single and organized temporality. What happens to Romeo and Juliet, and which remains in effect an accident whose aleatory and unforeseeable appearance can not be effaced, at the crossing of several series and beyond common sense, can only be what it is, accidental, insofar as it has *already* happened, in essence, before it happens. The desire of Romeo and Juliet did not encounter the poison, the contretemps of the detour of the letter by chance. In order for this encounter to take place, there must *already* have been instituted a system of marks (names, hours, maps of places, dates and supposedly 'objective' place-names) to thwart, as it were, the dispersion of interior and heterogeneous durations, to frame, organize, put in order, render possible a rendezvous: in other words to deny, while taking note of it, non-coincidence, the separation of monads, infinite distance, the disconnection of experiences, the multiplicity of worlds, everything that renders possible a contretemps or the irremediable detour of a letter. But the desire of Romeo and Juliet is born in the heart of this possibility. There would have been no love, the pledge would not have taken place, nor time, nor its theater, without discordance. The accidental contretemps comes to *remark* the essential contretemps. Which is as much as to say it is not accidental. It does not, for all that, have the signification of an essence or of a formal structure. This is not the abstract condition of possibility, a universal form of the relation to the other in general, a dialectic of desire or consciousness. Rather the singularity of an imminence who "cutting point" spurs desire at its birth—the very birth of desire. I love because the other is the other, because its time will never be mine. The living duration, the very presence of its love remains infinitely distant from mine, distant from itself in that which stretches it toward mine and even in what one might want to describe as amorous euphoria, ecstatic communion, mystical intuition. I can love the other only in the passion of this aphorism. Which does not happen, does not come about like misfortune, bad luck, or negativity. It has the form of the most loving affirmation—it is the chance of desire. And it not only cuts into the fabric of duration, it spaces. Contretemps says something about topology or the visible; it opens theater.

13. Conversely, no contretemps, no aphorism without the promise of a now

in common, without the pledge, the vow of synchrony, the desired sharing of a living present. In order that the sharing may be desired, must it not first be given, glimpsed, apprehended? But this sharing is just another name for aphorism.[7]

14. This aphoristic series crosses over another one. Because it traces, aphorism lives on, it lives much longer than its present and it lives longer than life. Death sentence [*arrêt de mort*]. It gives and carries death, but in order to make a decision on a sentence [*arrêt*] of death, it suspends death, it stops it once more [*il l'arrête encore*].

15. There would not be any contretemps, nor any anachrony, if the separation between monads only disjoined interiorities. Contretemps is produced at the intersection between interior experience (the "phenomenology of internal time-consciousness"[8] or space-consciousness) and its chronological or topographical marks, those which are said to be "objective," "in the world." There would not be any series otherwise, without the possibility of this marked spacing, with its social conventions and the history of its codes, with its fictions and its simulacra, with its dates. With so-called proper names.

16. The simulacrum raises the curtain, it reveals, thanks to the dissociation of series, the theater of the impossible: two people each outlive the other. The absolute certainty which rules over the *duel* (Romeo and Juliet is the mise-en-scène of all duels) is that one must die before the other. One of them must see the other die. To no matter of whom, I must be able to say: since we are two, we know in an absolutely ineluctable way that one of us will die before the other. One of us will see the other die, one of us will live on, even if only for an instant. One of us, only one of us, will carry the death of the other—and mourning. It is impossible that we should each survive the other. That's the duel, the axiomatic of every duel, the scene which is the most common and the least spoken of—or the most prohibited—concerning our relation to the other. Yet *the impossible happens*—not in 'objective reality', which has no say here, but in the experience of Romeo and Juliet. And under the law of the pledge, which commands every given word. They live *in turn* the death of the other, for a time, the contretemps of their death. Both are in mourning—and both watch over the death of the other. Double death sentence. Romeo dies before Juliet, whom he has seen dead. They both live, outlive the death of the other.

17. The impossible—this theater of double survival—also tells, like every aphorism, the truth. Right from the pledge which binds together two desires, each is already in mourning for the other, entrusts death to the other as well:

if you die before me, I will keep you, if I die before you, you will carry me in yourself, one will keep the other, will already have kept the other from the first declaration. This double interiorization would be possible neither in monadic interiority nor in the logic of 'objective' time and space. It takes place nevertheless every time I love. Everything then begins with this survival. Each time that I love or each time that I hate, each time that a law engages me to the death of the other. And it is the same law, the same double law. A pledge which keeps (off) death can always invert itself.[9]

18.   A given series of aphorisms crosses over into another one, the same under different names, under the name of the name. Romeo and Juliet love each other across their name, despite their name, they die on account of their name, they live on in their name. Since there is neither desire nor pledge nor sacred bond (*sacramentum*) without aphoristic separation, the greatest love springs from the greatest force of dissociation, here what opposes and divides the two families in their name. Romeo and Juliet bear these names. They bear them, support them even if they do not wish to assume them. From this name which separates them but which will at the same time have tightened their desire with all its aphoristic force, they would like to separate themselves. But the most vibrant declaration of their love still calls for the name that it denounces. One might be tempted to distinguish here, another aphorism, between the proper forename and the family name which would only be a proper name in a general way or according to genealogical classification. One might be tempted to distinguish Romeo from Montague and Juliet from Capulet. Perhaps they are, both of them, tempted to do it. But they don't do it, and one should notice that in the denunciation of the name (Act 2, scene 2), they also attack their forenames, or at least that of Romeo, which seems to form part of the family name. The forename still bears the name of the father, it recalls the law of genealogy. Romeo *himself*, the bearer of the name is not the name, it is *Romeo*, the name which he bears. And is it necessary to call the bearer by the name which he bears? She calls him by it in order to tell him: I love you, free us from your name, Romeo, don't bear it any longer, Romeo, the name of Romeo:

JUL. O Romeo, Romeo, wherefore art thou Romeo?
Deny thy father and refuse thy name.
Or if thou wilt not, be but sworn my love
And I'll no longer be a Capulet. (2.2.33–36)

She is speaking here, in the night, and there is nothing to assure her that she is addressing Romeo himself, present in person. In order to ask Romeo to re-

Jacques Derrida

fuse his name, she can only, in his absence, address his name or his shadow. Romeo—himself—is in the shadow and he wonders if it is time to take her at word or if he should wait a little. Taking her at her word will mean committing himself to dissolving his name, a little later on. For the moment, he decides to wait and to carry on listening:

> ROM. [*Aside*] Shall I hear more, or shall I speak at this?
> JUL. 'Tis but thy name that is my enemy;
> Thou art thyself, though not a Montague.
> What's Montague? it is nor hand, nor foot,
> Nor arm, nor face, nor any other part
> Belonging to a man. O, be some other name!
> What's in a name? that which we call a rose
> By any other name would smell as sweet;
> So Romeo would, were he not Romeo call'd,
> Retain that dear perfection which he owes
> Without that title. Romeo, doff thy name,
> And for that name which is no part of thee
> Take all myself.
> ROM. I take thee at thy word:
> Call me but love, and I'll be new baptized;
> Henceforth I never will be Romeo.
> JUL. What man art thou that thus bescreen'd in night
> So stumblest on my counsel?
> ROM. By a name
> I know not how to tell thee who I am:
> My name, dear saint, is hateful to myself,
> Because it is an enemy to thee;
> Had I it written, I would tear the word.
> JUL. My ears have not yet drunk a hundred words
> Of that tongue's utterance, yet I know the sound:
> Art thou not Romeo and a Montague?
> ROM. Neither, fair saint, if either thee dislike. (2.2.37–61)

19. When she addresses Romeo in the night, when she asks him "O Romeo, Romeo, wherefore art thou Romeo? / Deny thy father and refuse they name," she seems to be addressing *him, himself*, Romeo bearer of the name Romeo, the one who is not Romeo since he has been asked to disown his father and his name. She seems, then, to call him beyond his name. He is not present, she is not certain that he is there, *himself*, beyond his name, it is night and this night

176

screens the lack of distinction between the name and the bearer of the name. It is in his name that she continues to call him, and that she calls on him not to call himself Romeo any longer, and that she asks him, Romeo, to renounce his name. But it is, whatever she may say or deny, he whom she loves. Who, him? Romeo. The one who calls himself Romeo, the bearer of the name, who calls himself Romeo although he is not only the one who bears this name and although he exists, without being visible or present in the night, outside his name. *[handwritten: ja Shadow— Murmured idea]*

20. Night. Everything that happens at night, for Romeo and Juliet, is decided rather in the penumbra, between night and day. The indecision between Romeo and the bearer of his name, between "Romeo," the name of Romeo and Romeo himself. Theater, we say, is visibility, the stage [*la scene*]. This drama belongs to the night because it stages what is not seen, the name; it stages what one calls. Theater of the name, theater of night. The name calls beyond presence, phenomenon, light, beyond the day, beyond the theater. It keeps—whence the mourning and survival—what is no longer present, the invisible: what from now on will no longer see the light of day.

21. She wants the death of Romeo. She will have it. The death of his name ("'Tis but thy name that is my enemy"), certainly, the death of "Romeo," but they will not be able to get free from their name, they know this without knowing it [*sans le savoir*]. She declares war on "Romeo," on his name, in his name, she will win this war only on the death of Romeo himself. Himself? Who? Romeo. But "Romeo" is not Romeo. Precisely. She wants the death of "Romeo." Romeo dies, "Romeo" lives on. She keeps him dead in his name. Who? Juliet, Romeo.

22. Aphorism: separation in language and, in it, through the name which closes the horizon. Aphorism is at once necessary and impossible. Romeo is radically separated from his name. He, his living self, living and singular desire, he is not "Romeo," but the separation, the aphorism of the name remains impossible. He dies without his name but he dies also because he has not been able to set himself free from his name, or from his father, even less to renounce him, to respond to Juliet's request ("Deny thy father and refuse thy name").

23. When she says to him: my enemy is only your name, she does not think "my" enemy. Juliet herself has nothing against the name of Romeo. It is the name which she bears (Juliet and Capulet) that finds itself at war with the name of Romeo. The war takes place between the names. And when she says it, she is not sure, in the night, that she is making contact with Romeo himself.

She speaks to him, she supposes him to be distinct from his name since she addresses him in order to say to him: "You are yourself, not a Montague." But he is not there. At least she cannot be sure of his presence. It is within herself, deep down inside, that she is addressing him in the night, but still him in his name, and in the most exclamatory form of apostrophe: "O Romeo, Romeo, wherefore art thou Romeo?" She does not say to him: why are you called Romeo, why do you bear this name (like an article of clothing, an ornament, a detachable sign)? She says to him: why *are you* Romeo? She knows it: detachable and dissociable, aphoristic though it be, his name is his essence. Inseparable from his being. And in asking him to abandon his name, she is no doubt asking him to live at last, and to live for his love (for in order to live oneself truly, it is necessary to elude the law of the name, the familial law made for the survival and constantly recalling me to death), but she is *just as much* asking him to die, since his life is his name. He exists in his name: "wherefore art thou Romeo?" "O Romeo, Romeo." Romeo is Romeo, and Romeo is not Romeo. He is himself only in abandoning his name, he is himself only in his name. Romeo can (be) call(ed) himself only if he abandons his name, he calls himself only *from* his name. Sentence of death and of survival: twice rather than once.

24. Speaking to the one she loves within herself and outside herself, in the half-light, Juliet murmurs the most implacable analysis of the name. Of the name and the proper name. Implacable: she expresses the judgment, the death sentence [*l'arrêt de mort*], the fatal truth of the name. Pitilessly she analyzes, element by element. What's Montague? Nothing of yourself, you are yourself and not Montague, she tells him. Not only does this name say nothing about you as a totality but it doesn't say anything, it doesn't even name a part of you, neither your hand, nor your foot, neither your arm, nor your face, nothing that is human! This analysis is implacable for it announces or denounces the inhumanity or the ahumanity of the name. A proper name does not name anything which is human, which belongs to a human body, a human spirit, an essence of man. And yet this relation to the inhuman only befalls man, for him, to him, in the name of man. He alone gives himself this inhuman name. And Romeo would not be what he is, a stranger to his name, without this name. Juliet, then, pursues her analysis: the names of things do not belong to the things any more than the names of men belong to men, and yet they are quite differently separable. The example of the rose, once more. A rose remains what it is without its name, Romeo is no longer what he is without his name. But, for a while, Juliet makes out as if Romeo would lose nothing in losing his name: like the rose.

But like a rose, she says to him in short, and without genealogy, "without why." (Supposing that the rose, all the roses of thought, of literature, of mysticism, this "formidable anthology," absent from every bouquet . . .)

25. She does not tell him to lose all names, rather just to change names: "O be some other name." But that can mean two things: take another proper name (a human name, this inhuman thing which belongs only to man); *or*: take another kind of name, a name which is not that of a man, take the name of a thing then, a common name, which, like that of the rose, does not have that inhumanity which consists in affecting the very being of the one who bears it even though it names nothing of himself. And the colon, there is the question.

> O, be some other name!
> What's in a name? That which we call a rose
> By any other name would smell as sweet;
> So Romeo would, were he not Romeo call'd,
> Retain that dear perfection which he owes
> Without that title.[10]

26. The name would only be a "title," and the title is not the thing which it names, any more than a title of nobility participates in the very thing, the family, the work, to which it is said to belong. *Romeo and Juliet* also remains the surviving title of an entire family of plays. We must apply what goes on in these plays also to the plays themselves, to other genealogy, their idiom, their singularity, their survival.

27. Juliet offers Romeo an infinite deal, what is apparently the most dissymmetrical of contracts: you can gain all without losing anything, it is just a matter of a name. In renouncing your name, you renounce nothing, nothing of you, of yourself, nor anything human. In exchange, and without losing anything, you gain me, and not just a part of me, but the whole of myself: "Romeo, doff thy name, / And for thy name, which is no part of thee, / Take all myself." He will have gained everything, he will have lost everything: name and life, and Juliet.

28. The circle of all these names in *o: words, Romeo, rose, love*. He has accepted the deal, he *takes her at her word* ("I take thee at thy word") at the moment where she proposes that he take her in her entirety ("Take all myself"). Play of idiom: in taking you at your word, in taking up the challenge, in agreeing to this incredible, priceless exchange, I take the whole of you. And in exchange for nothing, for a word, thy name, which is nothing, nothing human, nothing of myself, or else nothing for myself. I give nothing in taking you at

your word, I abandon nothing and take absolutely all of you. In truth, and they both know the truth of aphorism, he will lose everything. They will lose everything in this aporia, this double aporia of the proper name. And for having agreed to exchange the proper name of Romeo for a common name: not that of a *rose*, but of *love*. For Romeo does not renounce all of his name, only the name of his father, that is to say his proper name, if one can still say that: "I take thee at thy word. / Call me but love, and I'll be new baptis'd: / Henceforth I never will be Romeo." He simultaneously gains himself and loses himself not only in the common name, but also in the common law of love: *Call me love*. Call me your love.

29. The dissymmetry remains infinite. It also hangs on this: Romeo does not make the same demand of her. He does not request that this woman who is secretly to be his wife renounce her name or disown her father. As if that were obvious and there was no call for any such rift [*déchirement*] (he will speak in a moment of tearing [*déchirer*] his name, the writing or the letter of his name, that is if he had written it himself, which is just what is in principal and originally excluded). Paradox, irony, reversal of the common law? Or a repetition which on the contrary confirms the truth of this law? Usually, in our cultures, the husband keeps his name, that of his father, and the wife renounces hers. When the husband gives his name to his wife, it is not, as here, in order to lose it, or to change it, but to impose it by keeping it. Here it is she who asks him to renounce his father and to change his name. But this inversion confirms the law: the name of the father should be kept by the son, it is from him that there is some sense in tearing it away, and not at all from the daughter who has never been put in charge of it. The terrible lucidity of Juliet. She knows the two bonds of the law, the *double bind*, which ties a son to the name of his father. He can only live if he asserts himself in a singular fashion, without his inherited name. But writing of this name, which he has not written himself ("Had I it written, I would tear the word"), constitutes him in his very being, without naming anything of him, and by denying it he can only wipe himself out. In sum, at the very most he can deny it, renounce it, he can neither efface it nor tear it up. He is therefore lost in any case and she knows it. And she knows it because she loves him and she loves him because she knows it. And she demands his death from him by demanding that he hold onto his life because she loves him, she knows, and because she knows that death will not come to him by accident. He is doomed [*voué*] to death, and she with him, by the double law of the name.

30. There would be no contretemps without the double law of the name.

The contretemps presupposes this inhuman, too human, inadequation which always dislocates a proper name. The secret marriage, the pledge (*sacramentum*), the double survival which it involves, its constitutive anachrony, all of this obeys the same law. This law, this law of contretemps, is double since it is divided; it carries aphorism within itself, as its truth. Aphorism is the law.

31.   Even if he wanted to, Romeo could not renounce his name and his father *of his own accord*, even though this emancipation is nevertheless being presented to him as the chance of at last being himself, beyond the name the chance of at last living, for he carries the name as his death. He could not want it himself, in himself, because *he is not without* his name. He can only desire it from the call of the other, in the name of the other. Moreover he only hates his name starting from the moment Juliet, as it were, demands it from him: *∫*

> My name, dear saint, is hateful to myself
> Because it is an enemy to thee.
> Had I it written, I would tear the word.

32.   When she thinks she recognizes him in the shadow, by moonlight, the drama of the name is consummated (Juliet: "My ears have yet not drunk a hundred words / Of thy tongue's uttering, yet I know the sound. / Art thou not Romeo, and a Montague?" Romeo: "Neither, fair maid, if either thee dislike"). She recognizes him and calls him by his name ("Are you not Romeo and a Montague?"), she *identifies* him on the one hand by the timbre of his voice, that is to say by the words she hears without being able to see, and on the other hand at the moment when he has, obeying the injunction, renounced his name and father. Survival and death are at work, in other words the moon. But this power of death which appears by moonlight is called Juliet, and the sun which she comes to figure all of a sudden carries life *and* death *in the name of the father*. She kills the moon. What does Romeo say at the opening of the scene (which is not a scene since the name destines it to invisibility, but which is a theater since its light is artificial and figurative)? "But soft, what light through yonder window breaks? / It is the east, and Juliet is the sun! / Arise fair sun and kill the envious moon, / Who is already sick and pale with grief" (2.2.2–5).

33.   The lunar face of this shadow play, a certain coldness of Romeo and Juliet. Not all is ice or glass, but the ice on it does not come only from death, from the marble to which everything seems doomed (*the tomb, the monument, the grave, the flowers on the lady's grave*), in this sepulchrally statuesque fate which entwines and separates these two lovers, starting from the fact of their names. No, the coldness which little by little takes over the body of the play and, as if

in advance, cadaverizes it, is perhaps irony, the figure or rhetoric of irony, the contretemps or ironic consciousness. It always places itself disproportionately between finitude and infinitude, it makes use of inadequation, of aphorism, it analyzes and analyzes, it analyzes the law of misidentification, the implacable necessity, the machine of the proper name that obliges me to live through precisely that, in other words my name, of which I am dying.

34.   Irony of the proper name, as analyzed by Juliet. Sentence of truth which carries death, aphorism separates, and in the first place separates me from my name. I am not my name. One might as well say that I should be able to survive it. But firstly it is destined to survive me. In this way it announces my death. Non-coincidence and contretemps between my name and me, between the experience according to which I am named or hear myself named and my "living present." Rendezvous with my name. *Untimely*, bad timing, at the wrong moment.

35.   Changing names: the dance, the substitution, the masks, the simulacrum, the rendezvous with death. *Untimely. Never on time.*

36.   Speaking ironically, that is to say in the rhetorical sense of the figure of irony: conveying the opposite of what one says. Here, the *impossible* then: (1) two lovers both outlive each other, each seeing the other die; (2) the name constitutes them but without being anything of themselves, condemning them to be what, beneath the mask, they are not, to be merged with the mask; (3) the two are united by that which separates them, etc. And they state this clearly, they formalize it as even a philosopher would not have dared to do. A vein, through the shard tip of analysis, receives the distilled potion. It does not wait, it does not allow any time, not even that of the drama, it comes at once to turn to ice the heart of their pledges. This potion would be the true poison, the poisoned truth of this drama.

37.   Irony of the aphorism. In the *Aesthetics*, Hegel pokes fun at those who, quick to heap praises on ironists, show themselves not even capable of analyzing the analytical irony of *Romeo and Juliet*. He has a go at Tieck: "But when one thinks one has found the perfect opportunity to show what irony is, for example in *Romeo and Juliet*, one is disappointed, for it is no longer a question of irony."[11]

38.   Another series, which cuts across all the others: the name, the law, the genealogy, the double survival, the contretemps, in short the aphorism of *Romeo and Juliet*. Not of Romeo and Juliet but of *Romeo and Juliet*, Shakespeare's play of that title. It belongs to a series, to the still-living palimpsest, to the open

theater of narratives which bears this name. It survives them, but they also survive thanks to it. Would such a double survival have been possible "without
that title," as Juliet put it? And would the names of Matteo Bandello or Luigi da
Porto survive without that of Shakespeare, who survived them?[12] And without
the innumerable repetitions, each staked in its particular way, under the same
name? Without the grafting of names? And of other plays? "O be some other
name."

39. The absolute aphorism: a proper name. Without genealogy, without the
least copula. End of drama. Curtain. Tableau (*The Two Lovers United in Death*
by Angelo dall'Oca Bianca). Tourism, December sun in Verona ("Verona by
that name is known" [5.3.299]). A true son, the other ("The sun for sorrow will
not show his head" [5.3.305]).

14   "Poetic Truth and Historical Truth,"
from *The Time Is Out of Joint:*

This is a postscript and not a conclusion, for the presentation of Shakespeare's poetic truth about history speaks for itself; it does not require, or even allow for, a conclusion. Nonetheless, the expression "poetic truth about history" calls for clarification. Poetic truth about history is unlike factual truth. It is also unlike a theory of history, a historical narrative, or a theoretical interpretation of a historical narrative. The interest of the latter is unearthing and understanding the past from the perspective of the present. The past can be changed. One changes the past not solely by reinterpreting it but also by discovering new facts, inserting them into a theory, revising the theory, or devising—in view of them—a new theory. Historical fictions are approximations. They want to tell us the story as it really happened. One will never know how something really happened, first and foremost because nothing "really" happened in any one fixed way. Everything happens in different ways for different people; thus the 'real' happening is not a fact but already an interpretation. Still, one can approximate, in various ways, what really happened. There are many different stories told about the same historical event, although—if they are true—there must also be some agreement among them. One can always write a new historical narrative about the same event. The past remains always open, *as the past*, in the present and the future. Aristotle was the first to remark that tragedy is unlike historiography, for it presents us with the way in which a thing could have happened or might have happened, and not how it happened in fact. This is why tragedy is a sibling of philosophy. The truth of tragedy is *revelatory*. In Shakespeare it is revelatory in a way that is different from that of the Greeks.

What is "revelatory" is the truth that we *accept as it is.* When we read the story of Richard III in a history book, we always ask the question, Did it happen this way or that way? Is it true? But when we watch Shakespeare's *Richard III* on the stage, we do not ask this question. For the question itself is external to the play. In historiography or even in the chronicle, the question concerning the truth of facts is, on the contrary, internal to the genre. Shakespeare's tragedies reveal both what has happened and how it has happened. They do not ask the question of why something has happened in this specific way, or what will be the consequences. The categories of causality and determination are alien to the genre of tragedy, and especially to Shakespearean tragedy. The plot develops in this way and that way, the development itself—namely, that men and women of a certain kind are acting in certain ways in certain situations—is self-explanatory. This is one reason why I called the tragedy of truth revelatory.

Philosophers have accounted for the experience of revelatory character of truth in art in several ways. In the hylomorphic tradition (for example, in Hegel), one could say that the content disappears entirely in the form. In a prosaic manner, one could add that the work of art is perfect, since nothing can either be added or taken away from it. But what is the message of such a commonplace wisdom? We know, for example that many of Shakespeare's plays were staged in shortened versions, and that sometimes even their endings were changed. Yet the revelatory character of the truth of the artwork does not change simultaneously. If one experiences *Hamlet* first in the presentation of Laurence Olivier's film, one will also feel that the play is perfect in the above-described sense. Whenever we are watching a play, its truth reveals itself. The truth, the perfection, will be exactly what we see and experience. The knowledge that something has been abbreviated does not annul the revelatory experience. For it is always there whenever a work and its listener/watcher are tuned in to one another. The truth of an artwork is revelatory, for the artwork has no 'before' and 'after'. It speaks for itself. Nothing can be added or taken away in the *present time*, when we are sitting in the theater and when the truth is going to be revealed. Let me give an example. The first performances of Mozart's *Don Giovanni* in Prague and Vienna were not exactly the same. Mozart composed an additional aria and left out one scene completely, if I remember correctly. But in both Prague and in Vienna, the opera revealed the truth. From this one should not conclude that to return to the original texts of Shakespeare (as we now know them) and to refrain from abbreviating them is futile, or that all possible changes in the text would be acceptable. Not all alterations or changes come across effectively, and some leave the spectator feeling dissatisfied. But this is also true of many presentations of the uncut versions of Shakespearean (or other) dramas.

Since historical truth is about the approximation of "what really happened" from the position of various theories and from the perspective of different presents, the interpretive work of history changes the fiction. However, if one presents a Shakespearean drama on the stage (presupposing that the whole drama is staged and that the end remains unchanged), the interpretative work does not change the fiction but the understanding of the fiction (causes, motivations, characters, and their relations). Moreover, the idea of "approximation" is entirely absent in the interpretation and in the staging of revelatory truth. There is nothing to approximate, because the drama itself *is* the truth. One is confronted with the question of what exactly this truth is, not with the question of whether this is the truth. As a result, all interpretations interpret the *that* and not the what of the truth. This has some significance for the question concerning the self-referentiality of the work of art. To remain with the tragedy, and more precisely with the historical tragedies of Shakespeare, the question is wrongly put. Since the so-called plot of Shakespeare's historical tragedies is taken from literary sources—from chronicles or from Plutarch, from historians who wanted to tell us how and what really happened—Shakespeare's historical tragedies are in this sense not self-referential. But as far as truth is concerned, they are. For revelatory truth is self-referential. The truth that is referential is true knowledge or true theory about something that combines and orders the truth of facts interpretively. But revelatory truth is not related to anything external, as such it is self-referential.

Almost all dramatic theories place great emphasis on the fact of 'presencing'. The drama does not take place in the past, but in the present. In the historical tragedies of Shakespeare, similar to Greek tragedies, the plot and the material are taken from the past. What the drama refers to has taken place in the past. However the presentation of the truth of history, that is, the truth of history as it appears in poetic truth, is always in the present. In historical tragedy, the past is presencing. It is not only interpreted from the standpoint of the present, but it *is* eternally present. Any time that a tragedy is staged—or when we read it—it is and will be the time of *now*.

In this sense, historical tragedy, particularly that of Shakespeare, preserves and reinforces one essential feature of *mystery plays*. The truth of the Jewish and Christian religions (and some other religions as well, which have no bearing on my topic) is revelatory truth. One can speak about revelatory truth authentically in one way alone: in revealing it. The repetition of revelation is the presentation of revelatory truth. That is, truth of the past is the truth of the present; it is constant presencing. Jesus is born every Christmas, although he was born two thousand years ago. We know that he was born roughly two thousand years ago, just as we know when Augustus Caesar was born and became the first man of Rome. But each and every Christmas, the birth of Jesus is repeated. And Christ is crucified every Good Friday, and every Easter he will be resurrected. In the *pravoslav* ceremony, everyone repeats: "Christ is resurrected, he is indeed resurrected," and they kiss one another on their lips. So is it in the Jewish religion. On the Seder evening of Passover, the Haggadah is read. Every year, every Seder evening, the story of the wicked boy is told. The boy asks his father: "How does the whole concern me? It happened a long time ago!" To this the father ritually answers that it happens to us, it happens to you, it is now that God liberates us from Egyptian slavery. In the religious festivities, festivals, ceremonies, and rituals, truth dwells in revelation. Sure, one can also tell about the same events as historical narratives. One can tell that history has not proved that the Jews were in Egypt at all, or that we are (historically) absolutely sure that Jesus of Nazareth was not born in December, and not in Bethlehem. But the historically important addenda to true knowledge are entirely irrelevant when it comes to truth as revelation. This, however, does not mean that revealed truth cannot be interpreted. In fact, it is always interpreted. It belongs, for example, to the Passover ritual to reinterpret passages of the Haggadah. The priest or the minister constantly reinterprets the stories of Christ's birth, passion and resurrection. Those interpretations can differ. They differ less than the interpretations of the Shakespearean tragedies only because there is a religious canon that puts a limit to interpretation, whereas no such canon exists for the interpretation of Shakespeare's history plays. And, of course, Shakespeare's history plays can be staged in every season, and they do not need to be staged every year. (In the case of Greek tragedy there were still such regular occasions.)

Perhaps it is clear by now why I said that the truth of Shakespeare's history plays (tragedies) is revelatory truth. But the plot of his history plays is neither mythical nor mystical. Neither God nor any deities participate in the action, and no festive occasion colors the fibers of the revealed truth. Truth is revealed about history. Historical events happening, historical characters acting, without any kind of otherworld interference of protection, will be the carriers of the truth. *Truth about that, not truth about why and what for.*

Shakespeare's history plays (tragedies) are tragedies of revelatory truth about history. They reveal the covering and the hiding, for they reveal the truth that there always remains something unrevealed and unrevealable. The infinite interpretability of the Shakespearean drama is also connected with this troubling experience. In poetry there is no other truth about history than the one revealed, presenced before us in a history play, but it is revealed that there are secrets in history and historicity about which neither the poet nor his characters can speak. Perhaps it is not the cause of events or the motivation of the characters—which become irrelevant in the process of revealing—that remains a mystery, the internal reserves and sources of the characters and of their actions. Why is one person good and the other one wicked? Why is Cordelia good and Goneril and Regan wicked? To this question no answer is given. We take the men and women as given, we take the characters as they are presented in their relationships to others by the poet. But the characters are just put on the stage; they are presented as the *archai* of a finite world standing for truth as such. It is important in Shakespeare that they are the archai of a finite world. For it is not through the eternal, the immortal, and the infinite that truth about history is revealed in Shakespeare's historical plays and tragedies, but through finite and transient beings in a finite present time. It is through the finite and transient beings that truth is revealed to the finite and transient. In Shakespeare's revelatory truth we recognize ourselves. We are revealed to ourselves. The truth reveals to the transient its own transience, its own finitude; this is what I meant when I said that it reveals *that* something cannot be revealed, not *what* cannot be revealed. In the latter case, it would be a secret, but in a former case one does not even know whether there is a secret.

This duality of revelatory truth constitutes the doubling of the stages in Shakespeare's tragedies and history plays (but not in some of his comedies). As I discussed at some length in the first part of this book, Shakespeare's characters act on a historical stage and sometimes also on an existential stage. And the most complex of characters play their parts on both stages. It may happen that one character makes his or her first appearance on the historical stage and enters at a crucial moment the existential stage (like Lear, Coriolanus, Richard II, and others). And there are characters that play continuously on both stages (Hamlet, Henry IV, Richard III, and so on). But the presences of the two stages is all-important in Shakespeare's historical drama. Shakespeare formulates this succinctly in Hamlet's words addressed to the actors: "[T]he purpose of playing ... was and is, to hold ... the mirror up to nature, to show virtue her own feature, scorn her own image, and very age and body of the time his form and pressure" (3.2.20–24). Shakespeare makes the differentiation—in Hamlet's formulation—between virtue and scorn on the one hand, and age and the body of time on the other. When presenting virtue and vice, one mirrors nature; virtue and vice present themselves as such on the existential stage. But the play also wears the impress of age and time. And the impress of age and time are not 'independent' of the mirrored virtue and scorn. The king's face is pressed upon a coin. One time one king's face, another time another king's face is pressed on the coin. The mirror, the drama, shows virtue and vice, but the pressure of time modifies them. This is how there are two stages.

The two stages together are the revelatory truth, not the existential stage alone. On the existential stage men and women are standing naked, sometimes metaphorically naked, sometimes even literally naked, as in the case of King Lear. History fades away, the stamp or the pressure of time disappears, the form of time becomes invisible. But the truth of history revealed in Shakespeare's dramas points to the nakedness as to exceptional moments. They are the moments of truth about human existence, and as such also moments of truth about history, about its insignificance, about its transience. However, the historical stage also reveals its truth: the truth of the significance of life-in-time. For intemporality makes its appearance in temporality, and time can stand still where there is time, where time and 'the times' matter.

The truth of Shakespeare's plays is revelatory. I almost said that the truth in art is revelatory in general. But it is better to stay with Shakespeare. The specificity of Shakespeare's history plays is, as I have tried to show in my interpretation of several of his dramas, that he was conscious of his manner of presenting historical truth. In this he differs from the ancients. In Greek tragedy the question of good and evil, of vice and virtue, of the sacred and the profane, of knowledge and ignorance occupied the center point of the drama. In Shakespeare the axiological center of the drama condenses all the categories of 'orientation', such as good/evil, beautiful/ugly, useful/harmful, successful/unsuccessful, sacred/profane, true/untrue. They do not fit, they shift, they contradict one another, they constitute different hierarchies of values, and they can also overbalance one another. I have mentioned that the ladders of grandeur and of morality, of historical significance and of political relevance, are very different in Shakespeare, and that one character can step to the highest rung in one and remain on the lowest rung on another of those ladders. Shakespeare presents heterogeneous slabs of values. He does not present one as the true measure and the other as the untrue one. To the contrary, revelatory truth reveals the complexity of multiplicity of the measures in a finite world of axiological conflicts. All ladders participate in revelatory truth. Perhaps this is why the question of truth will also be constitutive in Shakespeare in the plot of the drama, in the development of characters, and in their relation to each other.

The question of truth appears in several forms in Shakespeare, but it always remains the question of truth. Being and remaining true to ourselves (whether we are good or evil) is a fundamental question of truth. Presenting ourselves as we are (as we believe ourselves to be) or hiding ourselves: this is also the question of truth. Whether we are able to disclose ourselves or not: this is also the question of truth. Lying or telling the truth (truthfulness): this is a fundamental question of truth. Betrayal or treason is untruth, whereas loyalty is the truth. The true man is loyal and faithful, the untrue disloyal and unfaithful. At this point the question of truth becomes the question of the good. But being able to foresee the consequences of our actions is also a question of truth. The knowledge of human character is also a question of truth. The distinction between mere facts, the concern about the thoughtful interpretation of a fact: this is also a question of truth. The ability or inability to understand the stranger is again a question of truth. Curiosity, thoughtfulness, caution, reflection on our situation and our action, mediation between thought and act: these are all questions of truth. To be able to select among information, to determine not to believe anyone but believe someone absolutely: these are also questions of truth. To abstract one's decisions from momentary interest, real or seeming: this is also a question of truth. These and similar questions are presented in Shakespeare, and all of them are decisive in all of his dramas. As I mentioned about *Hamlet* in the introductory chapter to this book, Hamlet and Claudius are each other's absolute opposites, for Hamlet wants the truth and nothing but the truth and Claudius wants the untruth and nothing but the untruth.

I was at first reluctant to bestow the ambiguous title of "philosopher of history" on Shakespeare. Now, I would be less reluctant to do so. Shakespeare's historical dramas (and most of his dramas are historical) reflect on issues and reveal puzzles that would not be reflected on seriously and philosophically before the nineteenth century. The relation between the two stages would not be examined until Kierkegaard; the difference between the truth of fact, theory, and interpretation and revelatory truth would not be considered until the twentieth century. Shakespeare anticipated postmetaphysical philosophy and its central concerns at a time when modern metaphysics had not yet reached its peak. Modernity recognizes itself in Shakespeare only from the time of Romanticism, perhaps also because modern philosophy and the speculative self-understanding of modern man in general resigned at that time the ambition of metaphysical system building. It was only [1800's] around this time that philosophy abandoned fixing its gaze on the eternal, unchangeable, infinite, the immortal alone. When modern man began to abandon not necessarily faith in an eternal, timeless, and absolute meaning, but at least in the accessibility of such a meaning, the revelatory character of Shakespeare's tragedies could be grasped by an audience to whom it was revealed. The Shakespeare cults grew out of this experience. This *cultus* might wither as every cultus does. Moreover, there is no revelation without congregation. The revelatory truth of Shakespeare can also prove transient. The audience to which Shakespeare's tragedies, history plays, and dramas reveal their truth is a congregation that bears testimony to an understanding of virtue, scorn, the age and body of the time: the human condition as historical condition, the historical condition as modern condition, the modern condition as life lived fully amid the constraints of transience and finitude.

Notes

Introduction

1. Specific interventions that treat some of the writings collected in this volume are referenced in the notes to this Introduction. There are, additionally, many noteworthy publications from the past few years that offer philosophical engagements with Shakespeare's work: Paul A. Kottman, *Tragic Conditions in Shakespeare* (Baltimore: Johns Hopkins University Press, 2009), and *A Politics of the Scene* (Stanford, CA: Stanford University Press, 2008); Michael Witmore, *Shakespearean Metaphysics*, stands out in the "Shakespeare Now!" series (New York: Continuum, 2008); Linda Charnes, *Hamlet's Heirs: Shakespeare and the Politics of a New Millennium* (New York: Routledge, 2006), stands out too in the series "Accents on Shakespeare" alongside the essays collected in *Philosophical Shakespeares*, edited by John J. Joughin (New York: Routledge, 2000); see also, Tzachi Zamir, *Double Vision: Moral Philosophy and Shakespearean Drama* (Princeton, NJ: Princeton University Press, 2007); and Margreta de Grazia, *Hamlet Without Hamlet* (Cambridge, UK: Cambridge University Press, 2007). See as well the essays collected and edited by Agnes Heller in a special edition of the *Revue Internationale de Philosophie* (63, no. 269, 2009) devoted to Shakespeare's work. Heller has also written two recent books in which Shakespeare figures prominently: *Immortal Comedy* (Lanham, MD: Rowman & Littlefield, 2005) and *The Time Is Out of Joint: Shakespeare as Philosopher of History* (Lanham, MD: Rowman & Littlefield, 2002). For another recent effort to forge a dialogue between Shakespeare studies and the kind of philosophical engagement collected in this volume, the student of Shakespeare could consult Julia Reinhard Lupton, *Citizen-Saints: Political Theology in Shakespeare* (Chicago: University of Chicago Press, 2004), as well as her *Thinking with Shakespeare* (University of Chicago Press, forthcoming). The Italian philosopher Adriana Cavarero has written on *Hamlet* in *Stately Bodies: Literature, Philosophy and the Question of Gender* (Ann Arbor: University of Michigan Press, 2002). Also worthy of mention are Stanley Stewart, *Shakespeare and Philosophy* (New York: Routledge, 2009); A. D. Nutall's *Shakespeare the Thinker* (New Haven, CT: Yale University Press, 2007); Colin McGinn, *Shakespeare's Philosophy* (New York: HarperCollins, 2006); Lawrence F.

Rhu and Stanley Cavell, *Stanley Cavell's American Dream: Shakespeare, Philosophy, and Hollywood Movies* (New York: Fordham University Press, 2006); and Millicent Bell, *Shakespeare's Tragic Skepticism* (New Haven, CT: Yale University Press, 2002). Two treatments of Hegel and Shakespeare can be found in Jennifer Bates, *Hegel and Shakespeare on Moral Imagination* (Albany: State University of New York Press, forthcoming); and Sara Macdonald, *Finding Freedom: Hegel's Philosophy and the Emancipation of Women* (Montreal: McGill-Queen's University Press, 2008). Andrew Cutrofello's *Continental Philosophy: An Introduction* (New York: Routledge, 2005) surveys trends in the continental tradition of philosophy since Kant, surprisingly and delightfully, through abbreviated readings of Shakespeare's plays as well as philosophers' writings on Shakespeare. Of abiding interest are the essays by Henry and Anne Paolucci on Shakespeare and Hegel recently reprinted in their *Hegelian Literary Perspectives* (Smyrna, DE: Griffon House, 2002).

2. Several of the texts included in this volume are explicitly concerned with the problems of history, historical context, and historicization—particularly those by Herder, Benjamin, Lukács, Schmitt, and Heller.

3. Freud's writings on Shakespeare are handily available in *Writings on Art and Literature* (Stanford, CA: Stanford University Press, 1997). Jacques Lacan's essay "Desire and the Interpretation of Desire" is published in English in *Yale French Studies*, nos. 55/56 (1977), 11–52. Jean-François Lyotard's essay "Jewish Oedipus" is published in English in *Genre* 10, no. 3 (Fall 1977), 395–411. For good accounts of Freud and Lacan on Shakespeare, see, as a start: Ernest Jones, *Hamlet and Oedipus* (New York: Norton, 1976); Julia Reinhard Lupton and Kenneth Reinhard, *After Oedipus: Shakespeare in Psychoanalysis* (Ithaca, NY: Cornell University Press, 1993); Julia Reinhard Lupton, "Tragedy and Psychoanalysis: Freud and Lacan" in *A Companion to Tragedy*, edited by Rebecca Bushnell (London: Blackwell, 2005), 88–105; and Jean-Michel Rabate, "Hamlet and the Desire of the Mother," in *Jacques Lacan: Psychoanalysis and the Subject of Literature* (London: Palgrave, 2001), 54–68.

4. Goethe quoted in Wolfgang Stellmacher, *Herders Shakespeare-Bild. Shakespeare-Rezeption im Sturm und Drang: dynamisches Weltbild und bürgerliches Nationaldrama* (Berlin: Rütten and Loening, 1978), 110; cited by Kristin Gjesdal, "Reading Shakespeare—Reading Modernity," *Angelaki* 9, no. 3 (December 2004), 22.

5. The text in question is no. 17 of *Briefe die neueste Literatur betreffend* (February 16, 1759); of interest, also, are Lessing's *Hamburgische Dramaturgie*, nos. 5, 11, and 15. Translations of the latter can be found in *Shakespeare in Europe*, edited by Oswald LeWinter (Cleveland: World Publishing, 1963).

6. A concise history of the reception of the *Poetics* can be found in Stephen Halliwell, *Aristotle's Poetics* (Chicago: University of Chicago Press, 1998), 286–323.

7. A new edition of Herder's essay edited by Gregory Moore, who also offers

a useful introduction, can be found in Johann Gottfried von Herder, *Shakespeare* (Princeton, NJ: Princeton University Press, 2008).

8.   I take my cue in the following paragraph from Kristin Gjesdal's excellent essay "Reading Shakespeare—Reading Modernity," cited above. See as well her essay "Hegel and Herder on Art, History, and Reason," *Philosophy and Literature* 30, no. 1 (April 2006), 17–32. For another perspective, which sees Herder's and Kant's disagreement over Shakespeare as prototypical of the split between the 'analytical' and the 'continental' traditions in academic philosophy, see Andrew Cutrofello, "Kant's Debate with Herder about the Philosophical Significance of the Genius of Shakespeare," *Philosophy Compass* 3, no. 1 (2008), 66–82.

9.   The quotation is Gjesdal paraphrasing Herder; ibid., 25.

10.   I am citing J. M. Bernstein; see his introduction to *Classic and Romantic German Aesthetics* (Cambridge, UK: Cambridge University Press, 2003), xxvii.

11.   This is not to say that Herder managed to close the debate. Whether, or how, Shakespeare conformed to an Aristotelian unity of time and place continued to be an important point of contention well into the next century; for example, among writers such as Stendhal and Alessandro Manzoni.

12.   For more on the thought that a philosophy of history and of art coincide in Herder's essay, see Daniel O. Dahlstrom, "The Aesthetic Holism of Hamann, Herder and Schiller" in *The Cambridge Companion to German Idealism*, edited by Karl Ameriks (Cambridge, UK: Cambridge University Press, 2000), especially 82–84.

13.   Peter Szondi, *An Essay on the Tragic*, translated by Paul Fleming (Stanford, CA: Stanford University Press, 2002), 1. The journal *Telos* has recently devoted an entire issue (no. 140, Fall 2007) to very fine essays on Szondi's work.

14.   Dennis Schmidt has observed that tragedy was understood in Idealist philosophy to constitute *the* thought for philosophy henceforth. See Dennis Schmidt, *Of Germans and Greeks: Tragedy and Ethical Life* (Indianapolis: Indiana University Press, 2001). That Schmidt's book, as its title indicates, equates the problems tragedy posed with Attic tragedy is symptomatic of a point I shall make in the following sentences.

15.   It should be quickly added here—as Szondi himself is careful to point out later in the text—that something of the concept of the tragic (in the German sense) already adhered in Aristotle's *Poetics*, particularly in his notion of *peripeteia* that occurs as a result of the transgressive potential of all actions; just as, obviously, it adhered in the dramaturgical plot structure of the ancient works themselves. See Szondi, *Essay on the Tragic*, 49–56.

16.   Ibid., 2–3.

17.   G. W. F. Hegel, *Aesthetics: Lectures on Fine Art*, translated by T. M. Knox, vol. 2 (Oxford, UK: Clarendon Press, 1998), 1218.

18.   In these two paragraphs I am following my colleague Jay Bernstein's read-

ing of this essay. See J. M. Bernstein, "Love and Law: Hegel's Critique of Morality," *Social Research* 70, no. 2 (Summer 2003), 394 and passim. Part of Bernstein's argument—and something I wish to underscore—is that Hegel's articulation of tragedy and ethical life in Hegel's subsequent work, *The Phenomenology of Spirit*, is anticipated in key ways by the earlier "Spirit" essay. If Bernstein is right, then this would also make Hegel's encounter with Shakespearean tragedy (*Macbeth*, in the case of the "The Spirit of Christianity and its Fate") formative for Hegel's thoughts on tragedy more broadly, and for the place that it occupies in *Phenomenology of Spirit*. Szondi suggests roughly the same, albeit with less elaboration; see Szondi, *Essay on the Tragic*, 17–19.

19. Bernstein, "Love and Law," 394. Although Hegel mentions Shakespeare's play by name only a couple of times in the essay, I have included more than those relatively small sections in this volume because—as is Hegel's style, also with *Antigone* in the *Phenomenology*—much of the essay could be read as a reflection on Shakespeare's play, even when the work is not named by title. Hegel later reiterated parts of this reading of *Macbeth* in his *Phenomenology of Mind*; see *Hegel on Tragedy*, edited by Anne and Henry Paolucci (New York: Anchor, 1963), 294–95.

20. Similarly, in his reading of *Macbeth*, Freud suggests that the suffering of Macbeth and Lady Macbeth is not only the result of their "impotence against the decrees of nature," but moreover it is "through [their] own fault" that they suffer such diremption—which, for Freud, is figured above all in the relation between their own childlessness and "their crimes against the sanctity of generation." See Freud, "Some Character-Types" in *Writings on Art and Literature*.

21. Szondi, *Essay on the Tragic*, 22.

22. Similarly, in his introduction to the French translation of Ernest Jones's *Oedipus and Hamlet*, Jean Starobinski noted that Freud's engagement with Sophocles' *Oedipus* was paralleled from the start by reference to Shakespeare's *Hamlet*, as if the latter determined the reading of the former. See Jean-François Lyotard's comments on Starobinski in his essay "Jewish Oedipus."

23. Again, Bernstein sees the "Spirit" essay in much the same way; namely, as expressive of "Hegel's great idea since it reveals how ethical life matters independent of any particular moral norms, laws, ideals, principles or ends." See Bernstein, "Love and Law," 394.

24. On Szondi's reading, Hegel sees that Sophocles' *Antigone* sublates the struggle between law and love that characterizes the (nontragic) opposition of Christianity to Judaism by showing its tragic, ethical side; namely, by placing the conflict of love and law, family and state, at the center of the tragedy. See Szondi, *Essay on the Tragic*, 21.

25. Johann Wolfgang von Goethe, *Wilhelm Meister* (New York: Collier, 1962), 234–36.

26. Calling this "the sentimental view of Hamlet," A. C. Bradley countered that "if the sentimental Hamlet had crossed [the real Hamlet], he would have hurled him from his path with one sweep of his arm."

27. Hegel, *Aesthetics: Lectures on Fine Art*, 1226.

28. Consider, for example, the exchange between Hamlet and Gertrude immediately following Hamlet's killing of Polonius—that is, before Hamlet discovers whose life he has taken. Gertrude: "Oh me, what hast thou done? / Hamlet: "Nay, I know not. Is it the King?" (3.4.24–26). Hamlet, that is, does not know what he is doing but rather looks to Gertrude's response or to ulterior consequences of other sorts for the meaning of his action.

29. See Stanley Cavell, *Disowning Knowledge in Seven Plays of Shakespeare* (Cambridge, UK: Cambridge University Press, 1987). See also Gjesdal, "Reading Shakespeare—Reading Modernity," 17–18. I have included Cavell's essay on *Othello* rather than his somewhat more famous essay on *King Lear*, called "The Avoidance of Love," in part for reasons of space (the *Lear* essay is significantly longer) and in part because it seems to me that Cavell's reading of Shakespeare and skepticism finds greater plausibility in his discussion of *Othello*.

30. Franz Rosenzweig, *The Star of Redemption*, translated by William W. Hallo (Notre Dame, IN: University of Notre Dame Press, 1985), 210.

31. Hegel, *Aesthetics: Lectures on Fine Art*, 1226.

32. Ibid.

33. Ibid., 1230.

34. In the chapter on *Hamlet* in my book *Tragic Conditions in Shakespeare*, I offer a reading of *Hamlet* that takes up, and contests, the Hegelian interpretation by considering Hamlet's fate in light of the insuperability of two competing principles of social organization: matrilineal descent and state-sanctioned property rights.

35. Hegel, *Aesthetics: Lectures on Fine Art*, 1229–30.

36. Ibid., 1229–30.

37. In addition to the remarks collected in the lectures that make up *Shakespearean Tragedy*, the interested reader could look to Bradley's essay "Hegel's Theory of Tragedy," which contains a series of reflections on Hegel's limits as a reader of Shakespeare. It is handily collected as the postscript to *Hegel on Tragedy*, edited by Anne and Henry Paolucci. See also Bradley's *Oxford Lectures on Poetry* (London: Macmillan, 1909).

38. This may explain W. H. Auden's assertion in his essay "The Joker in the Pack" in *The Dyer's Hand* (New York: Vintage, 1988) that "the wicked man" does not appear as a subject of "serious dramatic interest" before Shakespeare and the Elizabethans. In the mystery plays, wicked characters like Satan or Herod do not have the individuality of Iago; nor, as Auden underscores, does a wicked man *triumph*, as Iago does, prior to *Othello*.

39. I am not supposing here that Bradley had actually read Hegel's early essay; that essay was not published in German until 1907, whereas Bradley's lectures were published in 1904. In this light, it is perhaps even more significant that he chooses precisely *Macbeth* to, as he puts it, "restate" Hegel's theory at the end of his essay "Hegel's Theory of Tragedy."

40. Theodor Adorno, *Negative Dialectics*, translated by E. B. Ashton (New York: Continuum, 1966), 228.

41. This thought is elaborated with respect to both Levinas and *Hamlet* in an essay by Simon Critchley that also analyzes the Wooster Group's performance of Racine's *Phaedre*. See Simon Critchley, "I Want to Die, I Hate My Life—Phaedra's Malaise," *Theory and Event* 7, no. 2 (2004).

42. Schmitt posits, like many historians, that it was England's naval power, and the industrial revolution to which it gave impetus, that lifted it out of the Middle Ages. In general terms, as Schmitt himself avows in a footnote (included here), he follows Hegel in seeing artworks as dialectically bound to the historical moment to which they belong. What that 'belonging' means, of course, is the question his essay means to raise.

43. For more on this, the interested reader could consult Johannes Türk's essay "The Intrusion: Carl Schmitt's Non-Mimetic Logic of Art" in *Telos*, no. 143 (2008), 73–89. Readers interested in recent scholarship on Schmitt's *Hamlet or Hecuba* could consult Victoria Kahn, "Hamlet or Hecuba: Carl Schmitt's Decision," *Representations*, no. 83 (Summer 2003), 67–96; Horst Bredekamp, Melissa Thorson Hause, and Jackson Bond, "From Walter Benjamin to Carl Schmitt, via Thomas Hobbes," *Critical Inquiry* 25, no. 2 ("Angelus Novus": Perspectives on Walter Benjamin; Winter 1999), 247–66; and Julia Reinhard Lupton, "Hamlet, Prince: Tragedy, Citizenship, and Political Theology," *Alternative Shakespeares 3*, edited by Diana Henderson (New York: Routledge, 2007).

44. Schmitt comments at length on Benjamin's *Origin of German Tragic Drama* in an appendix to his remarks on *Hamlet*. For a good reading of Schmitt on *Hamlet*, see Johannes Türk's contribution to *Telos*, no. 142 (2008).

45. For the passage to which Lukács is referring, see Paolucci and Paolucci, *Hegel on Tragedy*, 117–18.

46. For Heller the distinction between Shakespeare's histories and tragedies, and his comedies, is essential—precisely because she identifies this "revelatory truth" primarily with the former. Noticeably absent from this volume are reflections on comedy or comedies. There are surprisingly few philosophical accounts of comedy in general, and almost none that deal in a sustained way with Shakespearean comedy. (Henri Bergson's *Laughter: An Essay on the Meaning of the Comic* has more to say about Molière.) Heller herself has attempted to redress this in her recent book

Immortal Comedy. Hegel also discusses Shakespearean comedy in his *Lectures on Aesthetics*. For a good reading of Hegel on this score, the interested reader could consult Rodolphe Gasche's essay "Self-Dissolving Seriousness: On the Comic in the Hegelian Conception of Tragedy" in *Philosophy and Tragedy*, edited by Miguel de Beistegui and Simon Sparks (New York: Routledge, 2000). For another recent effort to think about comedy's significance for philosophy and for psychoanalysis, see Alenka Zupančič, *The Odd One In* (Cambridge, MA: MIT Press, 2008).

Selections

Some of the notes for the selections are mine, as indicated with the initials PK. Other notes were provided by the authors themselves or by the translators or editors of the volumes from which the selections are reprinted, as indicated in the source note to each selection. I have omitted some of the annotations for the sake of clarity and coherence but have left a great many that provide useful information to the reader.—PK

1. Herder, "Shakespeare"

Johann Gottfried Herder's "Shakespeare" originally appeared in *German Aesthetic and Literary Criticism: Winckelmann, Lessing, Hamann, Herder, Schiller, Goethe*, edited and introduced by H. B. Nisbet (Cambridge, UK: Cambridge University Press, 1985); translated by Joyce P. Crick, with modifications by H. B. Nisbet. The appearance of Herder's essay on Shakespeare in 1773 heralded the emergence of a new form of aesthetic criticism, as well as a new appreciation for Shakespeare's work. I gratefully acknowledge the publisher for permission to reprint copyrighted material. All notes are H. B. Nisbet's.—PK

1. The image is taken from Mark Akenside's didactic poem *The Pleasures of the Imagination* (1744), III, 550–59, which Herder paraphrases.

2. The editors whom Herder has in mind probably include Alexander Pope, Samuel Johnson, and Christopher Martin Wieland (1733–1813), whose eight-volume translation of *Shakespears theatralische Werke* was published in Zurich in 1762–66.

3. Herder here is, without naming him, contradicting Lessing, who in Section 46 of his *Hamburg Dramaturgy* had declared that the Greek tragedies simplified originally complex plots in the interests of those unities of time and place which were necessitated by the constant presence of one and the same chorus on stage; see Gotthold Ephraim Lessing, *Werke*, edited by Herbert G. Gopfert, 8 vols. (Munich: Piper, 1970–79), IV, 443.

4. Herder's account of Greek tragedy in this paragraph closely follows that of Aristotle in Chapters 4 and 6 of his *Poetics*.

5. Herder's criticism is directed at the poetics of Corneille and French classical

tragedy and at its German imitators such as Johann Christoph Gottsched (1700–1766), whose *Critical Poetics* [*Kritische Dichtkunst*] of 1740 had attempted to legislate for the German stage.

6. Aristotle, *Poetics*, Chapter 7.

7. That is, the French. Herder's contemptuous remarks on French neoclassicism echo Lessing's strictures on it in his *Hamburg Dramaturgy* of 1767–69.

8. The reference is again to Lessing's *Hamburg Dramaturgy*, particularly Sections 46–48; see Lessing, *Werke*, IV, 443–56.

9. Prosper Jolyot de Crébillon (1674–1762), French tragedian, whose dramas include *Idoménéé* (1705), *Rhadamiste et Zénobie* (1711), and *Catilina* (1748).

10. *Astreé*, a pastoral romance in five volumes (Paris, 1607–28) by Honoré d'Urfé (1567–1625).

11. *Clélie*, a romance in ten volumes (Paris, 1654–60) by Madeleine de Scudéry (1607–1701).

12. *Aspasia*: the name of more than one French novel of the eighteenth century. It is uncertain whether Herder is referring to one of them in particular or to them all as a class. Aspasia is also, however, a character in Madeleine de Scudéry's romance of chivalry, *Artamène ou le Grand Cyrus* (1648).

13. "The Britons, divided from the rest of the world," from Virgil, *Eclogues*, I, 66.

14. Pupil (literally, "chicken") of Aristotle.

15. Henry Home (Lord Kames) (1696–1782); author of *Elements of Criticism* (Edinburgh, 1762).

16. Richard Hurd (1720–1808), editor of *Q. Horatii Flacci Ars Poetica. Epistola et Pisones* (London, 1749), the commentary to which contained an analysis of the different kinds of drama.

17. Aristotle, *Poetics*, Chapter 7: "a whole is that which has a beginning, middle and an end ... well-constructed plots must neither begin or end in a haphazard way, but must conform to the pattern I have been describing."

18. Aristotle, *Poetics*, Chapter 7: "in just the same way as living creatures and organisms of many parts must be of reasonable size, so that they can easily be taken in by the eye, so too plots must be of a reasonable length, so that they may easily be held in the memory."

19. In his comparison, in the *Hamburg Dramaturgy* (Sections 11–12), of the unconvincing ghost in Voltaire's *Semiramis* with the far more effective ghost in Shakespeare's *Hamlet* (Lessing, *Werke*, IV, 281–86).

20. The young Herder was already studying the much decried heretic Spinoza. Along with Lessing and Goethe, he was shortly to initiate a wave of enthusiasm in Germany for Spinoza's mature pantheism, an enthusiasm which was shared by Schelling, Novalis, and other German Romantics; see David Bell, *Spinoza in Germany from 1670 to the Age of Goethe* (London: Humanities Press, 1984), especially 38–70 and 97–146.

21. Herder's criticisms here are directed in particular at Pierre Corneille's *Discours des trois unites* in *Théatre de Pierre Corneille*, vol. 3 (Amsterdam, 1664).

22. Mohammed's dream of his assumption into heaven.

23. Order of succession and simultaneity (order in time and space); compare Lessing's use of these categories in Chapter 16 of his *Laocoon*.

24. The reference is to William Wharburton's (1698–1779) eight-volume edition of Shakespeare (London, 1747).

25. Elizabeth Montagu (1720–1800), *An Essay on the Writings and Genius of Shakespeare, Compared with the Greek and French Dramatic Poets, with Some Remarks upon the Misrepresentations of Mons. De Voltare* (London, 1769); Herder reviewed the German translation (by J. J. Eschenburg) of the work in 1771 (*Sämtliche Werke*, V, 312–17).

26. See n. 16, above.

27. Heinrich Wilhelm von Gerstenberg (1737–1823), "Versuch über Shakespears Werke und Genie" in Gerstenberg's periodical *Briefe über Merkwürdigkeiten der Literatur* 2, Letters 14–18 (1766); the classification after Polonius occurs in Letter 17, reprinted in *Sturm und Drang. Kritische Schriften*, edited by Erich Loewenthal, 3rd ed. (Heidelberg: Verlag Lambert Schneider, 1972), 27–30.

28. Johannes Stobaeus, Greek anthologist of the sixth century A.D., whose *Florilegium* contained numerous extracts from a wide range of Greek authors. The English anthology of Shakespeare to which Herder refers is William Dodd's *The Beauties of Shakespeare*, 2 vols. (London, 1752). J. J. Eschenburg (1743–1820), German translator of Shakespeare, planned a similar anthology in German.

29. Richard III and Falstaff.

30. *Hamlet*, 2.2.88.

31. The actor David Garrick (1717–79).

32. These words are addressed to the young Goethe, who had already been infected by Herder's enthusiasm for Shakespeare, and whose essay *Von deutscher Baukunst* [*On German Architecture*], in praise of Gothic architecture, was printed immediately after Herder's essay on Shakespeare in the collection *On German Character and Art* (1773), in which these works first appeared.

33. "He has striven, now he rests!"

2. Goethe, from *Wilhelm Meister's Apprenticeship*

This excerpt from Johann Wolfgang von Goethe's *Wilhelm Meister's Apprenticeship* originally appeared in *German Aesthetic and Literary Criticism: The Romantic Ironists and Goethe*, edited by Kathleen M. Wheeler (Cambridge, UK: Cambridge University Press, 1984). *Wilhelm Meister's Apprenticeship* was Goethe's second novel and was published in 1795–96. I gratefully acknowledge the publisher for permission to reprint copyrighted material.—PK

3. Hegel, from "The Spirit of Christianity and Its Fate"

This excerpt from G. W. F. Hegel's "The Spirit of Christianity and Its Fate" originally appeared in *Early Theological Writings*, translated by T. M. Knox (Philadelphia: University of Pennsylvania Press, 1996). "The Spirit of Christianity and Its
Fate" was written after Hegel moved to Frankfurt in 1797, although it was not published in Hegel's lifetime. I gratefully acknowledge the publisher for permission to
reprint copyrighted material. All notes are T. M. Knox's.—PK

1. Noah's (and Abraham's) ideal is conceived in thought, but it is more than a
concept, for he ascribes existence to it; i.e., he conceives of God as a thinker who, as
thinker, is lord of the realities which are the objects of his thought.

2. That is, capable of understanding a law and so of coming under its sway.

3. "But of flesh with the life thereof, which is the blood thereof, shall ye not
eat."

4. Eupolemus was a Jewish historian whose work survives only in five frag-
ments in the *Praeparatio Evangelia* of Eusebius of Caesarea. For the relevant passage here, see *Praeparatio evanagelica* ix, 17.

5. Hegel's term here is *Schönres*, a term which he tends to use in connection
with Greece.

6. "And Joshua said unto all the people . . . Your father dwelt on the other side
of the flood in old time, even Terah, the father of Abraham . . . and they served
other gods." In another draft, Hegel interprets this relationship of Abraham's for-
bearers to "other gods" as one "animated by imagination"; i.e., he assumes that their
religious life at that time was similar to the Greek.

7. *Angst*, or "dread."

8. Hegel is thinking of tragedy, where fate sometimes overtakes a hero (e.g.,
Oedipus) as a result of something he has innocently done. *Schuld*, "guilt," is used in
German either with or without a moral reference. The criminal has *Schuld* for his
crime, but the wind is also said to be *schuldig* for melting the snow, i.e., is the cause
of the melting, or is responsible for it.

9. That is, each quarreled with the other in the first place because each claimed
a right and neither would submit to the other or tolerate any infringement of his
right by the other.

10. That is, property relationships. But other relations with others are also
meant; e.g., X may try to alienate Y's friend, and Y may just withdraw out of this
friendship relation and make no resistance. But this is to "abstract from himself,"
i.e., to renounce part of his own being.

11. That is, in wishing to escape another's power, wishing to maintain his own
independence, he has to carry abstraction so far that he ultimately destroys himself.
With this account of the "beautiful soul" compare Hegel's *Phenomenology of Mind*,
English translation, 2nd ed., 663ff.

4. Hegel, "Dramatic Poetry," from *Aesthetics: Lectures on Fine Art*

"Dramatic Poetry," as excerpted here, originally appeared in *Aesthetics: Lectures on Fine Art, vol.* 2, translated by T. M. Knox (Oxford, UK: Oxford University Press, 1975). I gratefully acknowledge the publisher for permission to reprint copyrighted material. All notes are T. M. Knox's unless otherwise indicated.

These pages constitute the conclusion of Hegel's *Aesthetics,* lectures on fine art given by Hegel in the 1820s. Published posthumously in 1835, Hegel's *Aesthetics* stands at the center of the remarkable tradition of German aesthetic philosophy, from Baumgarten's *Aesthetica* in the 1750s, through Wincklemann, Lessing, Kant, Schiller, Hölderlin, Schelling, and Schopenhauer in Hegel's lifetime, and on to Nietzsche, Heidegger, Gadamer, and Adorno afterward. Readers interested in recent engagements with Hegel's *Aesthetics* as a whole could begin by consulting the superb essays collected in *Hegel and the Arts*, edited by Stephen Houlgate (Evanston, IL: Northwestern University Press, 2007), as well as Gregg M. Horowitz's chapter on Hegel's *Aesthetics* in his book *Sustaining Loss: Art and Mournful Life* (Stanford, CA: Stanford University Press, 2001), 56–90.—PK

1. This is a term drawn from Hegel's *Logic* (e.g., *Enc.* §147). What is 'really' possible is something possible in certain real circumstances, and, indeed, is really potent there. 'Pigs might fly' may be a possibility, but not a 'real' one.

2. A. Müllner, 1774–1829.

3. Two aspects of the substantial or ethical order are the law of the land and family love. If these are not differentiated and the order is regarded as a harmonious whole, then action may be difficult, for in practice these aspects may conflict. And to sense this possible conflict may be to shrink from action.

4. Ideally, or *sub specie aeternitatis*, these 'powers' are a unity. But in the real and therefore finite world the universal, or ideal, is necessarily differentiated, and some of these powers, in their realization, become opposed to others. The naïve consciousness is the undifferentiated basis and substratum of Greek ethical life from which the protagonist detaches himself, causes conflict, and has to suffer. In the ensuing struggle the naïve consciousness, half horrified and half admiring, can only oppose to the protagonist's energy its own knowledge of the moral substance of life.

5. See Part 2 of Hegel's *Aesthetics: Lectures on Fine Art.*—PK

6. The last line of Schiller's *Shakespeares Schatten*. "Is nothing great but only your own contemptible nature to be brought on the stage?" Shakespeare's ghost asks. Schiller sarcastically makes the reply that Kotzebue and others might make: "After giving vice more than its fill in the earlier scenes, the poet makes a bow to virtue at the end." See Hegel's remarks on plays by Kotzebue and Iffland (included here), where Schiller's poem is again in his mind.

7. Hegel simply means that as human beings ('concretely existent'), individuals

have an entirety of obligations (are under the dominion of *all* the 'ethical powers'), but their overmastering 'pathos' is identified with one obligation alone, with the result that when one individual fights against another individual who is similarly overmastered by a different obligation, they are both caught in a fight against themselves.

8. The boast is not unreasonable, as these lectures surely prove. "Of this kind," *nach dieser Seite*: The meaning of this qualification has been much disputed. Did Hegel merely mean that *Antigone* was the finest of Greek tragedies, or did he put it above Shakespeare? His meaning, however, is clear from what he says later when he contrasts Greek tragedy with modern. His point is that *Antigone* is the finest portrayal of what he regards as the greatest tragic conflict, i.e., one where the issue is not merely personal, arising from, e.g., jealousy, like Othello's, but one where both parties are under the necessity of transgressing; they are divided against themselves; neither of them can obey *both* the valid *laws* to which they are subject.

9. *The Clouds.*

10. *The Frogs.*

11. *The Knights.*

12. *Ecclesiazusae* and *Thesmophoriazusae.*

13. *Peace.*

14. That is, presumably, as meaning something suffered, or something to which a man succumbs, the opposite of action. Hegel seems here to be emphasizing the connection between *Leiden* (suffering) and *Leidenschaft* (passion). But he is soon using "passion" in the ordinary sense as meaning something driving a man to act.

15. That is, in Greek tragedy the 'pathos' or ruling passion is 'substantial', i.e., has a moral or objective basis. In the Spanish tragedies, love may be 'substantial' in a sense, but it is only subjective after all, and therefore, so to say, or 'as it were', subjectively substantial, and the substantiality inhibits romantic individualization.

16. *As You Like It*, 1.7.139.

17. In Hegel's *Aesthetics*, vol. 1, translated by T. M. Knox, 237–41.

18. 1773–78.

19. The son declined to follow his father's devious ways. He therefore openly deserted Wallenstein instead of pretending to follow him. He is then killed in action against one of Wallenstein's regiments.

20. Also in Goethe's *Götz*.

21. "Calm yourself sir, you've had a serious fright. We live under a prince who does not tolerate fraud, a monarch who can read the hearts of men, and who is not taken in by the wiles of hypocrites." Molière, *Tartuffe*, Act 5, Scene 8, in *The Misanthrope and Other Plays*, translated by John Wood and David Coward (New York: Penguin, 2000), 87.—PK

22. Harpagon in *L'Avare*.

5. Bradley, from *Shakespearean Tragedy*

This text was taken from the public domain: http://www.clicknotes.com/brad-ley/welcome.html. Bradley's major works, *Shakespearean Tragedy* (1904), from which this text is taken, and *Oxford Lectures on Poetry* (1909), were the product of his tenure as professor of poetry at Oxford University. All notes are Bradley's.—PK

1. *Julius Caesar* is not an exception to this rule. Caesar, whose murder comes in the Third Act, is in a sense the dominating figure in the story, but Brutus is the "hero."

2. *Timon of Athens*, we have seen, was probably not designed by Shakespeare, but even *Timon* is no exception to the rule. The subplot is concerned with Alcibi-ades and his army, and Timon himself is treated by the Senate as a man of great importance. *Arden of Feversham* and *A Yorkshire Tragedy* would certainly be excep-tions to the rule; but I assume that neither of them is Shakespeare's; and if either is, it belongs to a different species from his admitted tragedies. See, on this species, Symonds, *Shakespeare's Predecessors*, Chapter 11.

3. Even a deed would, I think, be counted an "accident" if it were the deed of a very minor person whose character had not been indicated; because such a deed would not issue from the little world to which the dramatist had confined our attention.

4. Comedy stands in a different position. The tricks played by chance often form a principal part of the comic action.

5. It may be observed that the influence of the three elements just considered is to strengthen the tendency, produced by the sufferings considered first, to regard the tragic persons as passive rather than as agents.

6. An account of Hegel's view may be found in my *Oxford Lectures on Poetry*.

7. The reader, however, will find considerable difficulty in placing some very important characters in these and other plays. I will give only two or three illustra-tions. Edgar is clearly not on the same side as Edmund, and yet it seems awkward to range him on Gloucester's side when Gloucester wishes to put him to death. Ophelia is in love with Hamlet, but how can she be said to be of Hamlet's party against the King and Polonius, or of their party against Hamlet? Desdemona wor-ships Othello, yet it sounds odd to say that Othello is on the same side with a per-son whom he insults, strikes, and murders.

8. I have given names to the "spiritual forces" in *Macbeth* merely to illustrate the idea, and without any pretension to adequacy. Perhaps, in view of some interpreta-tions of Shakespeare's plays, it will be as well to add that I do not dream of suggesting that in any of his dramas Shakespeare imagined two abstract principles or passions conflicting, and incorporated them in persons; or that there is any necessity for a reader to define for himself the particular forces which conflict in a given case.

9. Aristotle apparently would exclude them.

10. Richard II is perhaps an exception, and I must confess that to me he is scarcely a tragic character, and that, if he is nevertheless a tragic figure, he is so only because his fall from prosperity to adversity is so great.

11. I say substantially; but the concluding remarks on *Hamlet* will modify a little the statements above.

12. I have raised no objection to the use of the idea of fate, because it occurs so often both in conversation and in books about Shakespeare's tragedies that I must suppose it to be natural to many readers. Yet I doubt whether it would be so if Greek tragedy had never been written; and I must in candour confess that to me it does not often occur while I am reading, or when I have just read, a tragedy of Shakespeare. Wordsworth's lines, for example, about poor humanity's afflicted will struggling in vain with ruthless destiny do not represent the impression I receive; much less do images which compare man to a puny creature helpless in the claws of a bird of prey. The reader should examine himself closely on this matter.

13. It is dangerous, I think, in reference to all really good tragedies, but I am dealing here only with Shakespeare's. In not a few Greek tragedies it is almost inevitable that we should think of justice and retribution, not only because the dramatis personae often speak of them, but also because there is something casuistical about the tragic problem itself. The poet treats the story in such a way that the question, Is the hero doing right or wrong? is almost forced upon us. But this is not so with Shakespeare. *Julius Caesar* is probably the only one of his tragedies in which the question suggests itself to us, and this is one of the reasons why that play has something of a classic air. Even here, if we ask the question, we have no doubt at all about the answer.

14. It is most essential to remember that an evil man is much more than the evil in him. I may add that in this paragraph I have, for the sake of clearness, considered evil in its most pronounced form; but what is said would apply, *mutatis mutandis*, to evil as imperfection, etc.

15. Partly in order not to anticipate later passages, I abstained from treating fully here the question why we feel, at the death of the tragic hero, not only pain but also reconciliation and sometimes even exultation. As I cannot at present make good this defect, I would ask the reader to refer to the word *Reconciliation* in the Index. [Not included in this volume.—PK] See also, in *Oxford Lectures on Poetry*, "Hegel's Theory of Tragedy," especially pp. 90, 91.

6. Benjamin, from *The Origin of German Tragic Drama*

This text originally appeared in Walter Benjamin, *The Origin of German Tragic Drama* (London: Verso Press, 1998), 131–38. *The Origin of German Tragic Drama* was originally written in 1925 as Benjamin's Habilitation thesis [*Habilitationsschrift*], although it was not accepted by Benjamin's readers and thus marked the end of Benjamin's academic career. It was first published in 1928. I gratefully acknowledge the publisher for permission to reprint copyrighted material. All notes are Benjamin's unless otherwise indicated.—PK

1. *Trauerspiel* literally means "mourning-play"; Benjamin uses the term generally to denote modern, baroque tragedy as distinct from classical tragedy (*Tragödie*).—PK

2. Georg von Lukács, *Die Seele und die Formen. Essays* (Berlin, 1911), 352–53. [This text has been translated into English by Anna Bostock as *Soul and Form* (London: Merlin Press, 1974).—PK]

3. Lukács, *Die Seele und die Formen*, 355–56.

4. Walter Benjamin, "Zur Kritik der Gewalt," *Archiv für Sozialwissenschaft und Sozialpolitik*, 47 (1920/21), 828 (Heft 3, August 1921). [This text has been translated into English as "Critique of Violence" in Walter Benjamin, *Reflections: Essays, Aphorism, Autobiographical Writings* (New York: Harcourt Brace, 1978).—PK]

5. Hans Ehrenberg, *Tragödie und Kreuz*, vol. 2, *Tragödie und Kreuz*, 53.

6. Benjamin, "Schicksal und Charakter," 92. See also Benjamin, "Goethes Wahlverwandtschaften," 98ff; and "Schicksal und Charakter," 189–92. [The latter is translated into English as "Fate and Character" in *Reflections*.—PK]

7. Jacob Minor, *Die Schicksals-Tragödie in ihren Hauptvertretern* (Frankfurt a.M., 1883), 75–76.

8. Pedro Calderón de la Barca y Henao (1600–1681) was a dramatist of the Spanish Golden Age.—PK

9. August Wilhelm Schlegel, *Sämtliche Werke*, VI, 386; translated into English by John Black as *A Course of Lectures and Dramatic Art and Literature* (Philadelphia, 1833), 496.

10. Peter Berens, "Calderóns Schicksalstragödien," *Romanische Forschungen* 39 (1926), 55–56.

11. "If anyone should find it odd that we do not bring forth a god from the machine, like the ancients, but rather a spirit from the grave, then let him consider what has occasionally been written about ghosts." Andreas Gryphius, *Trauerspiele*, hrs. von Hermann Palm, Tübingen, 1882 (Bibliothek des litterarischen Vereins in Stuttgart), 162, 163 (Cardenio und Celinde, preface).

12. Kurt Kolitz, *Johann Christian Hallmanns Dramen. Ein Beitrag zur Geschichte des deutschen Dramas in der Barockzeit* (Berlin, 1911), 163.

13. Benjamin, "Schicksal und Charakter," 192.

14. *Hamlet*, 3.2.379–81.

15. "Alas I die, yes, yes, accursed one, I die, but thou hast still to fear my vengeance: even beneath the earth shall I remain thy bitter enemy and the vengeance-seeking tyrant of the kingdom of Messina. I shall shake thy throne, disturb thy marriage bed, thy love, and thy contentment, and in my wrath do the utmost harm to king and kingdom."

16. Hans Ehrenber, *Tragödie und Kreuz*, 2 vols. (Würzburg, 1920), 52.
17. Lukács, *Die Seele und die Formen*, 46.
18. "In three days they must be judged: they are summoned before God's throne; let them now consider how they will justify themselves."
19. Albert Ludwig, "Fortsetzungen. Eine Studie zur Psychologie der Literatur," *Germanischromanische Monatsschrift* 6 (1914), 433.
20. Leopold Ziegler, *Zur Metaphysik des Tragischen. Eine philosophische Studie* (Leipzig, 1902), 52.
21. Ehrenberg, *Tragödie und Kreuz*, vol. 2, 57.
22. Conrad Müller, *Beiträge zum Leben und Dichten Daniel Caspers von Lohenstein* (Breslau, 1882), 82–83.
23. Conrad Höfer, *Die Rudolstädter Festspiele aus den Jahren 1665–67 und ihr Dichter. Eine literarhistorische Studie* (Leipzig, 1904) (Probefahrten, I), 141.
24. "Nowhere do I find rest, I must even quarrel with myself. I sit, I lie, I stand, but am always in thought." Andreas Tscherning, *Melancholy Speaks Itself.*
25. *Hamlet,* 4.4.33–39.
26. "The world knows no greater book than itself; but the greatest part of this book is man, before whom, in place of a fine frontispiece, God has printed his own likeness, and, besides, God has made him into an abstract, kernel, and jewel of the other parts of this great book of the world."
27. "Considering that pyramids, pillars, and statues of all kinds of material became damaged by time, or destroyed by violence, or simply decay . . . that whole cities have sunk, disappeared and are covered with water, whereas writings and books are immune from such destruction, for any that disappear or are destroyed in one country or place are easily found again in countless other places, so that in human experience there is nothing more enduring and immortal than books."
28. Arthur Hübscher, "Barock als Gestaltung antithetischen Lebensgefüls. Grundlegung einer Phaseologie der Geistesgeschichte," *Euphorion* 29 (1922), 552.
29. Franz Boll, *Sternglaube und Sterndeuteng. Die Geschichte und das Wesen der Astrologie* (Unter Mitwirkung von Carl Bezold dargestellt von Franz Boll) (Leipzig, Berlin, 1918) (Aus Natur und Geisteswelt, 638), 46.
30. Rochus Freiherr von Liliencron, *Wie man in Amwald Musik macht. Die siebente Todsünde* (Leipzig: Zwei Novellen, 1903).

7. Szondi, "Othello," from *An Essay on the Tragic*

This text is from Peter Szondi, *An Essay on the Tragic*, translated by Paul Fleming (Stanford, CA: Stanford University Press, 2002). All notes are Peter Szondi's.—PK

1. Paul Ernst, *Der Weg zur Form*, 3rd ed. (Munich: G. Müller Verlag, 1928), 121.
2. *Othello,* 5.2.16–19.
3. *Othello,* 5.3.360–62.

4. Compare Hegel and Kierkegaard on Socrates.
5. *Othello*, 3.3.357.
6. *Othello*, 1.3.287–88.

8. Marx, from *Economic and Philosophical Manuscripts of 1844*

This text was taken from the public domain: http://www.marxists.org/archive/marx/works/1844/manuscripts/preface.htm. Marx's *Economic and Philosophical Manuscripts of 1844*, from which this selection was drawn, were not published in his lifetime and were not made public until the 1930s.—PK

9. Nietzsche, from *The Birth of Tragedy*

This text was taken from the public domain: http://arthursclassicnovels.com/arthurs/nietzsche/tragedy_all.htm. Trained as a classical philologist, Nietzsche first published *The Birth of Tragedy* under the title *The Birth of Tragedy from the Spirit of Music* [*Die Geburt der Tragödie aus dem Geiste der Musik*] in 1872; he later published a second edition—with an added prefatory essay called "An Attempt at Self-Criticism," in which he discusses the earlier publication. The title *The Birth of Tragedy, Or: Hellenism and Pessimism* [*Die Geburt der Tragödie, Oder: Griechentum und Pessimismus*] was given in 1886.—PK

10. Lukács, "Shakespeare and Modern Drama"

Georg Lukács's "Shakespeare and Modern Drama" originally appeared in English in *The Lukács Reader* (London: Blackwell, 1995). "Shakespeare and Modern Drama" was delivered as a lecture on January 31, 1909, before the Hungarian Shakespeare Society; it was subsequently published in 1911. I gratefully acknowledge the publisher for permission to reprint copyrighted material. All notes are those of the editor of the Blackwell edition unless otherwise indicated.—PK

1. Diego de Velazquez (1599–1660) made a deep impression on Edouard Manet (1832–83), the leading Impressionist painter.

2. Frans Hals (1580–1666) was without a doubt one of the greatest portrait painters of all times. Considered a forerunner to the Impressionist in the expressiveness of his brushwork, Hals excelled in the clarity and brightness of his flesh tones and the subtle characterization of his sitters.

3. Tolstoy's diaries contain fascinating, though mostly critical, remarks on Shakespeare. Tolstoy held that great talents—the Goethes, Shakespeares, Beethovens, Michelangelos—produced side by side with beautiful things not merely "mediocre ones, but repulsive ones as well." *Tolstoy's Diaries*, edited by R. F. Christian (London: Flamingo, 1994), 314.

4. In his devastating attack on Shakespeare, Shaw said, "With the single exception of Homer, there is no eminent writer, not even Sir Walter Scott, whom I de-

spise so entirely as I despise Shakespeare when I measure my mind against his. The intensity of my impatience with him occasionally reaches such a pitch, that it positively would be a relief to me to dig him up and throw stones at him, knowing as I do how incapable he and his worshippers are of understanding any less obvious form of indignity." Quoted in Stanley Wells, *Shakespeare* (London: Sinclair-Stevenson, 1994), 351.

5. Lord Byron (1788–1824) and Percy Bysshe Shelley (1792–1822) engaged in a dialogue on *Hamlet*. Byron wondered how one can read *Hamlet* and still call Shakespeare a "thoughtful artist whose whole story, the action, after the first prologue and preparation of this ghost, remains stagnant; all the rest is stationary, episodical, useless." Thereupon Shelley read out a brilliant defense of *Hamlet,* and when he finished, he found Lord Byron fast asleep. *From Sensibility to Romanticism,* edited by F. W. Hilles and Harold Bloom (New York: Oxford University Press, 1965), 505–8.

6. Franz Grillparzer (1791–1872), Austria's leading poet and dramatist, admired Shakespeare's ability to penetrate the depths of human nature and to enter the very soul of its characters. Lukács's reference to Grillparzer's "secret" opposition to Shakespeare is mystifying, unless it implies envy. For Grillparzer's comments on Shakespeare, see *Sämthliche Werke,* vol. 3 (Munich: Carl Hanser, 1964), 642–59.

7. Otto Ludwig (1813–65), German novelist and dramatic theorist.

8. In his *Wilhelm Meister's Apprenticeship,* Goethe declared, among other things, that Shakespeare belongs "by necessity in the annals of poetry; in the annals of theater he appears only by accident."

9. Lukács refers to Grillparzer's plays that utilize Greek myths and legends. In the tragedy *Sappho,* Grillparzer depicts the Greek poetess Sappho, and in *Medea* he deals with the relationship of Medea and her husband.

10. In interpreting *Othello,* Lukács appears to ascribe to the Schlegel-Coleridge theory. According to this, Iago's action is not prompted by any plain motive like revenge, jealousy, or ambition. It springs from what Coleridge termed "motiveless malignity" or a disinterested delight in the pain of others. By contrast, Bradley argued that Iago by nature was not malignant, but an evil man. In fact, Iago combines intellect and evil; it is rare, but it exists, and Shakespeare represented it in Iago. A. C. Bradley, *Shakespearean Tragedy* (New York: Penguin, 1991), 233.

11. When Lukács enumerates 'chance' or 'accident' in most of Shakespeare's tragedies, he means any occurrence (not supernatural, of course) which enters the dramatic sequence neither from the agency of a character, nor from the obvious surrounding circumstances. To use Lukács's examples, it is an accident that Romeo never got the Friar's message about the potion (*Romeo and Juliet,* 5.2); an accident that Edgar arrived too late to save Cordelia's life (*King Lear,* 5.3); and an accident that Desdemona dropped her handkerchief at the most fatal of moments (*Othello,* 3.3).

12. Lukács dissented from William Hazlitt (1778–1830), who said that anyone

who studies *Coriolanus* "may save himself the trouble of reading Burke's *Reflections*, or Paine's *Rights of Man*, or the Debates of both Houses of Parliament since the French Revolution or our own." William Hazlitt, *On Theater*, edited by William Archer (New York: Hill and Wang, 1957), 112.

13. Lukács implies that in his historical plays, *Henry VI, Part One* and *Part Three*, along with *King John* and *Richard II*, Shakespeare treats his source material with characteristic freedom, shaping, omitting, altering, and adding.

14. Lukács's concept of 'necessity' is borrowed from Aristotle's *Poetics* and, applied to Shakespearean tragedy, it implies a power ordaining inevitably to the nature of what is, and controlling inevitably the sequence of what becomes.

15. See Paolucci and Paolucci, *Hegel on Tragedy*, 294. Lukács refers to Hegel's reading of *Macbeth* in a similar fashion in his book *The Historical Novel*, translated by Hannah Mitchell and Stanley Mitchell (Lincoln: University of Nebraska Press, 1983), 137–38. Also of interest in this regard is A. C. Bradley's riposte to Hegel's reading of *Macbeth* in his essay "Hegel's Theory of Tragedy," reprinted as the appendix to Paolucci and Paolucci, *Hegel on Tragedy*, 367–87.—PK

16. Walter Raleigh, *Shakespeare* (London: Macmillan, 1907). This influential book, twice printed in 1907, was diligently studied by Lukács.

17. Giotto (1267–1337) broke sharply with the past in portraying individuals. Representations of the human face in earlier paintings had given it an expressionless stare; he invested it with grief, fear, pity, joy, or other emotions to which the viewer could respond with instant understanding. Lukács always spoke in superlatives of Giotto, who "painted what no man could look upon without being the better for it."

18. Pieter de Hooch (1629–84) is celebrated for his delightful interiors and use of light. His real contribution to the development of painting lies in his revelation of the atmospheric life of these comfortable interiors.

11. Schmitt, "The Source of the Tragic," from *Hamlet or Hecuba*

Carl Schmitt's "The Source of the Tragic" will appear in Carl Schmitt, *Hamlet or Hecuba: The Intrusion of the Time into the Play*, translated by David Pan and Jennifer Rust (New York: Telos Press, 2009); translation authorized by George Schwab with permission from the Klett Cotta Verlag. I gratefully acknowledge these publishers for permission to reprint copyrighted material. All notes are Schmitt's unless otherwise indicated.—PK

1. In Chapter 1, "The Tabu of the Queen," Schmitt recapitulates the critical debate centering on the guilt of the queen in the murder of Hamlet's father. Considering the question irresolvable, Schmitt provides a historical explanation for the ambiguity. He elucidates the concrete situation during the years 1600–1603, which saw the first production of *Hamlet*—a time when London and all England was antici-

pating the death of Queen Elizabeth, and her successor had not yet been decided. Most important to Schmitt is the background of the situation, which concerned Mary, Queen of Scots. Her husband, Henry Lord Darnley, the father of James, was murdered by her lover, the Earl of Bothwell, in February 1566. In May of the same year, Mary Stuart married Bothwell. According to Schmitt, since James was the presumed successor to the throne, it was a tabu to establish the guilt of the mother for the murder of the father. Two supporters of James, the Earls of Southampton and Essex, were not only in disfavor with Queen Elizabeth but also patrons of Shakespeare's theater troupe, which was accordingly forced out of London. In order to regain a place for his plays in London, Shakespeare had to support James's bid for the throne. On this count, the queen in *Hamlet* had to be free of guilt. But in order to cater to the Protestant London audience, convinced of the Catholic Mary Stuart's guilt, the queen could not be portrayed as innocent. The combination of these two considerations dictated the queen's ambiguous status—the tabu of the queen.

In Chapter 2, "The Figure of the Avenger," Schmitt provides a similar explanation for Hamlet's indecisiveness—the distortion of the traditional figure of the avenger into a melancholic invert. In Schmitt's view, James stood at the center of the religious conflict between Protestants and Catholics and thus provided the model which distorted the figure of the avenger, the traditional man of action, into a Hamlet, whose action is inhibited by his contemplation. He lists as sources for his thesis: Lillian Winstanley, *Hamlet and the Scottish Succession* (Cambridge, UK: At the University Press, 1921); John Dover Wilson, *What Happens in Hamlet*, 3rd ed. (Cambridge, UK: At the University Press, 1951 [1935]); and Walter Benjamin, *The Origin of German Tragic Drama* (London: New Left Books, 1977).—Tr.

2. Richard Tüngel, an experienced journalist, has written, "One of the essentials of dramatic effect is that the spectators know and understand about what is happening or will happen on the stage. One could say that allowing the audience to know more than the performers is one of the most effective techniques of dramatic art. Shakespeare made use of this technique in many of his dramas and comedies. It is very possible that the historical presence of the Hamlet drama—its allusion to the Scottish tragedy—had such an effect upon the audience at that time." See *Die Zeit,* no. 45 (November 6, 1952).

3. See the essay on Paul Ernst, "The Metaphysics of Tragedy" in Georg Lukács, *Soul and Form* (Cambridge, MA: MIT Press, 1974).—Tr.

4. In Otto Ludwig's *Dramatishe Studien* he repeatedly emphasizes that a drama must be understood in terms of its "inner relationships," i.e., from within the drama itself. He is thus unrelenting in his criticism of Hegel, who was presumably too much of a sociologist to appreciate the process of a play in and of itself. Clearly irritated with the great philosopher-cum-sociologist, Ludwig cites what he calls "an almost comic example of the misunderstanding of the true nature of the drama

in his *Ästhetik* (vol. 1, p. 267)." From my point of view, I think Hegel is correct in arguing that Shakespeare (in *Macbeth*) conceded to King James by intentionally not mentioning the historical Macbeth's ancestral rights to the throne and thereby making him into a common criminal. In response to Hegel's reasonable arguments, Ludwig poses and answers a rhetorical question: "Can one even conceive of the idea that Shakespeare depicted Macbeth as a criminal in order to please King James? I cannot." In the context of German aesthetics in 1850, when Ludwig was writing, perhaps it was not possible. Today we can very easily conceive of it. Ludwig is a perfect example of the German cultural tradition—its conception of the dramatic playwright and its preconceived notions of Shakespeare the dramatist.

5. "In the end God puts all the dolls back in the box and begins a new game with Fortinbras." See Karl Kindt, *Der Spieler Gottes: Shakespeares Hamlet als christliches Welttheater* (Berlin: Wichern-Verlag Herbert Renner, 1949), 95. Together with the other merits of this excellent book, Kindt expands upon the objective (historical) action in the Hegelian Karl Werder's interpretation of *Hamlet*, which is an important step in overcoming the psychological interpretation. See Karl Werder, *Vorlesungen über Shakespeares Hamlet gehalten an der universitat in Berlin 1859–69* (Berlin: Hertz Verlag, 1875).

6. Chapter 8, 30–31. In the vulgate it reads, *ludens in orbe terrarum*. This is not the place to explicate this passage, nor to discuss the relation of church liturgy and its sacrifice to such a profound concept of play. In any case, Shakespeare's drama has nothing to do with church liturgy. Neither is it religious, nor does it exist (like classical French theater) in a framework determined by the sovereignty of the state. The idea that God plays with us can as well lift us up to an optimistic theodicy or lower us down into a despairing irony of bottomless agnosticism. It need not concern us here.

7. See Rüdiger Altmann's article "Freiheit im Spiel" in *Frankfurter Allgemeine Zeitung*, no. 100 (April 30, 1955). The entire passage reads, "play is the fundamental negation of the state of emergency. Therein lies its existential significance. One can only know what play is after experiencing the state of emergency. The fact that play is often fashioned after the state of emergency does not alter this fact." Formulated in Hans Freyer's concepts and terms, one could say that it belongs to the essence of the tragic not to be incorporated into a secondary system, even as the secondary system has its own rules which exclude intrusions of tragic action, perceiving such as disturbances if it notices them at all. Perhaps someday a legislator, realizing the relation between freedom and play or freedom and leisure will establish the simple legal definition: Play is everything that has to do with the structure and content of legally-sanctioned leisure.

8. Compare Caspar von Lohenstein's dedication to *Sophonisbe*, quoted in Benjamin, *Origin of German Tragic Drama*, 98.

9. Hamlet's Hecuba monologue precisely defines his true task, his cause, his

purpose, and he reproaches himself severely for being "unpregnant of my cause." But what is Hamlet's cause, his purpose? The question is all the more significant because in his Hecuba monologue Hamlet conceives the plan to capture the murderer through the play within the play—the plan of the "mousetrap." Here then, in this important question of Hamlet's purpose, we come across a curious discrepancy between the first edition of the play (Quarto I of 1603) and the later versions (Quarto II and Folio I), more commonly used today. According to the later versions, Hamlet has only *one* purpose: to revenge the king, who was rudely robbed of life and property. However, according to Quarto I, which originated *before* James I's accession to the throne in 1603, Hamlet suffers a double loss: his father murdered *and a Crowne bereft him* (Quarto I, 2, p. 587). It is clear that the young Hamlet was himself *bereft* or robbed of a crown. This second "motive and brand of suffering" was the call to the undecided James from the Essex-Southampton group. *After* the succession to the throne, it had to be left out.

10. Ulrich von Wilamowitz-Muellendorff, *Euripides Herakles*, vol. 1, *Einleitung in die Attische Tragödie* (Berlin: Weidemann Verlag, 1889), 43ff. What is "Attic Tragedy"? Wilamowitz-Muellendorff defines *legend* as "the sum of the living historical recollections of a people in a time when the people could only be conceived concretely as a history of a myth." According to Wilamowitz-Muellendorff, "An Attic tragedy is an internally self-contained part of heroic legend, poetically conceived in an elevated style for presentation by an Attic choir of citizens and two or three actors, designed as part of the public ritual in the shrine of Dionysus."

11. These lines are from Schiller's *Huldigung der Künste*: "*Wenn du das grosse Spiel der Welt gesehen, So kehrst du reicher in dich selbst zurück.*"

12. Wilhelm Wackernagel, *Über die dramatische Poesis* (Basel: Schweighauser Verlag, 1838). Nevertheless, the reality of tragedy is for Wackernagel only the reality of *past* history; the reality of the present belongs to *comedy*. He is thus already on his way to historicism. But his understanding is still considerable. Hegel's influence on his is enduring and significant, broadening his horizon. The very quality of insightful judgments is astonishing. One example is in his observations on the figure of Don Carlos in Schiller's drama. He emphasizes its historical falsehood, the extent of its deviation from historical reality, whereby "tragedy is displaced." He also cites Jean Paul's statement concerning the *cogito* of great historical names and the number of situations already named. Because he sees history not as present but only as past, it must ultimately become for him only a literary source. The same holds true for legend, similar to what we have already observed for Wilamowitz-Muellendorff. As a result, Wackernagel does not distinguish between *Trauerspiel* and tragedy, and ignores the problem between the relation of play and tragedy. In this respect, Benjamin's reference to Wackernagel must be refined. See Benjamin, *Origin of German Tragic Drama*, 89, 106.

12. Cavell, "Othello and the Stake of the Other," from *Disowning Knowledge*

Stanley Cavell's "Othello and the Stake of the Other" appeared in *Disowning Knowledge in Seven Plays by Shakespeare* (Cambridge, UK: Cambridge University Press, 1991). I gratefully acknowledge the publisher for permission to reprint copyrighted material. This essay on *Othello* first appeared as the conclusion of Cavell's book *The Claim of Reason* (Oxford, UK: Oxford University Press, 1979), just as his essay on *King Lear* concludes his *Must We Mean What We Say?* (Cambridge, UK: Cambridge University Press, 1969). All notes are Cavell's.—PK

1. Northrop Frye, *The Secular Scripture* (Cambridge, MA: Harvard University Press, 1976), 86.

2. "Knowing and Acknowledging" in *Must We Mean What We Say?* (Cambridge University Press, reprinted 1976), 263.

3. Compare "Aesthetic Problems of Modern Philosophy," ibid., 96.

13. Derrida, "Aphorism, Countertime"

Jacques Derrida's "Aphorism, Countertime" originally appeared in English in *Acts of Literature*, edited and translated by Derek Attridge (New York: Routledge, 1994). I gratefully acknowledge the publisher for permission to reprint copyrighted material. All notes are Derek Attridge's.—PK

1. The word *contretemps* signifies, in English as well as French, "an inopportune occurrence; an untoward accident; an unexpected mishap or hitch" (OED), but in French it also refers to being "out of time" or "off-beat" in the musical sense, to a sense of bad or wrong time, "counter-time."

2. References to Shakespeare's *Romeo and Juliet* are to the Arden text, edited by Brian Gibbons (New York: Methuen, 1980).

3. Derrida's text works with several senses of the verb *survivre*: "to survive," "to survive beyond" or "survive through," "to live on," and so forth. For a fuller account of "living on" and the related double-notion of "death-sentence" and "arrest of death" (*l'arrêt de mort*), see Derrida's "Living On/Borderlines."

4. The French phrase here is *caractère de sentence*, which can also mean "quality of judgment"; "*sentence*" carries the sense of "moral saying" as well as "judgment."

5. "Aphorism, Countertime" contains—or carries—a certain play on the verb *porter*, corresponding in some ways to the English verb "to bear" ("to carry" as well as "to wear [clothes]"). *Porter* is the verb used to designate, for example, being called by, having, or bearing a name (*porter le nom*), as well as being in mourning (*porter le deuil*). Derrida treats the idea of the name as bearing death within it—and as being structurally conditioned to survive its bearer—in several of his works: among others, *Signèpongel Signsponge*, "Otobiographies," and *Mèmoires*.

6. English in original. This is an allusion to Derrida's "Le facteur de la verité,"

a text concerned with Edgar Allan Poe's short story "The Purloined Letter," and Jacques Lacan's "Seminar on 'The Purloined Letter,'" the latter partly translated in *Yale French Studies* 48 (1973), 38–72. "Aphorism, Countertime" follows Shakespeare's text in focusing on the (tragic, comic, ironic, and above all *necessary*) possibility that a letter can always *not* reach its destination.

7. *Partage*, the usual word for "sharing," also signifies "division."

8. The reference is to Husserl. See, e.g., *The Phenomenology of Internal Time-Consciousness*, translated by James S. Churchill (Bloomington: Indiana University Press, 1964). See also Derrida's *Edmund Husserl's "Origin of Geometry": An Introduction,* 57; and Chapter 5 ("Signs and the Blink of an Eye") of his *Speech and Phenomena.*

9. The French text reads, *Un gage peut toujours s'inverser qui garde de la mort.* This double bind of what keeps off death and at the same time keeps it might be further elucidated by way of Derrida's *Mèmoires*, where for example he explores the notion that "*already* you are *in memory* of your own death; and your friends as well, and all the other, both of your own death and already of their own through yours" (87 n. 2).

10. I have followed the text of Derrida's quotation here, thus preserving the colon at the end of the first line. The Arden version, already cited, gives a full stop. As Brian Gibbons points out (Arden, 129), there have been several variants and varying hypotheses regarding these lines of the play. Confusingly perhaps, Q2–4 and F in fact give: "o be some other name / Belonging to a man."

11. See G. W. F. Hegel, *Aesthetics: Lectures on Fine Art*, translated by T. M. Knox, vol. 1 (Oxford, UK: Clarendon Press, 1975), 69.

12. Matteo Bandello and Luigi da Porto were the authors of two of the many earlier versions of the Romeo and Juliet story.

14. Heller, "Historical Truth and Poetic Truth," from *The Time Is Out of Joint*

Agnes Heller's "Historical Truth and Poetic Truth" originally appeared in *The Time Is Out of Joint: Shakespeare as Philosopher of History* (Lanham, MD: Rowman & Littlefield, 2002). I gratefully acknowledge the publisher for permission to reprint copyrighted material.—PK

Index